Towards Integration of Work and Learning

Marja-Leena Stenström · Päivi Tynjälä
Editors

# Towards Integration of Work and Learning

Strategies for Connectivity
and Transformation

 Springer

*Editors*
Prof. Marja-Leena Stenström
University of Jyväskylä
Institute for Educational Research
FI-40014 Jyväskylä
Finland
Marja-Leena.Stenstrom@ktl.jyu.fi

Prof. Päivi Tynjälä
University of Jyväskylä
Institute for Educational Research
FI-40014 Jyväskylä
Finland

ISBN: 978-1-4020-8961-9     e-ISBN: 978-1-4020-8962-6

Library of Congress Control Number: 2008933666

Printed on acid-free paper

9 8 7 6 5 4 3 2 1

springer.com

# Acknowledgements

Most of the chapters of this book are based on the research project Integration of Work and Learning: Strategies for Connectivity and Transformation, funded by the Academy of Finland (Project number 205922; see http://www.peda.net/veraja/ worklearn). The study described in Chapter 13 was partly funded by the EU Leonardo da Vinci programme (Leonardo da Vinci project QUAL-PRAXIS). Furthermore, the Finnish Ministry of Education financed part of the study reported in Chapter 12, whereas Chapter 6 is based on a study which was partly financed by the Aker Yards Ship Industry School in Turku and contributed by the Turku employment office. Furthermore, we wish to warmly thank Ms. M.A. Leila Leino for her good technical assistance in editing of the book and Mr. Michael Freeman, lecturer in the Department of Languages at the University of Jyväskylä, for his professional language checking. We also wish to thank our international partners who contributed to the volume and anonymous reviewers who gave us valuable feedback and suggestions to improve the work.

Marja-Leena Stenström and Päivi Tynjälä

# Contents

# Contributors

**Kaija Collin**, PhD, is a senior researcher at the Department of Educational Sciences, University of Jyväskylä, Finland. In her doctoral dissertation she focused on design engineers' learning at work as both individual and collective activity. She has published nationally and internationally in the area of workplace learning and adult learning and education. She has also been involved in editing two recent Finnish textbooks in the field of adult education and workplace learning. She is a member of the PROFID (Professional Identity in Working-Life Communities) research group, coordinated by Professor Anneli Eteläpelto, and a coordinator of her own research project The Innovative Learning Space – Intermediate Processes of Individual and Social Learning in the Workplace, funded by the Academy of Finland. E-mail: kaija.collin@edu.jyu.fi

**Ludger Deitmer**, PhD, is a senior research fellow and lecturer at the Institut Technik und Bildung (ITB) and deputy director of the Department of Innovation, HRD and Regional Development, both at the University of Bremen, Germany. He is also convenor for VETNET (Vocational Educational Training Network) which operates under the umbrella of EERA (European Educational Research Association). He has a diploma in electrical engineering, a master's degree in TVET, and his doctoral dissertation was on the management of regional innovation networks. In his research career he has been involved in a great number of pilot projects and research networks, such as the Design and Implementation of Curricula for Industrial Teachers and Trainers in German VET. He has been a coordinator in some of these projects. For several years he worked as a research coordinator in the regional innovation programmes, Work and Technology in the German fellow state of Bremen. He also coordinated the national programme New Learning Arrangements for Dual VET. He has published several books and a variety of articles, in particular on the relationship between organisational and technical change, vocational education and learning outcomes. This includes evaluation studies on the effects of regional and national innovation programmes on apprenticeship training. Together with other colleagues at ITB he works as a member of the INAP network on innovative apprenticeship (http://www.innovative-apprenticeship.net). E-mail: deitmer@uni-bremen.de

**Lars Heinemann**, PhD, is a senior researcher at the Institut Technik und Bildung (ITB) at the University of Bremen, Germany. He has worked in and coordinated various European and national research and development projects in the field of vocational education. Currently, he is researching cost–benefit relations and quality of vocational education in the German dual system of VET. His main areas of research and professional interest are vocational education and its formative effects on identity and commitment, evaluation and quality assurance, and learning with new media. E-mail: lheine@uni-bremen.de

**Kari Itkonen**, MA in Statistics, is a researcher in social sciences and entrepreneurship. He is currently working in the Expert Division of the School of Business and Economics at the University of Jyväskylä, Finland. His special interest is in SME (Small and Medium Sized Enterprises) policy and succession in firms. He has also conducted many studies on work-related learning, especially in the fields of vocational education. He has also produced a handbook on quality in vocational work-related learning. E-mail: itkonen@econ.jyu.fi

**Krista Loogma**, PhD, is currently the head of the Institute of Educational Research, Tallinn University, Estonia. She has academic qualifications in Electronic Engineering, Psychology, and Sociology and a PhD in Educational Sciences. She has worked in the field of management training and led a number of different research and development projects. In addition to education, labour market, and other social research areas she has also conducted interdisciplinary research and worked in the field of future studies in different scenarios and strategy projects at the national and European levels. She is also a member of various professional associations and networks, such as the European Association of Sociology, World Futures Studies Federation, European Education Research Association, VETNET network, and others. E-mail: krista.loogma@tlu.ee

**Fernando Marhuenda**, PhD, is a senior lecturer and researcher at the University of Valencia, Spain, and lectures on curriculum studies and training for employment and social inclusion at the School of Education. He has coordinated the research team on Transitions from Education and Access to Employment for Vulnerable Populations at the University of Valencia since 1996. He has directed and taken part in several research projects funded by regional and national governments as well as in the 4th and 5th EU Framework Programmes. He is currently supervising several PhD students and has authored number of national and international publications (Shaping Flexibility in VET, Reflections on Post-16 Strategies, Trabajo y Educación, Didáctica General, and others). He is a member and works with the Foundation Novaterra which supports the projects of Work Integration Social Enterprises and Social Inclusion of Vulnerable People through Work. E-mail: fernando.marhuenda@uv.es

**Mari Murtonen**, PhD, is as a senior researcher at the Centre for Learning Research, Department of Teacher Education, University of Turku, Finland. Her research topics include the development of expertise, learning and teaching in higher education, and the development of learning theory. She has published both internationally and nationally, edited books and acted as a guest editor in an international journal. She has worked in the project Integration of Work and Learning: Strategies for Connectivity and Transformation, funded by the Academy of Finland. She is currently involved in the education of university teachers. E-mail: mari.murtonen@utu.fi

**Pentti Nikkanen**, PhD, is a senior researcher at the Institute for Educational Research, University of Jyväskylä, Finland. He is also adjunct professor both in vocational education and training at the University of Tampere and in general education at the University of Oulu. His research interests are in the areas of work-related learning, transformation of individual learning into organisational learning, human resource development, effective school improvement, teacher effectiveness, curriculum development, empowerment, and tacit knowledge, among others. He has lately contributed research work in the following international projects: ESI (Effective School Improvement); FRONTEX (Common Core Curriculum for Training of Border Guards of the Member States of the European Union); ISTOF (International Study for Teacher Observation and Feedback); VIETVOC (Vocational Education Development Cooperation between Institutes in Vietnam and Finland). He has actively authored and co-authored many scientific books, articles, and research reports. He has also served as a member of the editorial board of The Finnish Journal of Vocational and Professional Education and Training (Ammattikasvatuksen aikakauskirja) since its inception. E-mail: pentti.nikkanen@ktl.jyu.fi

**Jeroen Onstenk**, PhD, is a social scientist. He worked from 1984 to 1999 as a senior researcher at the University of Amsterdam, the Netherlands. From September 1999 until the present he has been working as senior researcher at CINOP (Centre for Innovation of Education and Training), a major 'think tank' in Dutch vocational and continuing education and training. His research and consultancy topics include: new contents and new educational concepts in vocational training; apprenticeships in secondary vocational education; in-company training; concepts and good practices of on-the-job learning. His doctoral dissertation (1997) dealt with the intricate relations between working, learning and organisational innovation and the acquisition of key competencies, both in vocational education, apprenticeships, and professional practice. In 2004 he was appointed as the chair of Integrated Pedagogic Action, School of Education, Inholland Professional University. E-mail: jonstenk@inholland.nl

**Sari Sahlström**, MA in Education, was a research assistant at the University of Turku, Finland, during the project Integration of Work and Learning: Strategies for Connectivity and Transformation, funded by the Academy of Finland.

**Marja-Leena Stenström**, PhD, is a professor at the Institute for Educational Research, University of Jyväskylä, Finland, and an adjunct professor in vocational education both in the University of Tampere, Finland and University of Jyväskylä. Her research interests are vocational and higher education, and the relations between education and working life. She has led and coordinated several national and international research projects. She has also authored several scientific articles, research reports, and edited books. She has also served as a member of the editorial boards of the Journal of Career and Technical Education and The Finnish Journal of Vocational and Professional Education (Ammattikasvatuksen aikakauskirja), and as a member of the boards of The Finnish Association of Vocational Education and Training and VETNET (Vocational Education and Training Network) of EERA (The European Educational Research Association). E-mail: marja-leena.stenstrom@ktl.jyu.fi

**Päivi Tynjälä**, PhD, is a professor at the Institute for Educational Research, University of Jyväskylä, Finland. Her research has focused on teaching, learning and the development of expertise, especially in higher education but also in vocational education and training and in working life. In particular, she has specialized in studies of learning at the interface of education and work. She has led several large research projects in this field. She has published widely both internationally and nationally, and has edited the books Higher Education and Working Life (Eds. P. Tynjälä, J. Välimaa & G. Boulton-Lewis; Springer 2006) and Writing as a Learning Tool (Eds. P. Tynjälä, L. Mason & K. Lonka; Kluewer 2001). She has also served as an expert in many educational development and evaluation projects both nationally and internationally. She is a member of the editorial board of the two newly launched journals – Vocations and Learning: Studies in Vocational and Professional Education, and the Journal of Writing Research. She is also a member of the review panel of the British Journal of Educational Technology. Email: paivi.tynjala@ktl.jyu.fi

**Maarit Virolainen**, MA in Social Sciences, has been working as a researcher at the Institute for Educational Research, University of Jyväskylä, Finland since 1996. Her research interests relate to developing vocational education and training and professional higher education. She has recently been studying the cooperation with working life of the Finnish polytechnics in two research projects, Cooperation between Polytechnics and Working Life, funded by the Finnish Ministry of Education, and Integration of Work and Learning: Strategies for Connectivity and Transformation. E-mail: maarit.virolainen@ktl.jyu.fi

**Matti Vesa Volanen**, MA in Psychology and Philosophy, is a senior researcher at the Institute for Educational Research, University of Jyväskylä, Finland. He has worked on various projects including Transition from School to Work, organized by the Vienna Centre (1984–1986); Vocational and Technical Education in OECD Countries (VOTEC), organized by the OECD (1992–1995); Network on Transitions in Youth, organized by the European Science Foundation (1993–1996); Finding New Strategies for Post-16 Education by Networking Vocational and Academic/General Education (Leonardo project, 1996–1998); Social Individualization and *Poiesis* (Finnish Academy, 1998–2001); and Philosophy in Engineering (2005–2006). He has studied initial vocational education, the school-to-work transition, and the academic/vocational relationship in education, particularly their theoretical aspects. He is currently working on the topics of *philotechne* and the development processes of Finnish polytechnics. E-mail: matti.vesa. volanen@ktl.jyu.fi

# Part I
# Theoretical Perspectives: New Paradigms of Work and Learning

# Chapter 1
# Introduction

Marja-Leena Stenström and Päivi Tynjälä

## Changing Working Life as a Challenge to Education

Recent macro-level trends, such as economic globalisation, the development of the information society, changes in methods of production and the organisation of work, and the growing significance of knowledge as a factor of production, have created a new context for the relationship between education and working life. In this new context, the use of work experience as an educational and learning strategy has become one of the most important developments both in vocational education and training (VET) and in higher education. Although the tradition of making work an integral part of education has varied at different levels of the educational system, the challenges that systems of education currently face are very similar in many respects. These include the challenge of *equivalence* as regards the level of academic standards, the challenge of developing *pedagogical practices* for different forms of work-related learning, and the impact that work-related learning has on the *identity* of the educational organisation, the teacher, and the learner. The diversity of the systems through which work experience is realised, the varying levels of training of workplace trainers, and the lack of industrial experience of vocational school teachers have aroused discussion about how to guarantee and assess the quality of the learning taking place in different workplaces and of the work-based learning system as a whole. (See e.g. Boud & Solomon, 2001, p. 27; Griffiths & Guile, 2004; Guile & Griffiths, 2001.)

The key pedagogical question regarding collaboration between education and work is how to build a firm connection between theory and practice or abstract thinking and practical action – and between the development of general skills and specific vocational skills. In this book we suggest that connective learning situations involving individuals, work communities, organisations, and institutions constitute learning spaces which open up opportunities for transformations of various kinds (cf. Evans & Rainbird, 2002; Young & Volanen, 2000). The main idea underlying our book is that by connecting activities that have hitherto been kept separate we can create the potential for transformational processes.

M.-L. Stenström (✉)
Institute for Educational Research, University of Jyväskylä, Jyväskylä, Finland
e-mail: marja-leena.stenstrom@ktl.jyu.fi

M.-L. Stenström, P. Tynjälä (eds.), *Towards Integration of Work and Learning*,
© Springer Science+Business Media B.V. 2009

## Aims of the Book

The purpose of this book is to describe the learning taking place in the interface between education and working life: (1) at the level of the individual learning processes, (2) at the level of the organisational learning processes in educational institutions and work organisations, and (3) at the level of the educational system (see Fig. 1.1). The theoretical concepts uniting these different fields of learning are *connectivity* and *transformation*. These concepts are dealt with in more detail by Päivi Tynjälä in Chapter 2. In brief, by connectivity we refer to those processes which aim at creating close relationships and connections between different elements of learning situations, contexts of learning, and systems aiming at promoting learning. By transformation we mean the changes and developmental processes that flow from connecting different elements of learning.

The book provides a comprehensive introduction to the issue of the integration of work and learning, which is central to the current debate over the development of vocational and professional expertise. Different approaches from such disciplines as education, social science, and economics are presented. The contributors represent a broad range of experience in the field of work-related learning from VET to higher education and workplace training. The chapters are based on recent, wide-ranging empirical studies on work-related learning in Europe. According to the Lisbon strategy Europe is aiming at becoming "the most competitive and dynamic knowledge-based economy in the world capable of sustainable economic growth with more and better jobs and greater social cohesion". This means that European education systems need to adapt to the demands of the knowledge society. Here one

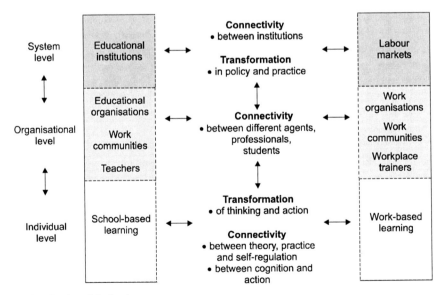

**Fig. 1.1** Design of the book

of the most important issues concerns how to enable lifelong learning, including both formal education and informal work-based learning. Social partnerships and co-operation between education and working life play a crucial role in this effort. The chapters that comprise this book present cases from five European countries of how partnerships have been organised and learning is connected with working to bring about transformation both in individuals' competencies and at the organisational and system level.

Many of the contributors come from Finland, a country which has been rated among the world leaders in international competitiveness. The Finnish model of the information and knowledge society has shown that a highly developed welfare state is not incompatible with technological innovation (Castells & Himanen, 2002). A high standard of education and a close relationship between education and industry are considered key factors in economic development. In this respect, the chapters present models of integrating work and learning in both Finnish VET and higher education.

While the Finnish VET system is a mainly school-based model in which workplace training is given as part of the qualifications, the German VET system rests on the dual model in which working life has a major responsibility for training the future workforce. Students are employees of the companies during their training. This presents a major challenge for partnerships in workplace learning: How can these partnerships provide the best possible conditions for developing vocational expertise with a high level of both theoretical and practical knowledge? The chapter on the German system presents a model for evaluating partnerships between education and work. The model can be applied in other school systems as well.

The third country represented here is the Netherlands, which is actively contributing to strengthening the European knowledge society. In the Dutch educational system combinations of school-based and work-based learning are integrated into a single national qualification structure. There is a full-time route that includes work placements and there is a part-time work-based route which combines part-time education with an apprenticeship in the company. Work experience is a compulsory component in Dutch adult education to guarantee the relevance of the courses and practice, and thus of the connection between education and working life. The chapter representing the Dutch system focuses, in particular, on apprenticeship in adult education.

The fourth European country which is represented in the book is Spain, where much effort has been put into developing social enterprises, that is, companies which aim not only to make a profit but also to diminish the marginalisation of uneducated people and to provide opportunities for them to join the labour market. Similar enterprises have been developed in many other European countries as well; here, they serve as a model for integrating work and learning for social purposes.

The rapid change taking place in working life is a reality all over the industrial world. One of the chapters is devoted to the issue of how workers adapt to these changes and what strategies they develop to cope with new conditions of work. An empirical study on this topic comes from Estonia, also a rising economy and a new EU member state.

With these cases representing different education systems and a variety of ways of organising work-related learning the book provides a collage of current models of integrating work and learning in European VET and higher education. Although several books (Boud & Solomon, 2001; Evans, Hodkinson, & Unwin, 2002; Illeris & Associates, 2004; Rainbird, Fuller, & Munro, 2004; Streumer, 2006; Tuomi-Gröhn & Engeström, 2003; Tynjälä, Välimaa, & Boulton, 2006) have been published recently that relate to the present topic (work and learning), the focus of our book is specially the ideas of connectivity and transformation.

## Structure of the Book

Part I introduces readers to the main ideas of the book and presents the *general theoretical framework common to all chapters*. In addition to this common framework, each chapter draws on theoretical or practical models specific to the educational system in question.

This *introductory* chapter written by Marja-Leena Stenström and Päivi Tynjälä describes the background of the book and presents an overview of each chapter at a general level. It is emphasised that, owing to rapid changes in society and working life, learning at the workplace has become a necessity for both individuals and organisations.

In Chapter 2 Päivi Tynjälä introduces the general *theoretical foundations* of the book by analysing the key concepts of *connectivity and transformation*. The idea of transformation is present in most learning theories, although different approaches use different theoretical concepts. These vary from those which refer to changes in thinking, such as conceptual change and transformative learning, to those which emphasise changes in actions or practices, such as expansive learning or innovative learning. The principle of connectivity refers to making connections at both individual and institutional levels. In connective learning situations, connections are made between different forms of knowledge, between different actors, and between learning that takes place in different contexts. It is shown how connectivity may contribute to the transformation of learning at the level both of individual learning and of organisations and systems.

Chapter 3 by Matti Vesa Volanen presents *a paradigm for the connective curriculum* through the concepts *being, doing, and making*. The starting point of this chapter is the notion of vocational competence as a combination of three basic elements, theory, praxis, and poiesis, which can be described as acts of being, doing, and making. The basic intention in this chapter is to analyse all three elements together – thereby showing the connective relationships between structures, policy, and curriculum. Thus a new perspective can be opened up on the relationship between the vocational and academic traditions. As we see, it is possible to integrate them in such a way that they enrich each other.

In Part II "*Integrating Work and Learning in Individual Experiences*", research findings from studies on individual learning at work are presented. First, the nature of workplace learning is described through the voices of employees – on the one hand those who are in a regular position and on the other those who experience a threat of marginalisation. Second, examples of how the integration of work and learning can be realised in educational contexts are presented.

Chapter 4, *"Connecting Work and Learning in Industrial Design and Development"*, by Kaija Collin discusses individual learning at the workplace in the light of a study of Finnish design engineers' and product developers' learning through their work. The work practices and learning of these occupational groups in the course of their everyday work are described as they themselves perceive them. The chapter also examines their learning through the various individual and social processes transpiring at the workplace. The findings suggest that in redefining designers' work and learning, four central themes are important: (1) design practice is learning in itself; (2) there is a close relationship between formal and practical knowledge in designers' learning at work; (3) previous work experience plays an essential role in learning; and (4) design practices and learning should be seen as shared, situated, and contextualised. It is concluded that vocabulary borrowed from formal education is not always necessarily appropriate suited to describing learning at work.

Chapter 5 also describes learning at work, but from a different point of view. Fernando Marhuenda's chapter deals with *Work Integration Social Enterprises (WISE)*, which are companies set up in Spain with the main purpose of providing jobs for people who have not been able to find employment in an ordinary firm even if they have the capacity to be productive. Marhuenda points first to the main results of the research done on WISEs, in order to put them into an educational perspective. Second, he introduces two organisations promoting WISEs, paying particular attention to the work processes they use in order to achieve their goal of social integration and to perform their related tasks. Third, he examines the work of one WISE organisation to show how they address educational processes.

Chapter 6 *"Educating Novices at the Workplace: Transformation of Conceptions and Skills of Students on a Metal Industry Course"* contributed by Mari Murtonen, Sari Sahlström, and Päivi Tynjälä also presents an example of individual learning but now from the perspective of students. The chapter examines the case of a company-based training programme for shipyard workers from the viewpoint of expertise development. The authors look at whether the connective model of work experience is present in a metal industry course run by the company at the workplace and how in this authentic work environment the vocational expertise of students is developed. In their analyses they utilise ideas drawn from two different lines of research: the classical studies of expertise and studies of conceptual change. This is a new way to approach vocational development as the theory of conceptual change has hardly been applied in research on work-based learning.

Part III *"From Individual Learning to Organisational Development"* turns the focus from individual learning toward organisational learning. It is important to consider how work organisations function because it is the larger work communities that broadly define the conditions for individual learning.

Chapter 7 *"Transformation of Individual Learning into Organisational and Networked Learning in Vocational Education"* by Päivi Tynjälä and Pentti Nikkanen describes the basic elements of organisational learning and its most recent form, network learning. Networked organisational learning is illustrated with an example from a recent study on networking and collaboration between vocational education institutions and working life organisations in Central Finland. In particular, the aim was to examine whether such co-operation generates innovative practices and leads to functioning networks with knowledge-creation capacity. Can these networks be characterised as "innovative knowledge communities"?

Chapter 8 *"Evaluation Approaches for Workplace Learning Partnerships in VET: Investigating the Learning Dimension"* by Ludger Deitmer and Lars Heinemann analyses the role of system evaluation and evaluation methods current in the field of VET in Germany. It is argued that the adaptation of newer evaluation approaches could be helpful in seeking to optimise the learning processes underlying successful VET, where this is implemented in collaboration with other regional stakeholders, such as workplace learning partners in local industries. First, the article briefly discusses the role evaluation used to play (and still plays) in VET. It also takes up the question of how networks of learning partnerships could be evaluated. Typically, these networks cross organisational boundaries and involve many different actors, and thus cannot be evaluated by instruments which centre on individual learner/teacher frameworks. The chapter then presents an overview on what evaluation methods are being used and from what perspectives for what purposes. In addition, aspects of VET that could be interesting subjects of evaluation are considered, including the dimension of collaborative learning in a workplace learning partnership. An example of a formative method of evaluation is given to show the potential of such evaluation instruments for VET. Finally, the authors offer suggestions as to how these evaluation methods could be put into practise.

Chapter 9 *"Developing Entrepreneurship in Small Enterprises – The Succession Process Supported by Apprenticeship Training as a Context for Learning"* by Kari Itkonen describes the ownership change process in a family firm as an example of integrating work and learning. This topic is dealt with from the perspective of theories of entrepreneurship and learning and on the basis of an empirical study of an apprenticeship training course tailored to meet the needs of entrepreneurs who were going through a succession process. Special attention is paid to the learning process connected with change of ownership and to the transformation achieved through the succession process on the three levels of the individual, the group, and the organisation.

In Part IV the transformational and connective processes are examined at the level of education systems. The focus is on the connection between education and working life and on the transformations that are currently taking place in this connection.

In Chapter 10, *"How Workers Cope with Changes in Working Life: Adaptation Strategies"*, by Krista Loogma the aim is to explain by what mechanisms workers cope with changes in working life driven by transformation processes at the societal level. The main question is how employees have coped with the contradictory demands of the labour market and what strategies they have applied. The principal change processes are described within the Estonian context. Transformation is treated as a combination of "revolutionary" transition processes (accompanied by the discontinuity of many trends in the economy and society) and "evolutionary" transformation processes (caused by the global-scale need to move into the knowledge/information era). The fast process of transformation, involving changes in the labour market, enterprises, and educational institutions, has implications for the demand and supply of skills and competencies as well as on the career and mobility patterns of labour.

Chapter 11, by Jeroen Onstenk, deals with *"Connections of School- and Work-Based Learning in the Netherlands"*. The Dutch VET system offers students a choice between school-based and work-based pathways. During recent years attempts have been made to establish models of vocational education which are more connective and which are characterised by the new practice- and competence-oriented approach introduced across the whole curriculum. Pedagogical solutions emphasise self-directed learning, the development of problem-solving competences, and individual coaching and guidance rather than frontal teaching in the classroom or simply launching students into the workplace. Onstenk examines the ways in which workplace learning is organised in both pathways and analyses the quality both of workplace learning and of the connections between school and work. He concludes that quality is not always guaranteed and that there is room for improvement in the integration of school-based and workplace learning.

In Chapter 12, *"Work Experience Constructed by Polytechnics, Students, and Working Life: Spaces for Connectivity and Transformation"*, by Maarit Virolainen the concepts of connectivity and transformation are discussed in the context of organising workplace placements as part of professional higher education. The chapter discusses the idealism of the connective model with respect to the results of empirical studies in Finnish polytechnics (or universities of applied sciences; equivalent to the German Fachhochschule). The aim of the chapter is to examine how well patterns of professional higher education conform to the model of connectivity. First, the relevance of paying attention to the model of connectivity on the level of higher education is discussed. Second, the concepts of integration and transformation are specified. The differences between them are found to be important because they are related to longstanding questions regarding differences between learning at school and learning at work. Third, the framework for organising placements in the interface of school and work in the Finnish polytechnics is discussed.

While Chapter 12 focussed on the connection between higher education and working life, Chapter 13, *"Connecting Work and Learning Through Demonstrations of Vocational Skills – Experiences from the Finnish VET"*, by Marja-Leena Stenström seeks to illuminate the relationships between vocational education and the world of work, especially in Finnish vocational education. With a view to developing co-operation between vocational education and working life and assuring the quality of vocational education, a system of workplace learning was recently introduced along with vocational skills demonstrations in Finland. In this country, VET has traditionally mainly been school-based, which means that these developments mark a radical change in this field of education. Competence-based examinations have been used mostly in countries where vocational education is driven by working life. Enhancing the work-related learning system through pilot projects on the implementation of vocational skills demonstrations is a development that reflects the current process of change in the relationship between working life and VET.

Altogether, the different perspectives on work-related learning presented by case studies in this book indicate that the relationships between education and the world of work are going through a fundamental transformation. Changes are taking place in educational policies, in the structure of education systems, in the form and content of curricula, and in pedagogical practices. The work of teachers has moved outside classroom instruction to networking with workplaces and collaborating with workplace instructors. It is important for the research community to subject these developments to critical analysis. This book is one attempt in this direction, and we hope that it will stimulate further research into new perspectives and questions as well as into this fascinating field of study.

# References

Boud, D., & Solomon, N. (2001). Repositioning universities and work. In D. Boud & N. Solomon (Eds.), *Work-based learning. A new higher education?* (pp. 18–33). Buckingham, England: Society for Research into Higher Education & Open University Press.

Evans, K., & Rainbird, H. (2002). The significance of workplace learning for a "learning society". In K. Evans, P. Hodkinson, & L. Unwin (Eds.), *Working to learn: Transforming learning in the workplace* (pp. 7–28). London: Kogan Page.

Evans, K., Hodkinson, P., & Unwin, L. (Eds.). (2002). *Working to learn: Transforming learning in the workplace*. London: Kogan Page.

Castells, M., & Himanen, P. (2002). *The information society and the welfare state: The Finnish model*. Oxford: Oxford University Press.

Griffiths. T., & Guile, D. (2004). *Learning through work experience for the knowledge economy: Issues for educational research and policy*. CEDEFOP. Luxembourg: Office for Official Publications of the European Communities.

Guile, D., & Griffiths, T. (2001). Learning through work experience. *Journal of Education and Work 14*, 113–131.

Illeris, K., & Associates. (2004). *Learning in working life*. Frederiksberg: Roskilde University Press.

Rainbird, H., Fuller, A., & Munro, A. (Eds.). (2004). *Workplace learning in context*. London: Routledge.

Streumer, J. N. (Ed.). (2006). *Work-related learning*. Dordrecht: Springer.

Tuomi-Gröhn., T., & Engeström, Y. (Eds.). (2003). *Between school and work. New perspectives on transfer and boundary-crossing*. Amsterdam: Pergamon.

Tynjälä, P., Välimaa., J., & Boulton-Lewis, G. (Eds.). (2006). *Higher education and working life: Collaborations, confrontations and challenges*. Advances in Learning and Instruction Series. Amsterdam: Elsevier.

Young, M., & Volanen, M.V. (2000). Towards a vocational curriculum and pedagogy of the future: Taking the post-16 strategies and SPES-NET project findings forward for future research. In M.-L. Stenström & J. Lasonen (Eds.), *Strategies for reforming initial vocational education and training in Europe* (pp. 258–265). Institute for Educational Research. University of Jyväskylä.

# Chapter 2
# Connectivity and Transformation in Work-Related Learning – Theoretical Foundations

Päivi Tynjälä

## Introduction: Connectivity and Transformation as Principles of Work-Related Learning

Traditionally the concept of "learning" has been related to formal education, whereas its use in the context of work is quite a new phenomenon. The interest of researchers and work organisations in learning taking place at the workplace has expanded since the beginning of 1990s, and the research on this area is now very extensive and interdisciplinary. The reason for this expansion is the unprecedented rapid change in society and working life during the past few decades. The fast pace of development of information and communications technology, the growing production of knowledge in the economy, increasing internationalisation and globalisation as well as changes in occupational structures and contents and in the organisation of work have challenged not only educational institutions but also work organisations to find new ways to ensure that the level of competence of the workforce meets the demands of the changing world of work. Thus, continuous learning has become important both for individuals operating in the learning society and for organisations competing on international markets.

Recent research on the outcomes of education, particularly at the tertiary level, has shown that there is a gap between the knowledge needed at work and the knowledge and skills produced through formal education. For example, Eraut (2004a) has questioned the transfer of knowledge from education to the workplace. Empirical studies support Eraut's critical view. Two separate studies on university and polytechnic graduates with 2–10 years work experience produced surprisingly similar findings: both university and polytechnic graduates found their working life skills inadequate, and the majority of them stated that they had learnt the necessary skills at work and not during their formal education (Stenström, 2006; Tynjälä, Slotte, Nieminen, Lonka, & Olkinuora, 2006). In this book we argue that the major source

P. Tynjälä (✉)
Institute for Educational Research, University of Jyväskylä, Jyväskylä, Finland
e-mail: paivi.tynjala@ktl.jyu.fi

M.-L. Stenström, P. Tynjälä (eds.), *Towards Integration of Work and Learning*,
© Springer Science+Business Media B.V. 2009

of the problem is the traditional separation between work and learning and that the remedy for the problem is the better integration of these domains.

This chapter presents the theoretical foundations of our argument for the integration of learning and work, and collaboration between schools and workplaces. The core concepts are *connectivity*, which refers to bringing together things that have earlier been separated, and *transformation*, which refers to the changes that take place through connective activities. Our ideas about these concepts can be summarised in three statements which we then examine in detail: (1) development of vocational and professional expertise requires integration of different forms of knowledge; (2) the connective model of work experience presented by Guile & Griffiths (2001) supports the integration of knowledge; and (3) connectivity leads to transformations at the level both of individual learning and of the learning of organisations and systems. Our conclusion is that it is important to consider the workplace as a learning environment for both employees and students, in order to ensure the continuous development of competence. This requires close collaboration and partnership between education and work.

## Vocational Expertise Requires Integration of Knowledge

In this section, on the basis of recent accounts on the components of vocational and professional expertise, we describe what elements expertise consists of and how it is constructed. We begin by presenting in detail these accounts of the components of expert knowledge and go on to compare and summarise them. Finally, on the basis of our analysis, we present a model of vocational expertise that emphasises the integration of different forms of knowledge.

### *An Analysis of Expert Knowledge by Carl Bereiter*

The first psychological studies on expertise divided expert knowledge into two basic categories, *declarative knowledge* and *procedural knowledge* (Anderson, 1983). The concept of declarative knowledge refers to explicit knowledge that can be expressed in words, figures, numbers, or other symbols. Procedural knowledge, in contrast, finds its expression in practical skills. Ryle (1949) and Bereiter and Scardamalia (1993, p. 49) labelled declarative knowledge *knowing-about* and procedural knowledge *knowing-how*. Declarative knowledge can be described as factual, conceptual or theoretical knowledge, while procedural knowledge is practical and often implicit in nature. Both forms of knowledge are important but, as Bereiter (2002, p. 132) has stated, they are not enough; people also need knowledge that links knowing-about and knowing-how together. This kind of knowledge can arise only in situations where declarative knowledge is used to solve practical problems. We shall discuss this issue later on.

According to Bereiter (2002), although the categories of declarative and procedural knowledge can usefully be applied to the different components of expertise, this dichotomy leaves out a vast range of knowledge that does not clearly belong in either category. Consequently, he presents a broader classification of types of expert knowledge:

1) Statable knowledge. This category largely corresponds to the concept of declarative knowledge in the previous typology by Bereiter and Scardamalia (1993), and thus refers to knowledge that can be put into some explicit form.

2) Implicit understanding. As the label indicates, this type of knowledge is unstated, tacit knowledge. We acquire implicit understanding through our experience, not through reading from books. That is why it remains implicit. The role of experiential tacit knowledge is very important in high level expertise (Dreyfus & Dreyfus, 1986).

3) Episodic knowledge. This type of knowledge is also born out of experience. Studies on human memory have made a distinction between semantic memory and episodic memory, and Bereiter (2002, p. 140) applies this to the analysis of expert knowledge. In the episodic memory are the different episodes, events, cases and narratives from our past. Research on expertise has shown that much of the reasoning and decisions made in occupational situations is based on repertoires of previous cases.

4) Impressionistic knowledge. Beyond statable knowledge and implicit understanding lie many kinds of feelings and impressions that also influence our actions. Impressionistic knowledge can be seen as extremely vague implicit understanding, and it is expressed in feelings or intuitions. Bereiter (2002, p. 131) refers to a line by a young stockbroker in Walker Percy's *The Movie Goer*: "I woke up that morning with a good feeling about American Motors". A prerequisite for having such feelings is a great amount of experience in the field in question.

5) Skill. In Bereiter and Scardamalia (1993) previous classification this category was labelled procedural knowledge, but in the revised taxonomy Bereiter (2002, pp. 137, 143) sees "procedural" as a particular class of skills characterised by explicit steps. Skills have a cognitive and sub-cognitive component, although intertwined. The cognitive component is knowing-how – being able to do things – while the sub-cognitive part is the improvement in skill that comes with practice.

6) Regulative knowledge. In their previous version, Bereiter and Scardamalia called this type of knowledge self-regulative knowledge. Now, however, they extend the scope of knowledge beyond the regulation of one's own activities. Self-regulative knowledge involves metacognitive knowledge about one's own ways of doing and thinking, strengths and weaknesses, while regulative knowledge pertains to collective activity as well, involving the principles and ideals which certain professional groups pursue in order to accomplish their work.

According to Bereiter (2002, p. 148), competence in any domain involves all six kinds of knowledge. However, Bereiter emphasises that in high level expertise these types of knowledge are not separate but they are tightly integrated into a whole: the per the expertise is, the deeper the integration between the forms of knowledge becomes.

In addition to the forms of personal knowledge described above there is also socio-cultural knowledge that is embedded in the tools and practices of social communities (Bereiter, 2002; Wenger, 1998). This knowledge is often tacit but it can be explicated as well. For example, written rules of action and procedures documented in quality manuals represent explicit socio-cultural knowledge.

## A Typology of Knowledge Demonstrated by Beginning Professionals

Le Maistre and Paré (2006) investigated the transition from university to workplace in four professions: education, occupational therapy, physiotherapy, and social work. On the basis of their interviews with final year students, recently graduated students in their first two years at work, and their experienced colleagues they presented a typology of professional knowledge (Fig. 2.1).

The model posits two main categories of knowledge: *professional knowledge* and *personal knowledge*. Personal knowledge corresponds to Bereiter and Scardamalia (1993) self-regulative knowledge including self-knowledge (knowledge of one-self as a performer and learner) and metacognition (involving self-knowledge and self-assessment). Professional knowledge is divided into three categories: *content knowledge* (that corresponds to declarative knowledge), *procedural knowledge*, and *knowledge about one's profession*. Procedural knowledge includes knowledge about implementing different procedures, knowledge about clients and psychomotor knowledge which pertains to, for example, touch in physiotherapy, or the stance or voice of a teacher in front of the class. Knowledge about one's profession concerns the attributes of that profession and knowledge of the organisation. The

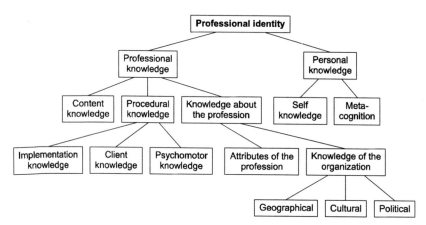

**Fig. 2.1** The knowledge involved in the development of professional identity (Le Maistre & Paré, 2006, p. 107)

latter is further divided into three sub-categories: geographical, cultural and political knowledge. When the categories by Le Maiste and Paré are compared with those of Bereiter (2002), strong resemblances can be seen: professional content knowledge resembles statable knowledge, procedural knowledge resembles skill, and personal knowledge resembles regulative knowledge. Like Bereiter, the authors emphasise that the acquisition of professional expertise requires the integration of all identified types of knowledge.

## Transfer of Knowledge from School to Work: Michael Eraut's View

Eraut (2004a) has examined the types of knowledge used in the educational context and in the workplace, and has suggested the following categorisations.

The kinds of knowledge which *vocational and professional education programmes* claim to provide are:

1) *Theoretical knowledge*, which introduces concepts and theories;
2) *Methodological knowledge* about how evidence is collected, analysed and interpreted;
3) *Practical skills* acquired through laboratory work, project work etc;
4) *Generic skills* claimed to be acquired during education, either through direct teaching or as a side-effect of academic work. These include basic skills in number, language and information technology, communication skills, learning skills and self-management skills;
5) *General knowledge about occupation.*

Eraut (2004a, p. 206) claims that although most of these types of knowledge are described as transferable, there is little evidence of the extent to which types 2, 4 and 5 are acquired by students and about the chances of 1 and 3 being subsequently transferred (or not) to the workplace. Eraut continues his analysis by presenting *the modes of knowledge found in the workplace*:

1) *Codified knowledge* acquired during initial professional training and further episodes of formal learning or in the workplace itself. The former includes codified academic knowledge and concepts, theories and methodology. The latter includes job-specific technical knowledge and knowledge of systems and procedures.
2) *Skills* needed in the job: technical, interpersonal, thinking and learning.
3) *Knowledge resources* including materials and on-line resources, and especially other people, i.e. colleagues, clients, networks, etc.
4) *Understanding*, involving understanding of other people, situations and contexts, strategic understanding etc.
5) *Decision making and judgement* which vary with the context: decisions may be rapid, with little time for analysis or consultation, or deliberative and consultative.

Comparison of the knowledge used in education and the workplace reveals that education programmes pay little attention to many forms of knowledge important at work. One reason for this is that these forms of knowledge are largely context-specific and their acquisition requires participation in workplace practices. Therefore Eraut (2004a, p. 220) criticises separation of theory and practice in many programmes and calls for more integrated models.

## *Summary of the Components of Expertise*

The accounts of the elements of vocational and professional expertise are summarised in Table 2.1. In the bottom row of the table are gathered the features that are common to each type of knowledge described by the different authors. On the basis of this summary we can conclude that vocational and professional expertise is constructed of the following elements:

I. Personal knowledge:

1. *Factual, conceptual and theoretical knowledge*, this is universal and explicit knowledge;
2. *Experiential and practical knowledge*, this concerns particular cases and is often implicit but may be also explicit. This knowledge finds its expression in skills and to some extent in narratives;
3. *Regulative knowledge*, including metacognition and self-reflection. This knowledge may be either implicit or explicit, and it includes both "knowledge" and "skills" components.

II. Socio-cultural knowledge

Knowledge embedded in social practices, environments, tools and devices.

Common to all the analyses of expert knowledge described above is that although the components of expertise can be analytically discerned, they are not to be seen as separate parts of expertise. Instead, all the authors emphasise that in high level expertise the different components are tightly interwoven. This notion has important implications for pedagogical practices: Since expertise consists of integrated elements of theoretical, practical and regulative knowledge, the development of expertise also requires the integration of these elements. A model of integrative pedagogy is presented in Fig. 2.2.

The pedagogical model presented in Fig. 2.2 is based on the analysis of expert knowledge outlined in the previous section (Bereiter, 2002; Bereiter & Scardamalia, 1993; Eraut, 2004a; Le Maistre & Paré, 2006) and the notion of the situated nature of learning (Lave & Wenger, 1991; Wenger, 1998). In Fig. 2.2 the basic elements of expertise, that is, theoretical knowledge, practical knowledge and regulative knowledge, are presented in shaded boxes. As described above, theoretical knowledge is universal, formal and explicit in nature. It can be easily explicated, for example in

Table 2.1 Recent descriptions of the components of vocational and professional expertise

| Author | Forms of personal knowledge | | | | | | |
|---|---|---|---|---|---|---|---|
| | Declarative knowledge | Procedural knowledge | Episodic knowledge | Implicit understanding | Impressionistic knowledge | Regulative knowledge | Socio-cultural knowledge |
| Anderson | Declarative knowledge | Procedural knowledge | | | | | |
| Bereiter | Statable knowledge | Skill | Episodic knowledge | Implicit understanding | Impressionistic knowledge | Regulative knowledge | Knowledge embedded in socio-cultural practices and devices used |
| Le Maistre and Paré | (Professional) content knowledge Knowledge about occupation: geographical, cultural, political | Procedural knowledge, implementation knowledge, client knowledge, psychomotor knowledge | | | | Personal knowledge: Self-knowledge + metacognition | |
| Eraut: Knowledge at the workplace | Encoded knowledge | Skills | | Understanding | | Decision making and judgement | Knowledge embedded in resources and materials |

**Table 2.1** (continued)

| Author | Forms of personal knowledge | | | | | Socio-cultural knowledge |
|---|---|---|---|---|---|---|
| Eraut: Knowledge in educational contexts | Theoretical knowledge, methodological knowledge, general knowledge about occupation | Practical skills, generic skills | | | | Socio-cultural knowledge |
| Summary | Explicit, factual, conceptual and theoretical knowledge | Practical and experiential knowledge (often tacit) = skills | Experiential, explicit knowledge | Experiential, intuitive, tacit knowledge | Regulative knowledge metacognition and reflection) | Socio-cultural knowledge |

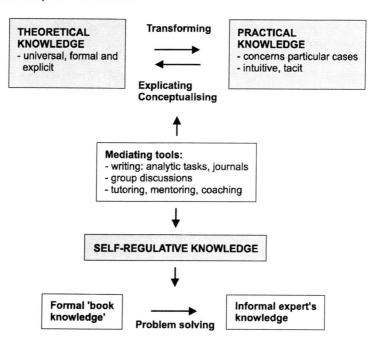

**Fig. 2.2** The model of integrative pedagogy (Tynjälä et al., 2006)

books and lectures. In contrast, practical knowledge that we gain through hands-on experiences concerns particular cases – it is not universal in the sense that theoretical knowledge is. Practical knowledge (often referred to as procedural knowledge or simply as skills) is often not easy to explicate; it is rather intuitive, implicit or tacit in nature. The arrows running between the boxes symbolising theoretical and practical knowledge in Fig. 2.2 illustrate the significance of interaction and integration of these different types of knowledge. For example, Gaie Leinhardt and her colleagues (Leinhardt, McCarthy Young, & Merriman, 1995) have emphasised that professional education should involve, on the one hand, the transformation of theoretical knowledge into a form where it becomes available for use in particular cases, and, on the other hand, the explication and conceptualisation of tacit knowledge derived from work experience. In other words, theories should be considered in the light of practical experiences and practical experiences in the light of theories. While traditional education has treated them separately (e.g. theoretical courses and practice periods have been carried out separately without any purposive link between them), modern pedagogical thinking emphasises the unity of theory and practice (Griffiths & Guile, 2003; Guile & Griffiths, 2001; Tynjälä, Välimaa, & Sarja, 2003).

Besides theoretical and practical knowledge, the third constituent of expertise is regulative knowledge, which includes metacognitive and reflective skills and the more general regulative principles in each domain (Bereiter and Scardamalia, 1993; Bereiter, 2002). Linking the development of self-regulation with theory and practice is shown at the center of Fig. 2.2. To integrate theory and practice *mediating tools*

needed. All the activities that enable students to make tacit knowledge explicit
analyse theoretical knowledge and practical experience are potential mediating
tools. These include, for instance, discussions with a tutor, mentor or a small group,
or such writing assignments as analytic tasks, portfolios, and self-assessment tasks.
During their apprenticeship students may also write a learning journal to reflect on
their work and learning. These kinds of activities allow students to develop their
self-regulatory knowledge in the context provided by the knowledge and problem
domain of their future profession.

According to Eraut (2004a, p. 215) recognising what theory is needed in any
particular situation is mainly learned through participation in practice and getting
feedback on one's actions. Most components of a practitioner's theoretical repertoire
remain dormant until triggered by a very specific aspect of the situation. Therefore
it is important that theoretical knowledge is used in solving practical problems.
Bereiter and Scardamalia (1993) have stated that *problem-solving* is the very essence
of developing expertise. According to them, formal knowledge is turned into skills
when it is used to solve practical problems and into informal knowledge when it is
used to solve problems of understanding (Bereiter & Scardamalia, 1993, p. 66). The
process of integrating theory, practice, and self-regulation can be seen as a problem-
solving process where students simultaneously need to solve practical problems and
related conceptual problems, that is, problems of understanding. This is illustrated
at the bottom of Fig. 2.2. Eraut (2004a, p. 220) has pointed out that in some professional training programmes the separation of theory and practice components
over time and space militates against their integration. Vocational programmes are
often organised around qualification frameworks that specify knowledge and competence separately, without giving any attention to the linkage between them or to
how knowledge use might be assessed. According to Eraut, more integrated programmes could make a real difference. In particular the introduction of a practice
development role that incorporates responsibility for both students and new staff
and the facilitation of continuing learning in the workplace by experienced staff
should be considered. Eraut states that until the nature and importance of transfer
is recognised and supported in this way, the impact of education on the workplace
will continue to be lower than expected and the quality of work will suffer from the
limited use of relevant knowledge.

## The Connective Model of Work Experience Supports Integration of Knowledge

In the previous section it was shown that studies on expertise consistently suggest
that profound vocational and professional expertise is based on the tight integration of different kinds of knowledge. In this section we present the connective
model of work experience proposed by Guile and Griffiths (2001) and Griffiths and
Guile (2003) which in our view represents a promising approach to an integrative
pedagogy targeted at developing vocational and professional expertise.

Guile and Griffiths (2001) have analysed the different models of the relationship between learning that occurs within and between education and work and have identified five main models of work experience. In brief, they are:

*The traditional model*: The students are simply "launched" into the workplace where they have to adjust to the requirements of the job. In this model it is assumed that learning occurs automatically, so there is no need for any special guidance or facilitation. Instead, work experience is managed through traditional supervision. There is only minimal amount of co-operation between vocational institutions and the workplace, the role of the education and training provider being purely to deliver a formal preparation programme. There is a sharp division between formal and informal learning.

*The experiential model*: In this model, and according to the experiential learning theories (Kolb, 1984), reflection on the work experience has an important role in the learning process. However, rather than reflection here Guile and Griffiths emphasise the student's interpersonal and social development, setting this at the forefront of the work experience agenda. (Probably they see reflection here as an inherent element in supporting the student's development). Positing the student's development as the central aim of work experience has led to greater dialogue and co-operation between education providers and workplaces. The aim is not only to adapt students to the world of work but also to support their self-awareness, and economic and industrial awareness. Supervision can be described as arms-length supervision, and the role of the education provider is in briefing and de-briefing students regarding their of work-experience placements.

*The generic model*: In this model work experience is seen as an opportunity for developing and assessing the generic skills needed in working life. Thus, the emphasis is on learning outcomes. Students build a personal portfolio to show their development in acquiring key skills. Students also take part in the assessment of their skills. The teachers' and education provider's role is to facilitate this process. The aim is to support students' self-management. This outcome-based model is recognisable in the vocational education and training system used in the UK.

*The work process model*: Here the aim is that the students develop a holistic understanding of the work process and work context. The idea is that the students adjust themselves to the changing context of work through the opportunity to participate in different communities of practice and this way to develop the capacity to transfer knowledge and skills gained in one work context to another. The model requires the integration of theoretical and practical learning, and hence collaboration between vocational institutions and the workplace is important. Work experience is managed by coaching students, and the role of the education and training provider is to support reflection-in and -on-action.

*The connective model*: On the basis of the socio-cultural learning theories Guile and Griffiths present the connective model as an ideal model of utilising work experience. The core of this model is the reflexive connection making between formal and informal learning, and between "vertical" and "horizontal" learning, the former referring to students' conceptual development, the latter referring to the development of the capacity to work in different contexts. The idea is to resituate learning in a way that requires students to draw upon their formal and conceptual learning. Through working collaboratively the aim is to develop polycontextual and connective skills which enable "boundary crossing", that is, the ability to work in new and changing contexts. This requires close co-operation between vocational colleges and workplaces, and therefore the central role of the education and training provider is to develop partnerships with workplaces to create environments for learning.

According to Guile and Griffiths (2001), all these models, except for the ideal connective model, can be recognised in existing European VET systems. However, the classification is more analytical than descriptive: no specific work experience programme fits neatly into any particular models and some programmes may contain elements of more than one model. The fifth model, the connective model, represents a new curriculum framework in which emphasis is on connecting learning that takes place in different education and work contexts.

Following the work by Sfard (1998), Hakkarainen and his colleagues (Hakkarainen, Palonen, Paavola, & Lehtinen, 2004; Paavola, Lipponen, & Hakkarainen 2004) have presented three metaphors of learning: the acquisition metaphor, the participation metaphor, and the knowledge creation metaphor. As regards these metaphors, the traditional, experiential and generic models of work experience represent the traditional knowledge acquisition metaphor or standard paradigm of learning (Hager, 2004). The work process model, in contrast, seems to emphasise the participation metaphor, i.e. the view of learning as participation in communities of practice, while the connective model, with the aim of developing working life in collaboration with educational institutions and workplaces, goes very well together with the knowledge creation view of learning.

*The connective model of work experience* proposed by Guile and Griffiths is based on the Cultural Historical Activity Theory (Engeström, 2000; Vygotsky, 1978) which defines learning as a socially and culturally determined phenomenon. The term connectivity "defines the purpose of that pedagogical approach which educators would adopt in order to take explicit account of the relationship between theoretical and everyday knowledge in their attempt to mediate the different demands arising in the contexts of education and work" (Griffiths & Guile, 2003, p. 59). In work experience programmes following the connective model the learners are supported to

- understand and use the potential of school subjects as conceptual tools for seeing the relationship between their workplace experience and the study programmes as a whole;
- develop the intellectual foundation for criticising existing work practices and taking responsibility for working with others to conceive and implement, where possible, alternatives;
- develop the capability of resituating existing knowledge and skill in new contexts as well as being able to contribute to the development of new knowledge, new social practices and new intellectual debates;

- become confident about crossing organisational boundaries or the boundaries between different, and often distributed communities of practice; and
- connect their knowledge to the knowledge of other specialists, whether in educational institutions, workplaces or the wider community (Griffiths & Guile, 2003).

Griffiths and Guile (2003) emphasise the importance of four practices of learning: *thinking, dialogical inquiry, boundary crossing*, and *resituation of learning*. In developing thinking, dialogue and argumentation are central activities. Dialogic inquiry refers to the practices which allow students to appropriate the cultural resources afforded by the environment, including assistance from more experience others, and the provision of tools, such as computers, to resolve a problem. Language here is the principal mediating tool. Boundary crossing (Beach, 2003; Engeström, Engeström, & Kärkkäinen, 1995) means that students move across different learning environments and different workplaces, and negotiate between these different contexts. It is assumed that in this way students not only add to their knowledge and skills (vertical development) but also develop the capacity to work in different contexts (horizontal development). The fourth practice, resituation of knowledge and skill involves using and transforming knowledge and skills in different contexts.

One of the assumed advantages of the connective model is its potential in developing what is called work process knowledge (Boreham, Samucay, & Fischer, 2002). This term refers to an overall understanding of one's work processes including not only personal skills but also the broader context of that work. Work process knowledge arises from the combination of theoretical and practical knowledge (Boreham, 2002). Griffiths and Guile (2003, p. 62) describe this process as follows: "First, the movement from experience to understanding starts with practical experience: the latter paves the way for understanding and enables individuals to integrate theoretical knowledge into practical understanding. Second, the development of work process knowledge constitutes the link between experience and scientific knowledge because it is in the work context that the two different modes of knowing ("practical knowledge" and "theoretical knowledge") are called forth and hence become meaningful in relation to one another." Griffiths and Guile present *kernel concepts* as theoretical or conceptual tools for learners for overcoming the separation of theoretical and practical knowledge and for integrating them. Kernel concepts are concepts which help learners to identify relationships between theoretical knowledge and the events that occur in the real world, and thus everyday experience can be used to revise, amend, or transform theoretical knowledge. Bereiter and Scardamalia (1993) describe exactly the same process in their depiction of the development of expertise, but they label the process problem solving. According to them, "Formal knowledge is converted into skill by being used to solve problems of procedure" and "Formal knowledge is converted into informal knowledge by being used to solve problems of understanding" (Bereiter and Scardamalia, 1993, p. 66). What these ideas share is what Leinhard et al. (1995) have described as the reciprocal and interactive process of "theorising practice" and "particularising theory". In other words, at the core of developing vocational and professional competence is the integration of theory and practice, as suggested earlier by the model of integrative pedagogy. Thus the connective model of work experience provides a promising framework for realising an integrative pedagogy in collaboration with educational institutes and workplaces.

Some recent studies have examined the extent to which the different models of work experience described by Guile and Griffiths (2001) are recognisable in educational practices. For example, studies in Finnish vocational education and training and polytechnics have shown differences between fields of study in the models used to organise students' learning at work (Tynjälä, Virtanen, & Valkonen, 2005; Virolainen, 2004, 2007; Virtanen & Tynjälä, in press). For example, in a study by Virtanen & Tynjälä (2008) it was found that all models described by Guile and Griffiths could be recognised in Finnish VET and that there was a clear shift in process away from the traditional model towards the other models. School-based learning and work-based learning were most closely connected with each other in the field of social and health care, while features of the traditional model were most often observed in the field of technical education. Furthermore, social and health care students gave higher self-ratings of their boundary crossing skills than students in other fields, which finding is consistent with the findings about connectivity.

In sum, our idea of connectivity refers to the integration of work and learning in various contexts and environments. It involves the tight integration of the different forms of knowledge used, dealt with and created in the interface between education and work. Connectivity concerns also people. Work-related learning connects students and workers, tutors and workplace trainers, teachers and workplace partners, and so on. Similarly, it connects educational institutions and work organisations, experience and analysis, feeling and thinking, the present and the future (Eyler & Giles, 1999, p. 183). In sum, the principle of connectivity refers to both individual and institutional connection-making between what is learnt in different contexts and the reflective processes which make further learning possible (Young, 1998, 1999).

## Connectivity Leads to Transformations

So far, we have dealt with one basic concept, connectivity, related to the theme of this book, the integration of work and learning. The second basic concept, transformation, is examined in the following sections. The main idea underlying our framework is that by *connecting things what have earlier been seen as separate entities it is possible to create potentials for transformational processes*. In other words, connectivity leads to transformations. This idea is supported by studies in many different fields such as learning and education, innovation, and organisational development. The principle applies at all levels, from individuals up through organisations and larger systems of education to the world of work. What follows is a brief review of how the idea of transformation has been dealt with in research on individual learning, how it appears in studies of organisational learning, and how it is expressed at the level of educational systems.

## The Concept of Transformation in Research on Individual Learning

The idea of transformation as a result of the learning process is present in most recent learning theories, although in different approaches to research on learning it has been described by recourse to a variety of theoretical concepts. Some theories, such as Mezirow's (1991) theory of transformative learning, speak explicitly about transformation, while in other theories the transformative dimension is an implicit one. For example, cognitive constructivists describe learning as a process of conceptual change (Vosniadou, 1994), while socio-cultural theories see learning as changes in the learner's participation in a community of practice (Lave & Wenger, 1991; Wenger, 1998), or as the development of an activity system (Engeström, 2000). However, despite the different foci and emphases of these theories, they all deal with a phenomenon that is basically a process of transformation: a change in the ways in which people think and act. Thus, the idea of transformation emphasises that learning is seen as a creative or innovative activity rather than a reproductive activity.

Mezirow's (1991) theory of transformative learning was developed in the context of adult education. The basic elements of the theory are *meaning perspectives* and *critical reflection*. By meaning perspective Mezirow refers to structure of assumptions that constitutes a person's frame of reference for interpreting the meaning of experiences and the world. Critical reflection is a process through which the person assesses the validity of those assumptions. In the transformative learning process critical self-reflection results in the reformulation and transformation of these assumptions and of the person's meaning perspective. In other words, people begin to see and think about things in a different way than before.

The theory of transformative learning describes the change in the way the learner thinks as a result of the learning process. Similarly, cognitive research on learning has examined the learning process and learning outcomes as changes in individuals' thinking. The studies of conceptual change (Vosniadou, 1994) have indicated that very often students have misconceptions about the phenomena they are studying. For example, it is typical for students to think that plants draw their energy with their roots from the earth, although the scientific explanation is that the plants create energy themselves in the process of photosynthesis. In these kinds of cases a radical conceptual change is needed in students' conceptions in order to transform an incorrect everyday way of thinking into a scientific one. Research has indicated that bringing about radical changes in students' thinking is hard and it requires that students are made aware of their false thinking and provided with conceptual tools such as metaphors or analogies which help them to understand scientific explanations of phenomena.

The theories of transformative learning and conceptual change derive from different theoretical backgrounds. While the notion of transformative learning draws on the ideas of the critical theory and of emancipatory education, studies on conceptual change are based on the cognitive constructivist view of learning. Despite these differences in theoretical viewpoints, both theories describe learning as a process through which changes take place in the learners' thinking. Both theories also emphasise the role of critical reflection in this process. As described earlier, thinking in general and critical reflection in particular are seen as central in the connective model of work experience. By practising critical thinking students can become aware not only of their own competence development needs but also of defects in workplace practices, which may pave the way to transforming these practices.

While cognitive approaches to learning research conceptualise learning as a phenomenon that takes place mainly through thinking processes supported by social interaction, socio-cultural theories describe learning as participation in communities of practice (Billett, 2004; Lave & Wenger, 1991; Wenger, 1998). The idea that a novice proceeds towards expertise through what Lave and Wenger (1991) have called *legitimate peripheral participation* is often seen as the basis for students' work experience. At the very beginning novices work in the peripheral, less critical, areas of practice, and gain more responsibility as their competence develops. Of crucial importance in the learning process is interacting and working under the guidance of more competent workers, observing their ways of doing the job, and participating in the community of practice.

With regard to our present discussion of transformation as an outcome of learning the notion of legitimate peripheral participation can be criticised. As a result of the process of legitimate peripheral participation some transformation, indeed, takes place. What is transformed is the learner's position in the community of practice: the novice becomes gradually an expert. However, because the model appears to emphasise socialisation into the existing practices of the community, these practices are taken for granted, and, thus the need to question or develop them is ignored. Thus, the model of legitimate peripheral participation does not seem to provide a basis for developing work practices. Instead, it seems to support reproductive rather than transformative learning. Another limitation in the model is the question of whom it recognises as a learner. This model depicts learning processes at work mainly as a novitiate activity while experts inhabit a role of a kind of a teacher, facilitator or coach. However, it is not only novices in the modern workplace who learn. Fuller and Unwin (2002) showed in their study that in their daily work people teach each other across the traditional workplace boundaries of age, experience and status. Old-timers guide beginners in some activities, while new-comers may guide experts in some other things. Thus, Fuller and Unwin argue that the concept of pedagogy and pedagogic practice is relevant to all types of employee and workplace and that organisations need to find ways of encouraging people to share their expertise.

Although the notion of legitimate peripheral participation has been criticised for its bias towards reproductive learning it can be seen to provide a context for transformative learning when combined with the connective model of work experience. Then the core of the learning process moves from a socialising towards a development orientation: through practices of thinking, dialogical inquiry, boundary crossing and resituating learning students, teachers and workers together develop work. There are many applications of the notion of legitimate peripheral participation which go beyond the limitations of the model and support the idea of learning as transformative or even as creative and innovative activity. These models expand the scope of learning to the organisational perspective, to which we turn to next.

## Transformations in Organisations

One of the main ideas of the connective model of work experience by Guile and Griffiths (2001) is that workplaces and educational institutions together create learning environments and that the learners include not only students but also regular employees and whole work organisations. The idea is to critically question and analyse work processes and collaboratively develop new practices. In this way student-placements, internships, apprenticeships, project-based learning and the like can serve the larger aims of organisational learning and development.

Several theoretical frameworks and conceptualisations have been employed to examine transformational processes in organisations. We briefly review the following: (1) *Communities of practice* (Wenger, 1998), (2) *Learning organisation* (Argyris & Schön, 1996; Nikkanen, 2001; Senge, 1990), (3) *Expansive learning* (Engeström, 1987; 2004), (4) *Ba* – a space for learning (Nonaka & Konno, 1998), and (5) Innovative knowledge communities (Hakkarainen et al., 2004).

1) By *communities of practice*, Wenger (1998) refers to the informal communities that people form as they pursue joint enterprises at work and during their leisure time. Through participation in these communities people share their knowledge, negotiate meanings, form their identities, and develop their work practices. Conceptualising learning as participation in communities of practice has important implications for the developing of organisations. In many traditional organisations, learning is the province of the training department, as a unit separated off from actual practice. Training departments deliver courses, document procedures and prepare manuals for learners – but do not engage learners in the organisation's most valuable learning resource, that is, practice itself. In contrast, the model Wenger presents is an integrative approach to training. Newcomers are seen as an integral part of a community of practice from which it follows that old-timers and newcomers work and learn together. These generational encounters bring about processes of reflection that serve both newcomers and the community. Thus, Wenger recommends that organisations arrange their learning processes as participatory processes, whether the learners be newcomers or old-timers, and that they place their emphasis on learning, rather than teaching, by using the learning opportunities offered by practice.

Considering learning as a participatory process is consistent with recent accounts of the nature of expertise as a collective rather than individual phenomenon. Bereiter and Scardamalia (1993) emphasise that expertise is not confined to the individual but may also be applied to groups that function as units. For example, scientific research teams, sport teams, surgical teams and teams of air traffic controllers form units that carry out joint enterprises. In Wenger's (1998) terms, they form communities of practice. From the viewpoint of developing and transforming workplace practices it is therefore important to pay attention not only to learning of individuals but also to the learning and development of the units (collectives of individuals) that constitute the actual practice in the workplace.

2) Another concept describing learning at the collective level is that of the *learning organisation* which gained much popularity in the 1990s. Various definitions of a learning organisation emphasise "conscious collaborative change and objective-oriented influence on the future" (Nikkanen, 1998, pp. 96–100). A learning organisation encourages and facilitates the learning of its members and transforms itself by structuring its policy and strategy formation, evaluation, implementation, and improvement processes. (Argyris & Schön, 1996; Nikkanen, 2001; Senge, 1990; Slotte & Tynjälä, 2003). According to Senge (1990) a learning organisation is continually expanding its capacity to create its own future. This capacity is grounded on the ability of employees and the organisation to change and become more effective, and on the fact that change requires open communication, a culture of collaboration and the empowerment of all the members of the work community. Thus, the learning organisation can be defined as "an organisation that facilitates the learning of all its members and continuously transforms itself" (Pedler, Boydell, & Burgoyne, 1991).

Appelbaum and Reichart (1998) suggest that organisational learning has three overlapping stages. The first stage is a cognitive one – members of learning communities expand their thinking and create new knowledge. The second stage is related to how workers perform their work. Employees begin to internalise their new insights and adjust their work practices. The last stage is improvement in performance, with changes in practices leading to measurably better results, superior quality, an increased market share or other tangible gains. The core of organisational development is the learning of the kind that Senge (1990) calls generative. The processes of generative learning or creating new knowledge are highly social in nature: collaboration and interaction among co-workers is essential. For this reason, many researchers have argued that organisational learning goes beyond individual learning, which is not to deny the obvious fact that organisations can learn only through the experience and actions of individuals (Argyris & Schön, 1996; Senge, 1990).

3) The concept of *expansive learning* (Engeström, 1987, 2004) also refers to collective learning that goes beyond individual learning and beyond acquisition of existing knowledge. The expansive learning process starts with the work community questioning their existing practices and analysing the historical background of these practices: What was the situation when these practices started, and is the situation now different? The process continues with modelling and implementing new practices developed through dialogue between the members of the community. New practices are then consolidated and reflected on, which eventually may lead to the questioning of them and to starting a new phase of developing practices. In this way expansive learning produces new modes of action and radical changes in a work community of an organisation.

In his analysis of expertise in modern working life Engeström (2004) goes still further suggesting that expertise may be located and distributed not only in communities of practice but in multiple interacting communities. He argues that expansive learning producing radical transformations in and between organisations is a key process of expertise and involves what he calls *negotiated knotworking* as the defining characteristic of collaborative and transformative expertise. Knotworking is characterised by a pulsating movement of tying, untying, and retying together otherwise separate threads of activity. People who work in separate departments or organisations come together for certain purposes, to negotiate meanings, solve problems, and then continue with other partners for other purposes, maybe to re-form again later on. Engeström argues that knotworking is a significant new form of organising and performing expert work activity.

4) Organisational studies on workplace learning have emphasised that it is the responsibility of a work organisation to create a propitious climate and other pre-requisites for the learning of individuals, groups and whole work communities (Argyris & Schön, 1996; Lähteenmäki, Toivonen, & Mattila, 2001; Nikkanen, 2001; Senge, 1990). Space for learning and thinking is often called for. Nonaka and Konno (1998) have described such learning space with the Japanese concept *ba*, which means a shared space for emerging relationships. *Ba* can consist of physical, virtual or mental spaces or combinations of these, and it provides a forum for developing individual and collective knowledge. For example, a team can be a *ba* for the individuals in it and a network of organisations can be a *ba* for those organisations. The benefit of *ba* is that by participating in it individuals or teams or organisations can transcend their own perspectives or boundaries. The idea is very much the same as in Vygotsky's (1978) well known notion of the zone of proximal development: in collaboration one can advance to higher level outcomes than by working alone.

Nonaka and Takeuchi (1995) have described different modes of knowledge transformation. According to them, knowledge creation in organisations takes place through the following forms: (1) *socialisation*, which refers to the sharing of tacit knowledge, e.g. through apprenticeship; (2) *externalisation*, involving the expression and explication of tacit knowledge to convert it to explicit knowledge, e.g. through narratives; (3) *combination*, involving the conversion of explicit knowledge into more complex explicit knowledge, e.g. through documents; and (4) *internalisation* which means converting explicit knowledge into the organisation's tacit knowledge, e.g. through learning-by-doing. Eraut (2004b, p. 263) has criticised the model proposed by Nonaka and Takeuchi, asserting that the knowledge they describe as tacit knowledge being transformed into explicit knowledge was already explicit knowledge, but, in a mode of personal knowledge which was not shared with others before. As a response to this critique it can be said that what is important is less whether the personal knowledge was explicit or implicit but more that knowledge which hitherto had been only the property of an individual becomes shared.

On the basis of the types of knowledge transformation described above Nonaka and Konno (1998) have distinguished between different types of learning space, *ba* (Fig. 2.3). There is an *originating ba* for socialisation, a space where people can meet face-to-face and share feelings, experiences and mental models. This is the primary *ba* where the knowledge creation process begins. *Interacting ba* provides a space for externalisation, that is, for making tacit knowledge explicit. Here people share their mental models and reflect and analyse them. *Cyber ba* represents the

**Fig. 2.3** Different forms of learning space, *ba* (modified from Nonaka & Konno, 1998)

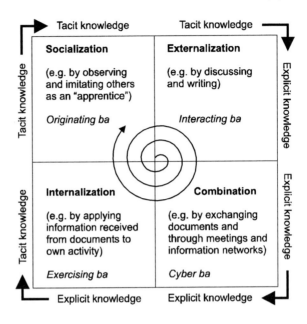

combination phase of knowledge creation: explicit knowledge is combined with other explicit knowledge. This can take place, for example, in on-line networks, documentations and databases. Finally, *exercising ba* supports the internalisation of explicit knowledge to tacit knowledge in a process where explicit knowledge is used in action. If we examine any workplace from the framework of *ba*, it will soon be seen that some workplaces and networks provide different forms of "*ba*", while similarly there are workplaces where these kinds of learning space and time cannot be found. For example, in some workplaces the practices for externalising tacit knowledge may be almost non-existent. From the point of view of students this situation would make learning more difficult because they would have to rely solely on the process of socialisation, which does not provide much explicit knowledge.

5) Common to the models of expansive learning (Engeström, 1987, 2000) and knowledge creation (Nonaka & Konno, 1998; Nonaka & Takeuchi, 1995) is that both of them emphasise the collaborative nature of transforming knowledge and developing practices in organisations and that they recognise the role of informal activities and practices in bringing about creative learning. Hakkarainen and his colleagues (2004) have described such collective endeavours as *innovative knowledge communities*, by which they mean communities that intentionally aim to create new knowledge. These communities base their potential for transformation on collaborative knowledge building (Bereiter, 2002). Peculiar to these communities is dynamic expertise which is linked with a broad range of networking connections inside and outside the organisation, open communication, knowledge sharing, and people engaging what Bereiter and Scardamalia (1993) call progressive problem-solving.

This is the process in which people set themselves challenges and problems that are more complicated than the ones they have already solved, and in this way they can go beyond previous solutions and surpass the limits of their existing knowledge.

On the basis of the theoretical models presented above the prerequisites for organisational transformation can be summarised as follows. First, perhaps the most essential aspect of the organisational learning process is *interaction* between the members of the community. Learning in organisations is possible only through interactive processes. Second, the interaction should occur around and through *shared goals* (Billett & Seddon, 2004; Paavola et al., 2004; Senge, 1990). This means that the participants have a shared view or vision of the aim of the activities and that the personal aims of individuals and the visions of groups and of the company are consistent and aligned (cf. Vesalainen & Strömmer, 1999). Third, it is important that the members of the organisation and its outside networks are aware of the knowledge and expertise that is distributed in the organisation and those networks (Hakkarainen et al., 2004). In other words, *meta-knowledge*, that is, knowledge of who knows what and where the information can be found, makes it possible to fully utilise the different and complementary expertise of people. Fourth, the community members' *willingness to share their knowledge* with others is an important determinant for initiating learning processes. Knowledge sharing does not happen automatically but requires a fifth prerequisite of organisational development, *trust and a collaborative climate* (Sveiby & Simons, 2002). Finally, bringing about transformational processes seems to require *progressive problem solving* (Bereiter & Scardamalia, 1993). In other words, when an individual, team or organisation has produced a solution to a given problem, they do not get into a rut but are already setting another problem which is more complex than the previous one. In this way individuals and organisations constantly redefine their tasks and challenges, work at the edge of their competence and surpass themselves.

How these prerequisites of transformation are fulfilled in an organisation is also reflected in the way the organisation provides a learning environment for students. Realising the connective model of work experience requires close interaction, trust and collaboration between the education providers and the workplaces as well as a shared vision of the task of enhancing learning and developing work practices.

## *Transforming Educational Systems*

The broadest interpretation of connectivity and transformation involves the level of the educational system. Today's society and working life is marked by a rapid change as can be seen, for example, in globalisation, the growing production of knowledge, changes in work contents, occupational structures and the organisation of work. As the society changes, it is important that the education system changes as well. The traditional structures and practices do not necessarily function well in the changing world. Indeed, many transformative trends are globally visible in educational policy and systems.

The earlier industrial society relied heavily on routine production whereas the production and service systems of the contemporary information society are based on the continuous flow of information and the development of processes. This presents challenges to the existing structures and quality of work practices (Kauppi, 2004). Theorists of the information society or the network society (Castells, 2000; Reich, 1991) have forecast an increase in the role of symbolic analytic jobs and person-to-person services and decrease in the amount of routine workers in the society of the future. VET, in particular, faces the challenge of how to create learning environments which can simultaneously combine the development of routine skills and the prerequisites for transformation.

High competence requirements have lead to the massification of secondary and higher education. Recent European trends in educational policies, such as the Bologna process in higher education and the Copenhagen process in vocational education and training, are good examples of how the economy shapes the development of education systems. (For more information on the Bologna process, see Bologna process, 2007 and for more information on the Copenhagen process, see Copenhagen Decraration, 2007). Both processes are part of the Lisbon strategy, which has the aim of making Europe "the most competitive and dynamic knowledge-based economy in the world capable of sustainable economic growth with more and better jobs and greater social cohesion". Among the current targets are to enhance quality assurance systems of education, to increase the mobility of students and the workforce across Europe, to establish a common credit system and to homogenise degrees and degree structures.

The goals of the Bologna and Copenhagen processes are also related to the European policy to promote life-long learning and enhance the standard of qualifications within of a common European framework. The aim of this policy is to create a system which will increase transparency in qualifications and support mutual trust between different stakeholders, such as educational institutes, educational administration, employers and employees transferring within the European Community. For this purpose, the EU Heads of Government has initiated the creation of a European Qualification Framework (EQF, 2007). The aim of the EQF is to enable the qualification systems on the national and sectoral levels to be related to each other, thus facilitating the transfer and recognition of the vocational and professional qualifications of individual citizens. The proposal for the EQF is for eight levels of qualification on the basis of learning outcomes. As many of the generic skills needed in working life are learnt only at work (Stenström, 2006; Tynjälä et al., 2006), one aim of the EQF system is to support the recognition of informal learning outside education systems and to promote lifelong learning.

The challenges presented by the changing working life and the trends in European educational policies are clearly visible in national policies as well. For example, the Development Plan for Education and Research by the Finnish Ministry of Education emphases the importance of a close relationship between industry and education both at the secondary and at the tertiary level (Ministry of Education, 2007). An interesting example of the education system responding to the needs of society in

Finland was the establishment of the polytechnics[1] as a new second sector of higher education, alongside the universities. One of the main objectives of the reform was to enhance the structure of higher education and make it more responsive to the needs of working life and society (Välimaa, 2006, p. 40). Originally, the polytechnics only provided professional bachelors' level degrees, but few years ago new masters' level degrees were established. What distinguishes these new degrees is that they are strongly working life oriented. First, applicants are required to have at least 3 years of work experience after finishing their bachelors' degree. Second, most students work and pursue their studies at the same time, which means a considerable amount of evening and weekend classes as well as distance learning. Third, polytechnic studies include co-operation with workplaces throughout so that, finally, to gain their master's thesis students carry out a development project in working life, usually at their own workplace where they also have a mentor for the project. Altogether, the masters' degree studies in the polytechnic utilise a fair amount of work-related learning.

Similar examples of the establishment of working life oriented university degrees can be found in other countries. For example, in the UK a new Foundation Degree was established at the beginning of the new millennium. A key aim was to advance and formalise the inroads that work-based learning had increasingly made into higher education curricula during the previous decade (Zamorski, 2006). According to the then Minister of Higher Education, Tessa Blackstone, the foundation degree has the potential to raise the skill level of the workforce, particularly in the new industries and forge new alliances between universities, colleges, and employers (Zamorski, 2006, p. 58). Foundation degrees are tailored specifically to the needs of industry and they aim to dissolve the historical divide between vocational and academic education by integrating theory and practice through work-based curricula. Similar examples of new, business life oriented forms of education are presented later in this book.

In many countries, reforms which aim to establish a closer relationship between education and work have been carried out in vocational education and training (VET) as well. In countries where the VET system is largely driven by working life, as in Germany and Austria, special attention has recently been paid to developing new forms of quality assurance and assessment for apprenticeships (Tutschner & Grollmann, 2006). In countries with a school-based VET system, as in Finland, workplace learning systems have been improved. This has been followed by the development of competence-based assessment which requires the creation of close connections between educational institutions and working life

---

[1] The Finnish polytechnic system is equivalent to the German Fachhochschule and thus serves as an alternative sector of higher education, parallel to the universities. As a consequence of the Bologna process and to indicate the polytechnic education is part of the higher education system, polytechnics have now started to translate the Finnish word 'ammattikorkeakoulu' (Fachhochscule, polytechnic), as "University of Applied Sciences". However, the Finnish Association of Finnish University Rectors does not approve of this translation and recommends a translation such as "College of Professional Higher Education". The debate over the translation continues

organisations (Stenström, 2006; see also Stenström's Chapter 13 in this volume). All these developments reflect the current global process of change in the relationship between working life and vocational education.


# Conclusion

The need for a closer relationship between education and working life expressed in governmental policies globally has led to transformations and reforms of the VET and higher education systems in many countries. The reforms have been both structural – such as the establishment of new qualifications – and pedagogical – such as the development of workplace learning and approaches to the assessment of learning. Common to these recent educational developments is the aim of integrating work and learning. This integration is about connecting activities that have been treated separately in the era of the industrial economy: learning in school and work at the workplace. The era of the knowledge society, in turn, has presented people, organisations, and societies with the challenge of continuous learning, which is not possible when learning is separated from the world of work. In this chapter we have presented the concept of connectivity as the key to promoting transformations in educational systems and working life in creating learning environments for students, employees, employers, organisations, and economies. The following chapters will present models and examples of how the principle of connectivity can be applied in the individual, organisational and system levels, and what kinds of transformations connecting work and learning may bring about.


# References

Anderson, J.R. (1983). *The architecture of cognition.* Cambridge, MA: Harvard University Press.
Appelbaum, S. H., & Reichart, W. R. (1998). How to measure an organization's learning ability: The facilitating factors – Part II. *Journal of Workplace Learning 1*,15–28.
Argyris, C., & Schön, D. A. (1996). *Organizational learning II: Theory, method and practice.* Reading, MA: Addison-Wesley.
Beach, K. (2003). Consequential transitions: a developmental view of knowledge propagation through social organizations. In T. Tuomi-Gröhn & Y. EngeStöm (Eds), *Between school and work. New perspectives on transfer and boundary crossing* (pp. 39–61). Amsterdam: Pergamon.
Bereiter, C. (2002). *Education and mind in the knowledge age.* Mahwah, NJ: Erlbaum.
Bereiter, C., & Scardamalia, M. (1993). *Surpassing ourselves: An inquiry into the nature of expertise.* Chicago: Open Court.
Billett, S. (2004). Learning through work: Workplace participatory practices. In H. Rainbird, A. Fuller & A. Munro (Eds.), *Workplace learning in context* (pp. 109–125). London: Routledge.
Billett, S., & Seddon, T (2004) Building community through social partnerships around vocational education and training, *Journal of Vocational Education and Training, 56*(1), 51–67.
Bologna process (2007). *The Bologna Process. Towards the European higher education area.* Retrieved September 17, 2007, from http://www.aic.lv/ace/ace_disk/Bologna/index.htm

Boreham, N. 2002. Work process knowledge in technological and organizational development. In N. Boreham, R. Samurcay & M. Fischer (Eds.), *Work process knowledge* (pp. 1–14). London: Routledge.

Boreham, N., Samucay, R., & Fischer, M. (Eds.). (2002). *Work process knowledge*. London: Routledge.

Castells, M. (2000). *The rise of the network society* (2nd ed.). Oxford: Blackwell.

Copenhagen Decraration (2002). *Enhanced European cooperation in vocational education and training – the "Bruges-Copenhagen process"*. Retrieved September 17, 2007, from http://ec.europa.eu/education/copenhagen/index_en.html

Dreyfus, H. L., & Dreyfus, S. E. (1986). *Mind over machine. The power of human intuition and expertise in the era of the computer*. Oxford: Blackwell.

Engeström, Y. (1987). *Learning by expanding*. Helsinki-Orienta-Konsultit.

Engeström, Y. (2000). Expansive learning at work: Toward an activity-theoretical reconceptualisation. *Journal of Education and Work, 14*(1), 133–156.

Engeström, Y. (2004). The new generation of expertise. Seven theses. In H. Rainbird, A. Fuller, & A. Munro (Eds.), *Workplace learning in context* (pp. 145–165). London: Routledge.

Engeström, Y., Engeström, R., & Kärkkäinen, M. (1995). Polycontextuality and boundary crossing in expert cognition: Learning and problem solving in complex work activities. *Learning and Instruction 5*(4), 319–336.

EQF (2007). *The European qualifications framework: A new way to understand qualifications across Europe*. Retrieved September 17, 2007 from http://ec.europa.eu/ education/policies/educ/eqf/index_en.html

Eraut, M. (2004a). Transfer of knowledge between education and workplace settings. In H. Rainbird, A. Fuller & A. Munro (Eds.), *Workplace learning in context* (pp. 201–221). London: Routledge.

Eraut, M. (2004b). Informal learning in the workplace. *Studies in Continuing Education, 26*(2), 247–273.

Eyler, J., & Giles, D.E. Jr. (1999). *Where's the learning in service-learning?* San Francisco: Jossey-Bass Publishers.

Fuller, A., & Unwin, L. (2002). Developing pedagogies for the contemporary workplace. In K. Evans, P. Hodkinson & L. Unwin (Eds.), *Working to learn* (pp. 95–111). London: Kogan Page.

Griffiths, T., & Guile, D. (2003). A connective model of learning: The implications for work process knowledge. *European Educational Research Journal, 2*(1), 56–73.

Guile, D., & Griffiths, T. (2001). Learning through work experience. *Journal of Education and Work, 14*(1), 113–131.

Hager, P. (2004). The conceptualization and measurement of learning at work. In H. Rainbird, A. Fuller, & A. Munro (Eds.), *Workplace learning in context* (pp. 242–258). London: Routledge.

Hakkarainen, K., Palonen, T., Paavola, S., & Lehtinen, E. (2004). *Communities of networked expertise: Professional and educational perspectives*. Amsterdam: Elsevier.

Kauppi, A. 2004. Työ muuttuu – muuttuuko oppiminen? (Work changes – does learning change?). In P. Tynjälä, J. Välimaa, & M. Murtonen (Eds.), *Korkeakoulutus, oppiminen ja työelämä* (pp. 187–212). Jyväskylä: PS-kustannus.

Kolb, D. A. (1984). *Experiential learning. Experience as the source of learning and development*. Englewood Cliffs, NJ: Prentice Hall.

Lave, J., & Wenger, E. (1991). *Situated learning. Legitimate peripheral participation*. Cambridge: Cambridge University Press.

Le Maistre, C., & Paré, A. (2006). A typology of knowledge demonstrated by beginning professionals. In P. Tynjälä, J. Välimaa, & G. Boulton-Lewis (Eds.), *Higher education and work: Collaborations, confrontations and challenges* (pp. 103–113). Amsterdam: Elsevier.

Leinhardt, G., McCarthy Young, K., & Merriman, J. (1995). Intergrating professional knowledge: The theory of practice and the practice of theory. *Learning and Instruction, 5*, 401–408.

Lähteenmäki, S., Toivonen, J., & Mattila, M. (2001). Critical aspects of organizational learning research and proposals for its measurement. *British Journal of Management, 12,* 113–129.

Mezirow, J. (1991). *Transformative dimensions of adult learning.* San Fransisco: Jossey-Bass.

Ministry of Education (2007). *Development plan for education and research.* Retrieved September 17, 2007, from http://www.minedu.fi/export/sites/default/OPM/Julkaisut/2004/liitteet/opm_190_opm08.pdf?lang=en

Nikkanen, P. (1998). Learning organisation, organisational learning and human resource management. In W.Th.J.G. Hoeben (Ed.), *Effective school improvement: State of the Art. Contribution to a discussion* (pp. 95–118). CT 97/2027. University of Groningen, Institute for Educational Research. The Netherlands: GION.

Nikkanen, P. (2001). Effectiveness and improvement in a learning organization. In E. Kimonen (Ed.), *Curriculum approaches* (pp. 55–76). Jyväskylä: University of Jyväskylä, Department of Education & Institute for Educational Research.

Nonaka, I., & Konno, N. (1998). The concept of "ba": Building a foundation for knowledge creation. *California Management Review, 40*(3), 40–54.

Nonaka, I., & Takeuchi, H. (1995). *The knowledge-creating company. How Japanese companies create the dynamics of innovation.* New York: Oxford University Press.

Paavola, S., Lipponen, L., & Hakkarainen, K. (2004). Models of innovative knowledge communities and three metaphors of learning. *Review of Educational Research, 74*(4), 557–576.

Pedler, M., Boydell, T., & Burgoyne, J. (1991). *The learning company* (2nd ed.). London: McGraw-Hill.

Reich, R. B. (1991). *The work of nations.* New York: Vintage Books.

Ryle, G. (1949). *The concept of mind.* London: Hutchinson.

Sambrook, S., & Stewart, J. (1999, September). *Influencing factors on lifelong learning and HRD practices: Comparison of seven European countries.* Paper presented at the European Conference on Educational Research, Lahti, Finland.

Senge, P. M. (1990). *The fifth discipline: The art and practice of the learning organization.* New York: Doubleday Currency.

Sfard, A. (1998). On two metaphors for learning and dangers of choosing just one. *Educational Researcher, 27,* 4–13.

Slotte, V., & Tynjälä, P. (2003). Industry-university collaboration for continuing professional development. *Journal of Education and Work, 16*(4), 445–464.

Stenström, M.-L. (2006). Polytechnic graduates working life skills and expertise. In P. Tynjälä, J. Välimaa & G. Boulton-Lewis *(Eds.), Higher education and working life: Collaborations, confrontations and challenges* (pp. 89–102). Amsterdam: Elsevier.

Sveiby, K.-S., & Simons, R. (2002). Collaborative climate and effectiveness of knowledge work – an empirical study. *Journal of Knowledge Management, 6*(5), 420–433.

Tutscher, R., & P. Grollman (2006). Practice-oriented assessment and quality assurance in VET in the geriatric sector in Germany. In M-L. Stenström & K. Laine (Eds), *Quality and practice in assessment. New approaches in work-related learning* (pp. 67–88). Jyväskylä: University of Jyväskylä, Institute for Educational Research.

Tynjälä, P., Slotte, V., Nieminen, J., Lonka, K., & Olkinuora, E. (2006). From university to working life: Graduates' workplace skills in practice. In P. Tynjälä, J. Välimaa, & G. Boulton-Lewis (Eds.), *Higher education and working life: Collaborations, confrontations and challenges* (pp. 73–88). Amsterdam: Elsevier.

Tynjälä, P., Virtanen, A., & Valkonen, S. (2005). *Työssäoppiminen Keski-Suomessa. Taitava Keski-Suomi -tutkimus osa I* [Students' workplace learning in Central Finland. "Skilled Central Finland" research report. Part I]. Jyväskylä: University of Jyväskylä. Institute for Educational Research.

Tynjälä, P., Välimaa, J., & Sarja, A. (2003). Pedagogical perspectives into the relationship between higher education and working life. *Higher Education, 46,* 147–166.

Wenger, E. (1998). *Communities of practice. Learning, meaning and identity.* Cambridge: Cambridge University Press.

Vesalainen, J., & Strömmer, R. (1999). From individual learning to network learning – networks as learners and as forums for learning. In T. Alasoini & P. Halme (Eds.), *Learning organizations, learning society*. National workplace development programme yearbook 1999 (pp. 117–139). Helsinki: Ministry of Labour.

Virolainen, M. (2004). Työhön sopeutumisesta oppimisen tilanteiden luomiseen. Ammattikorkeakoulujen työelämäjaksot ja työstä oppimisen mallit [From adaptation to work towards developing learning situations at work. Workplace learning and its models at polytechnics]. In P. Tynjälä, J. Välimaa, & M. Murtonen (Eds.), *Korkeakoulutus, oppiminen ja työelämä. Pedagogisia ja yhteiskuntatieteellisiä näkökulmia* (pp. 213–233). Jyväskylä: PS-kustannus.

Virolainen, M. (2007). Workplace learning and higher education in Finland: Reflections on current practice. *Education + Training*, *49*(4), 290–309.

Virtanen, A., & Tynjälä, P. (2008). Students' experiences of workplace learning in Finnish VET. *European Journal of Vocational Training* 2008/2(44), 199–213.

Vosniadou, S. (1994). Capturing and modelling the process of conceptual change. *Learning and Instruction*, *4*, 45–69.

Vygotsky, L. S. (1978). *Mind in society*. Cambridge, MA: Harvard University Press.

Välimaa, J. (2006). Analysing the relationship between higher education institutions and working life in a Nordic context. In P. Tynjälä, J. Välimaa, & G. Boulton-Lewis (Eds.), *Higher education and working life. Collaborations, confrontations and challenges* (pp. 35–53). Amsterdam: Elsevier.

Young, M. (1998). *Curriculum of the future. From the new sociology of education to a critical theory of learning*. London: Falmer press.

Young, M. (1999). Knowledge, learning, and the curriculum of the future. *British Educational Research Journal*, *25*, 463–477.

Zamorski, B. (2006). Bringing industry and academia closer together: The introduction of the foundation degree in the UK. In P. Tynjälä, J. Välimaa, & G. Boulton-Lewis (Eds.), *Higher education and working life: Collaborations, confrontations and challenges* (pp. 57–72). Amsterdam: Elsevier.

# Chapter 3
# Being, Doing, Making – A Paradigm for the Connective Curriculum

Matti Vesa Volanen

## European Strategies for the Parity of Esteem in Post-16 Education

Some years ago the Leonardo – research project "Strategies for post-16 education in Europe" (Lasonen & Young, 1998; Stenström & Lasonen, 2000; Volanen, 1992) identified four strategies in eight European upper secondary education systems for promoting parity of esteem between vocational and academic education. These were (1) vocational enhancement, (2) mutual enrichment, (3) linkages, and (4) unification. I quote the summary of the project report (Lasonen & Young 1998) in the following paragraphs:

"*Vocational enhancement*: The strategy of vocational enhancement emphasizes the distinctive nature of vocational education on the basis of its characteristic content and links between employers and the providers of vocational education. Esteem for vocational education is linked with the high standard of the content and pedagogy offered in vocational education and training. The strategy is most closely associated with the systems in Germany and Austria. The reforms in these countries are based on a belief that vocational training can provide a path both to higher education qualifications and to employment. The conclusions drawn from the German strategy are based on a single local experimental reform, while the Austrian reforms are nationwide. In the German experiment an enhancement strategy is applied to the renewal of the pedagogy of vocational education by means of a "bottom–up" approach. In Austria, by contrast, the strategy involves a top–down reform of structures and certification.

*Mutual enrichment*: In the Finnish and Norwegian reforms, vocational education institutions, enterprises, and academic upper secondary schools cooperate with the aim of giving students a broader range of choices and offering them the stimulating learning methods and environments. The strategy brings together the different

M.V. Volanen (✉)
Institute for Educational Research, University of Jyväskylä, Jyväskylä, Finland
e-mail: matti.vesa.volanen@ktl.jyu.fi

M.-L. Stenström, P. Tynjälä (eds.), *Towards Integration of Work and Learning*,
© Springer Science+Business Media B.V. 2009

types of schools by encouraging cooperation while simultaneously preserving their distinctive character. In Norway the strategy is being applied on a national level, while in Finland it is pursued in 16 localities. In Norway the aim has been to create a comprehensive upper secondary school and ensuring vocational students a smooth transition from school to work on the system level. Teacher education has been reformed by combining the training of vocational and general subject teachers. Curriculum reform has led to a restructuring of study programmes and improved opportunities for vocational students through 1 year of on-the-job training. In Finland the strategy involves increasing student choice beyond the boundaries separating vocational and general upper secondary schools in the localities. The essential basis of the reform is to facilitate cooperation between vocational and general upper secondary schools. The practical implementation of the strategy depends on collaboration between schools and teachers and on attracting the interest of students and gaining the support of their parents.

*Linkages*: Countries representing the linkages strategy have made vocational and general education more formally equal by linking both to a common qualification structure. The English and French educational systems, which have traditionally fostered elitism by emphasising only academic studies for the few, are now attempting to make vocational education more attractive and to raise its status in relation to general education. In France the emphasis of the *Baccalaureat professionnel* is on improved employment prospects. In England, again, the main focus has been on enabling students on the new vocational programmes (GNVQs) to have access to university on terms similar to those available to A levels students.

*Unification*: Under the unification strategy vocational and general education are merged to create a single post-16 education system. It is believed that requiring all students to study certain common general subjects will provide them with equal opportunities to engage in further studies, a factor that determines the attractiveness of different qualifications. Sweden and Scotland represent unified systems where the aim is to abolish the distinction between vocational and general learning. However, unification strategies are not necessarily identical. The comparison demonstrates one possible dimension of their variation, for while Sweden emphasizes uniformity of treatment and outcomes for all students, in Scotland the stress is, instead, on providing choice among a flexible range of opportunities."

The analysis of the post-16 strategies was policy- and structure-orientated. The approach excluded the discussion on the relationship between the four strategies and the content of vocational education, the curriculum. The content of the strategies did not achieve sufficient definition. The other Leonardo project, INTEQUAL (Brown & Manning, 1998) paid more attention to the idea of *integrated learning* as a problem of the upper secondary curriculum, but did not answer structural or policy questions. My basic intention in this chapter is to analyse all three elements together – structure, policy, and curriculum. In this way we can then, I think, open up a new perspective on the relationship between the vocational and academic traditions. As we shall see, it is possible to integrate them in such a way that they enrich each other.

## Mutual Enrichment of Vocational and Academic Education: the Horizon of *philotekhne*

Differentiating between academic and vocational education is highly embedded in the European tradition and it is, therefore, impossible to eliminate it through according supremacy to the one type of education against the other, whether through the scientifization of vocational education or the vocationalization of academic education. Instead the mission is to create a new kind of interdependency between the two traditions so that we are able to generate a process of mutual enrichment.

The fundamental roots of this differentiation between academic and vocational education go back to classical Antiquity, but the Reformation, the birth of labour markets, the role of the state in the process of the formation of (civil) society have all contributed to determining how important and central the distinction between vocational and academic education has been as an influence on the structure of European educational systems.

Traditionally there has been a strong association between an academic education and knowledge and competencies related to life outside work, that is, the public life of a gentleman or a citizen. By the contrast, the work of a craftsman and the vocational tradition have been much more closely associated with skills belonging to the world of work. When we discuss the differentiation between vocational and academic education, we are at the same time discussing the differentiation between being a citizen and being a labourer.

In the Anglo-American tradition citizenship was seen in the terms of the marketplace. Following the Second World War, however, the concept of the citizen has been redefined from the point of view of the social state, which partly excludes questions linked with working life.[1] In the German tradition citizenship is represented by the traditional craftsman. The German concept of citizenship expresses the idea of community, of a shared "house" (i.e. socially meaningful space and time), not of the open, abstract marketplace. This means that the idea of the social state has not led to a purely market-based idea of citizenship; rather, the community has developed in the direction of society while still retaining some features of the traditional community, as is seen in the German system of vocational education.

In the history of the birth of labour markets in Europe we can see at least two very different kinds of mainstream: "vocationalization from above" (Germany, France) and "vocationalization from below" (England).[2] In the first case the state has exerted a very strong impact on the construction of the labour market, on occupations and on vocational education. In the second case market processes have been more decisive.

In the Nordic countries, at least in Finland, Sweden, and Norway, these two pairs of distinctions exist in peculiar combinations: characteristically, vocationalization from above together with the central planning of vocational education and the labour

---

[1] See the discussion on Marshall in Turner (1993).

[2] I use here the theory of professionalization on the assumption that the distinction between "from above" and "from below" is applicable to other types of occupation as well (Konttinen, 1991; Siegrist, 1990).

market has been quite a strong feature of Nordic societies, while at same time citizenship is understood in terms of the labour market and the state. This is possible only on the assumption that society is generated by the state to ensure general welfare. However, today differentiating between state and society is a powerful trend in the Nordic countries.

Three educational systems can be seen to emerge from these two pairs of distinctions, i.e. vocationalization from above vs. vocationalization from below and market-based vs. community-based society as the historical basis of citizenship (see Table 3.1).

**Table 3.1** Vocational education and citizenship

| Vocationalization | The basis of citizenship | |
| --- | --- | --- |
| | Community-based society | Market society |
| From below | D Mutual enrichment, "cultured experts" | B On-the-job training (England) |
| From above | A Dual education (Germany) | C School-based education (Nordic) |

My hypothesis is that to be able to approach the mutual enrichment of vocation and citizenship, vocational and academic education with the production of "cultured experts" (D) the other three approaches (A, B, C) all require, because of the following trends in the working and social life, a change in the relationship between vocational and academic education:

1. The idea of "the learning/knowledge society" implies that the process of reflection, some form of learning, is indispensable in all social activities.
2. The production and work process must be opened to learning. As regards production units, this is a question of survival.
3. New production concepts/models question the modern differentiation between citizenship and the labourer: every labourer is more or less required to work as a citizen.
4. Open and complex working situations, which cannot be prepared for beforehand by issuing rules and directives, are increasingly common. More versatile skills and more broad-based knowledge – concrete *and* general skills and knowledge – are needed to handle such situations. Thus mastering skills includes a new quality of *crafting* the content of work situations with concepts in a context.
5. Vocational competence means the ability to increase the output and quality of the commodities made by a production unit. An increasingly important question is how concrete and rich a concept is the term "productivity" that we are using; does it, for example, also embrace the questions involved in environmental, social, human and cultural capital, or in other words, epistemic, ethical and aesthetical questions?

If we then on this basis follow a variation on the Weberian way of thinking (Konttinen, 1991; Volanen, 2007, pp. 66–67), we can say that the premodern version of professions had at least three different ideas of knowledge: first, the *Kulturmensch* with scholarship, knowledge of the origin of the culture and of the essence and fate of man in the world; second, elementary instrumental knowledge as part of the

*Kulturmensch* or of craftsmen; and, third, traditional knowledge based on craft work as mediated in the craft tradition and as part of craft production. Profession in the modern version turns the knowledge of the *Kulturmench* and craftsmen into that of the *Fachmensch*, i.e. knowledge which is based on natural science and specialization. We can then form the grid presented in Table 3.2.

**Table 3.2**  Situating cultured experts (adapted from Volanen, 2007)

| Working horizon | Main orientation of work process | |
| --- | --- | --- |
| | Knowledge | Craft |
| Ensemble | Cultivated person *Kulturmensch* | Cultured expert *Gebildet expert* |
| Speciality | Overspecialized person *Fachmensch* | Professional worker *Berufmensch* |

The main question for the *Fachmensch* is the "How are things or processes?" and for the modern *Berufsmensch* "How can I make it?". The integration of formal and instrumental knowledge in the course of manipulating objects and symbols simultaneously is "precisely what makes technicians' work culturally anomalous" (Whalley & Barley, 1997, p. 49). A craftsman manipulates or transforms materials to produce artifacts. Instead, technicians manipulate materials to produces symbolic references. But technicians do not use these references to create new references, as in the academic professions. Technicians use these references to manipulate objects. Neither are technicians a kind of hybrid of craftsman and blue-collarworker. The work of technicians punctures the existing cultural bulwark; it is at once a synthesis of mental and manual, clean and dirty, white collar and blue-collar. Such a syntethetic melding of cultural opposites has been previously approximated only by engineering, surgery and other "manual" professions (Whalley & Barley, 1997, p. 49).

This synthesis between head and hand – *Being* and *Making, theoria* and *poiesis* – leaves out the third element, the heart, questions of *Doing, praxis* and *ethics*. To educate cultured experts we need a more profound footing. We need to pose *three* questions to open up the horizon of *philotekhne*: How are things? (theory), how are they when they are good (ethics) and how could we produce them according to the laws of beauty (aesthetics). This tradition of *philotekhne*, friendship for craft, is in fact older than the friendship for knowledge (philosophy), but its history is part of the history of craft work. The history of craft work is a fundamental part of the European tradition of work. In this tradition work is not a question of an occupation but question of a vocation. To open up this position, let us take craft work as methodological mirror for the development of labour and for the new connective vocational education curriculum (Volanen, 2005, 2006).

## Craft Work as a Methodological Mirror for the Development of Labour

The Developmental Labour Research programme, which has in the last few years served as a valuable organising point of reference in the field of Finnish labour research, buried craft work in the rubbish dump of history. According to the

programme, craft work was replaced by industrial labour, with humanistically oriented work evolving as a counterbalance to industrial labour. As a synthesis there
emerged the idea of theoretically mastered labour (Engeström, 1990, 1995; Kuutti, 1999; Toikka, 1982, 1984).

This interpretation of history views craft work from the presentist perspective
of the modern industrial society and wage labour, as it submerges itself almost un-
critically in the modernisation process that has reshaped work. A smooth production
process became a central, sometimes the sole criterion of the modernisation of work.

The concept of "theoretically mastered labour" places knowledge over skill.
Apart from making this epistemic postulation, it deconstructs the ethical and aesthetic moments of work as questions lying outside the manufacturing process. Modern notions of work push the concept of craft beyond the boundaries of labour and
out of reach of analysis. As such, it is impossible to assess wage labour as shaped
by industrialisation from the perspective of history and, as a result, also from the
perspective of the future.[3]

However, it is critical to examine the entire range of work forms, and for this
we need craft work as a mirror, a lens, or even a lantern. I am not speaking
about romanticising or idealising craft work but about methods of juxtaposing
the human being as a totality – as someone with a head, hands and a heart –
with an analysis of labour. In the cultural history of Europe, craft work has an
incomparably longer and richer history than industrial wage labour, whose short
and bleak history can scarcely be called rich, at least from the viewpoint of the
labourer.

We cannot return to craft work. However, we find ourselves obliged, in an emerging new production situation, to look for the conditions under which forms of work
take shape. If the *classical* economy was grounded in agriculture and craft tools, the
first *modern* economy was grounded in machines and machine systems. Since then,
machines have learned to use language, languages are learned to use machines, and
languages are central means of production. This has meant the formation of a *texture*
of machineries and languages. Machines cannot manage without languages, nor can
languages manage without machines. The tools of work activity and work-related
communication are becoming intertwined. They are metamorphosing into moments
of one and the same work process.

In many respects, the same technical process pushed the subjective agent of
production outside the manufacturing process proper, turning it into a monitoring
and regulating factor of production. In other words the role of *expertise* changed
in the economy. Expertise cannot be based adequately on merely knowing things.
During the last few years we have, as a part of globalisation, seen ownership, enterprises, and factories increasingly becoming differentiated as external preconditions.
It seems that as a result of this deepening split, the relationship between labour

---

[3] It is true that different researchers have different views on the subject, with Toikka in particular
elaborating his ideas in an expansive manner, including ethics, see Toikka (1982).

and entrepreneurship is also being restructured in crucial ways (Bsirske, Mönig-Raane, Sterkel, & Wiedemuth, 2004; Glissmann & Peters, 2001; Haug, 2003; Schmitthenner & Peters, 2003; Schumann, 2003; Wolf, 1999).

Having said this, we can begin our examination with the thesis that *craft*[4] is a richer and more concrete concept than knowledge. In classical philosophy, craft, the art of making things, posed a challenging conceptual problem: how to account for the fact that women and slaves engaged in craft work that produces, makes visible, something new and unprecedented. This had to be explained away, demanding super mundane ideas (Plato) or the supernatural productive ability of nature (Aristotle). Otherwise there would have been no escaping the admission that slaves and women were giving birth to something that was non-divine and/or non-natural, in other words human. This was, naturally, beyond the pale in a slave society. Thus, it was precisely the possession of concepts, or, more precisely, the mastery of the linguistic articulation of concepts and the associated social practices that distinguished a free man from a slave. Craftspeople of those times had – as ever – thoughts with hands and hands that thought, that is, abilities to make or craft things. For the purposes of making things, those concepts took the form of and had their mode of existence in a *feel for* the making of an artefact. The associated concepts often lacked even an oral, let alone a written expression. In those days craft was still mute.[5]

Nevertheless, even at that time craft was already a method, a means, a route from raw materials to making a product, an artefact. Unlike knowledge, craft refers to something that is immediately present, to a situation, a sphere of activity, a workshop. Where a knower is faced with a single question, i.e. How are things?, masters of a craft must ask themselves no fewer than three questions as they construct their sphere of activity: How are things? How are they when they are made well? How can they be made artfully? Thus, the master of a craft describes, evaluates, and changes the world in a beautiful manner, here and now, but in what is nevertheless a valid and universal way. The methodology of craft is nothing less than a general theory about world-making.

Thus, we can see that an analysis of work that relies primarily on a programme of 'theoretically mastered labour' pays little attention to the essential and central themes that emerge from the concept of craft. If we could restore the essential constituents of craft and work, however, we could reinterpret the concept of "mediated activity", adopted from the cultural-historical school of psychology, and congruent with its methodological core.

---

[4] *Craft* refers to pulling together, stretching, while *skill* (Swedish *skilja*) refers to separating.

[5] We should recall that in classical philosophy we find a metaphor that describes the public craftsman, the *demiurge*. The main distinctions among *theoria/praxis/poiesis* arise from the notion of craftpersons' activity sphere and how that was torn apart in a way that supported the ideology of a slave society. (See, for example, Agamben, 1999; Bartels, 1965; Blumenberg, 1957; Cahoone, 1995; Dabrowski, 1990; Riedel, 1973, 1976; Solmsen, 1963; Taminiaux, 1987; Thomsen, 1990; Ulmer, 1953.)

## *The Problem of Mediation in Work Activity*

Two key researchers behind the development of activity theory, Yrjö Engeström and Georg Rückriem, have both recently paid attention to the problem of mediation involved in the development of activity theory (Engeström, 1999; Rückriem, 2003). Engeström addresses the problem of mediation by inspecting multi-contextual issues of mediation. But he does not engage in general questioning about the fundamental philosophical nature of *activity*, as this is related to the changing role of mediation.

The concept of *activity* is used in at least two comparatively different senses. Activity (*Tätigkeit, energeia*) has, particularly in the modern period, developed into an ontologising concept. That is, activity is a precondition of existence. Viewed this way, the concept of activity is used variously, ranging from mundane to philosophic, as a serviceable general concept.

On the other hand, the epistemological aspect of the concept of activity, that is to say *object-oriented activity* (*Am-Werk-Sein*), assigns no advanced qualities to that which is to be its object. Instead, any attributes emerge only *after* the relevant activity has been completed. If activity involves reshaping the object, for example by using a tool, the object *informs* the agent, in one way or another, about its resistance. The object is recognized and identified only after the activity. This feedback, missing from classical philosophy, opens up the possibility of gaining an understanding of the *civilising* essence of (craft) work.[6] Moreover, this understanding is lacking in modern philosophy of the Enlightenment and, thus, in industrial wage labour and often also among those studying it.

In Hegelian terms, the concept of object-oriented activity is a phenomenological rather than a psychological notion. The concept of activity finds its psychological equivalent in *behaving oneself* or disposition (*sich verhalten/lassen können*).[7] Here the something that serves as the object, which stands before (*Gegenstand*), is given *in advance* some characteristic or feature that then becomes the focus of activity. Accordingly, when we rewrite mediating activity we are defining the relationship between *behaving oneself* and activity.

In psychological terms, the concept of mediating activity presupposes at least three things: There are two elements with something mediated between them by a third element. Vygotsky (1986) equated this mediating factor with the word or the tool, Leontjev (1978) with activity (subject–activity–object). However, mediating activity conceived as that which makes human mental activity possible left Vygotsky facing a formidable methodological dilemma, the logical structure of mediation alone divides the mental in two, into something that serves as the source and into something that serves as the target of mediation. This was against Vygotsky's endeavour to present human mental development as a unity (see Veresov, 1999).

---

[6] The idea of *Bildung*

[7] Thus, this is not a behaviourist S–R interpretation of human behaviour but a perspective revolving around "behaving oneself," a concern with our ability and willingness to behave. On the mutual relationship between behaviour and activity see, for example, Riedel (1976) and Rubinstein (1977).

Leontjev inherits the same problem; the agent and the object of an agent's activity have an external relationship with the activity and with each other. Rephrased in psychological terms this question becomes: are interpreting the world, *behaving oneself*, and changing the world, *object-oriented activity*, two different processes?

Culturally, as a fruit of the philosophy of the Enlightenment, we are under pressure to generate this split. We can even say that the first industrial revolution split the central moments of craft work apart, turning them into opposites, severing from craft work *theoria* (Being) and *praxis* (Doing) and the main part of *poiesis* (aesthetics), reducing wage labour to the use of physical force, the labour force. On the flip side, science and scholarship, politics, and the arts all acquired, in nation states, corresponding institutions, which became the loci of externally conducted research into and externally administered protection of labour. This led, among other things, to the emergence of scientific methodologies of work research such as Taylorism, humanistic work research and, more recently, the concept of theoretically mastered labour. It led also to the emergence of poor relief and – with time – the welfare state. Further, in the course of time there evolved a massive and relatively independent machinery for the industrial production of meanings.

Can we still accept this "object of thought" (*Gedankending*, Marx)? That is, can the abstraction of wage labour and its consequences, as it emanates from modern society, be an authentic starting point for work research and work development? As far as I can see, the answer is no.

It ceased to be an acceptable starting point when the external relationship between machine and language became intertwined in a single system, *a texture*, where it is no longer possible to make an unambiguous distinction between communication and activity. Accordingly, labour is increasingly a communicative activity or activity-oriented communication. Meaning production is no less an industry than is the production of artefacts, themselves invariably carriers of a varying weight of meanings. Thus, we are not speaking about a difference among meanings carried by language and meanings mediated by artefacts but – to put it briefly – of a power relationship. How much time and social space do we as employees, citizens, consumers, fathers, mothers, and children have to devote, diversify, enrich, in other words, individualize and localize, to produce artefacts/meanings? Whether during or outside working hours it is this process of individualisation and localisation that is the process par excellence in which the mental and the social are born. Individualisation means social production.

In psychology, the relationship between communicative activity and activity-oriented communication translates into the constant endeavour to define the relationship between *activity* and *behaving oneself* (*sich verhalten/lassen können*). What is the relationship between form (*behaving oneself*) and content (*object-oriented activity*)? The answer appears with increasingly clarity when we recognize that communication and activity can be understood as different power relations vis-à-vis the object. Before communication is made, at least in principle, there is recognition of the relative independence of an object (*Anerkennung*), while in activity it is only retrospectively that we can form an idea of the object's own character

(*Aneignung*).[8] A *deed* (*Tat*) is a fundamental act that determines the relationship between behaving oneself and activity that constitutes a social time/space locus, bringing together the agent and the object. Thus, mediation is not something to be finished but instead provides a setting for an enriching constitutive act, for the construction of a social time/space locus.

How does the work sphere appear to an expert, the modern craftsperson? Experts are, of course, given assignments. They do not get their hands dirty except in a metaphorical sense. The expert sets out to generate a sphere of activity that encompasses the object of his/her work as well as the expertise itself and those who possess it. This act of constitution, this sphere of activity thus established, is a social space that makes it possible to frame and solve the three questions mentioned above. Thus, activity is not about transferring something through the medium of something else but it is an act of constitution, the construction of a space/sphere of activity. This sphere is a mediating space. This constitutive act takes place every time work starts. When an employee goes to work or starts a new job, one asks, how do they do things here? What is it that one is supposed to get done? What's the way to get it done artfully?

Thus, vocational craft is *constitutive*. In principle craft creates the methodological field map or the framework within which the three questions are asked. It is these questions and the answers given to them that generate and shape the shared sphere, a social space for learning and activity that defines the basic character of the subject, the object and the mediating process alike. That is, it defines the content of the work. This is basically a matter of scale. Every labour situation involves, in one way or another, on one scale or another, all the three questions mentioned above. The challenge involved in work lies in the question, to what extent is it possible to clear away, while going about a job, "dead work" and social fetishes by drawing on 'living work?'

Even if work tasks must be carried out according to a particular schedule, it is possible to frame the questions in a rich and concrete manner. In other words, constitutive tasks are used to reveal as fully as possible what factors are *referentially* present within the *immediate* range of the sphere of activity (that is, what the relevant description or *theoria* is), what there is in *representation* (that is, what the relevant value judgment, the conception of a good outcome is, what it represents, *praxis*), how the outcome could be brought about artfully (*poiesis*).

This presupposes that work embraces – at its best – three different temporalities: productive *idleness*, exploratory, defining *play* and artful *production*. All have

---

[8] I have here in my mind, as a heuristic tool, the different stages of the development of Hegel's subjective spirit – *adaptation* (*Anpassung*, anthropology) – *assimilation* (*Aneignung*, the start of phenomenology) – *recognition* (*Anerkennung*, the end of phenomenology) – *development* (*Entwicklung*, psychology). Vygotsky's concept of mediating activity means a jump straight from anthropology to psychology with the result that it becomes impossible to overcome the duality of the theory (internal/external, high-level/primitive psychological processes) (see Keiler, 1999; Veresov, 1999). Leontjev's theory moves within a phenomenological circle (object-oriented activity and assimilation); its methodological core has nothing to say about recognising another human being or, hence, language.

their own characteristic rhythms and temporalities, porosity and liveliness. Doing concrete work on a human scale depends on how skilfully the mutual relationships are between these three temporalities, how they are organized and on what scale, in terms both of time and space, the three basic questions are framed and solved.

## *Modes of Learning Movement at Work*

Sfard (1998) foregrounds in her well-known article two highly different metaphors of learning, emphasising that we need both. Accordingly, learning must be seen as both acquisition (*theoria*, Being) and participation (*praxis*, Doing). She argues that learning is a unity of acquiring a theory and constructing oneself as the member of a community in *praxis*. The analysis above leads to the conclusion, that we need yet a third metaphor of learning, production (*poiesis*, *Making*). But just how do these three aspects of learning, being, and making relate to each other?

This is a matter of the relationship among concept formation, interpretation, and content production, or concept, context, and content. Concepts are not bricks or billiard balls, related only externally or peripherally. On the contrary, establishing a locus of learning brings into play a shared constellation of content, context, and concept, where each of the three movements influences the others. A classical example from the realm of art is taking a bottle rack (= concept) to an art exhibition (= context) and how this constitutive act transformed views (= content) of both bottle racks and art exhibitions.

As a rule, whenever learning is consciously organized, one of these three perspectives is adopted as a starting point. There is a simultaneous choice of the mode of movement considered most important in learning. Formal learning is traditionally associated with mastering concepts in a closed and regulated environment, such as in schools. The time/space locus of learning is set aside from other pursuits and separated from the immediate vicinity with a view to fostering internal, cognitively oriented learning. Thus, formal learning is a matter of concept formation, of searching for and defining levels of abstraction and concreteness through activity that is emphatically theoretical.

To promote and enliven this activity, a learning event is often augmented with opportunities for students to gain insights into the ways in which concepts are relative and open to a variety of interpretations. The most common solution is to use different presentational and representational methods to place the things being taught in various contexts. For example, if we want to get to know Mr. Schmidt, then by placing Mr. Schmidt in our imaginations, at an art exhibition, on a playing field, in a hospital, at home or at work, we see him every time in a different light, and we gain increasingly concrete ideas about the concept of Mr. Schmidt. When we succeed in this we arrive at an understanding of Mr. Schmidt as an example[9] of

---

[9] In the sense of a *para-deigma*, *Bei-spiel*, that which has been discussed in addition to something else; see, for example Agamben (1993, pp. 8–10).

a general phenomenon. Finally we can come back to Mr. Schmidt and understand him – and hence ourselves – more concretely as a person, Arnold Schmidt.

Thus, there are two interlinked learning movements: abstraction – concretization, which means ascending to concrete awareness *and* contextualization – individualization, meaning discovering individualization. At its best, this learning movement proceeds around the circle presented in Fig. 3.1.

The problem with this circle of movement is that those involved in it drift into a mode of work that foretells cognition. As a result, the process often – though not always – stops with the definition of a general but abstract model. A diagnosis about Mr. Schmidt is identified with Arnold Schmidt. From the perspective of this diagnosis, Schmidt's special personal characteristics are contingent, of secondary importance, and can be ignored when drawing conclusions about the activities to be undertaken. Our grounds for deciding which characteristics are significant are the powers we discover and represent through the *praxis* of our own context.

A central "reason" why a learning movement comes to a halt is because systems and model-theory bring into play the relationship between linguistic signs, words and reality, the Pandora's Box of semantics. As a result, ascending to the concrete, again with Mr. Schmidt as an example, the individualisation of meaning becomes unnecessary, even impossible. Why? Because Mr. Schmidt is a labour, health, social or educational policy *case*, and the practices of these institutions make no provision for ascending to the concrete. On the contrary, they often see it as a threat to

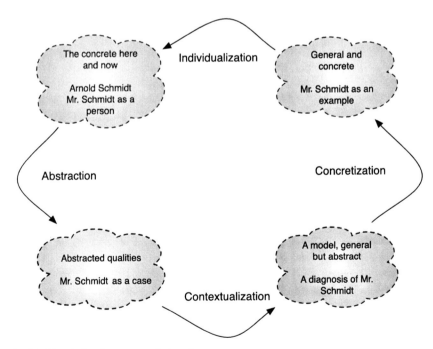

**Fig. 3.1** The circle of movements in learning

their mutual division of labour. The essential point is that Arnold Schmidt's and our prospects for growing into richer and more concrete personalities are narrowed down because we are unable to use these institutions to gain a *feel* of ourselves and other people.

The third mode of learning movement involves learning the making and learning by making. This introduces a completely different perspective – how do we as individuals, as Arnold, Peter or Mary, make our own worlds, both at work and in other areas of life? The movement of learning oscillates between me and the object. I cannot control the direction or rhythm of this movement by answering just one question, but instead I face, in my mind, all three questions.

If I were a potter shaping clay, I would give clay form and become *informed* myself. I would learn what can and cannot be done using a given type of clay and simultaneously I would learn about myself what I can or cannot do. And naturally I would – as I gained experience – learn to shift these limits in my own chosen directions. Thus, as a potter I would learn *by making*. Today, when activity and communication have – as I pointed out above – become intertwined in a single texture, this learning movement must be supported and accompanied by the two previously mentioned movement directions. Thus, the expert – today's craftsperson – moves simultaneously and separately in three different directions. From a research analytic perspective we can break this down as presented in Fig. 3.2.

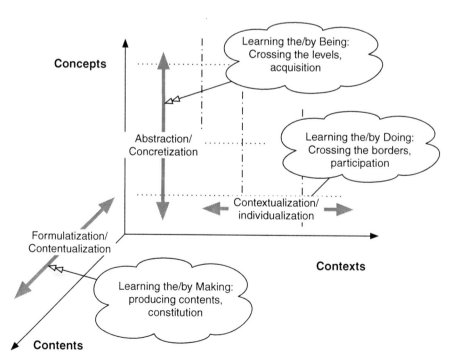

**Fig. 3.2** The three dimensions of learning

Figure 3.2 graphically represents how we read and write a work situation. Into what work situations can we read referential elements (theory), into what moments and with what elements can we write representation (*praxis*), and how are they manifested in activity? In other words, how do we describe, form value judgments and make things artfully as we work? The essential issue concerns the scale of the questions and answers in terms of time and place. Must we be content to challenge, as a part of our work, only the questions of this day, this week, or this month? Or can we, rather, address them from a long-term perspective, possibly even as problems of our age? Must we be content to frame these questions only in terms our own work, workplace, company or locality, or can we pose them nationally across Finland, pan-nationally across Europe or even globally across humanity? Thus, it is the economy of time that determines how much, and with what scope, we are able to embed into our work its epistemological, ethical, and aesthetic ideals. The main requirement of learning on the job – work as general civilizing education – presupposes placing time at the disposal of those doing the work.

## *Forms of Learning*

To summarize, we learn something in some particular context, through some particular process (*by* Being/Doing/Making) with some conceptual stake (*to Be/Do/Make*).

We can learn the concepts associated with some thing (Being), how to interpret it (Doing) or even the history of using it to make things/of making it. Learning what a hammer is and being given a description of how a hammer is used or even seeing someone using a hammer is not yet a guarantee that we would be able to hammer a nail into a wall. Playing a builder and using a toy hammer still does not get the job done.

However, we can concentrate, learn and apprehend how things are (by Being) by spending time in some environment without, properly speaking, engaging in conscious study. We can also study by playing, as a performance, the desired outcome of some activity (by Doing). We can also study by making something, thus becoming familiar with the preconditions of and the potentials for the existence of things. Table 3.3 is indicative of these possibilities.

In a concrete research and work development situation we must determine which mode of learning dominates a given situation, which mode has a supporting func-

**Table 3.3** On forms of learning

| Relationship with reality | Form | | |
|---|---|---|---|
| | In context | As a concept | As content |
| Being referentiality | Learning by being | Learning the Being | *Theoria* assimilating a phenomenon |
| Doing representation | Learning by doing | Learning the Doing | *Praxis* participation |
| Making Presence | Learning by making | Learning the Making | *Poiesis* content production |

tion, and what the scale is of each mode. Schools represent assimilative learning about things, as supported through forms of learning by doing. Coincidentally the hidden curriculum (learning by being) is in constant operation. At the workplace it is about making and experiencing accumulated learning as achieved through the process of making or producing. The question is about finding ways of embedding and situating into this form of learning other modes of the learning movement.

Using craft work as a methodological mirror which places epistemological, ethical and aesthetic before us challenges the methodological core of work development as an internal precondition of work. Concomitantly, this brings to light the need for three different metaphors of learning and for three directions of the learning movement, enabling us to gain also better understanding of their combined movement. The expert is revealed as a world-maker who establishes, constitutes a time/space locus where all three themes – epistemology, ethics, and aesthetics – are actualized and presuppose each other in the process of solving work-related problems. This means that we must in a new way think about the questions of learning in institutional settings, i.e. the question of the curriculum.

## A Paradigm for the Connective Curriculum

In Europe we have two main traditions of structuring the contents of education: *Lehrplan* and *Curriculum*. It is not possible here to go into the large spectrum of thinking, debate, and practices within and between the traditions. Let us say only this: With *Lehrplan* we open up the discussion on teaching and schooling, and with *Curriculum* that on learning and the life course. We find a lot of discussion in both traditions from the theoretical and practical points of view: deriving the content of learning from the chosen theoretical starting point opens up the spectrum of scholarship. On the other hand, taking the practical approach, we try to derive the content of learning mainly from working life.

In Finland, Pekka Ruohotie has recently made a proposal regarding the general qualifications and competences needed in working life (Ruohotie 1999; see Table 3.4).

Ruohotie's proposal is interesting. He is actually saying that *all* labour is embedded in a necessary process via which everyone personally and collectively evaluates and values the tasks that make up his/her work. In a way, he is transforming the traditional "best practices" of researches and officials into a fundamental aspect of all work. He is not only asking questions about *theory*: how does the world stand and what capabilities do we have to find out? He also asks questions of *praxis*: what should the world be like and what abilities one must have to be able, together with other workers, to conceptualize the idea of a good result?

In my view, there is one fundamental shortcoming in Ruohotie's proposal. How can we be sure that the qualifications and competences listed are learned during the course of education? For example, the structure of the Lehrplan/curriculum of upper secondary general education is not formed according to that structure but

**Table 3.4** The general qualifications and competences needed in working life (Ruohotie, 1999)

Mastery of life:
- Learning to learn
- Ability to organize and control time
- Personal strengths
- Problem solving and analysis

Communication:
- Human interaction
- Listening
- Verbal communication
- Written communication

Leading human and process:
- Coordination
- Decisions
- Handling conflicts
- Planning and organizing

Innovation and speeding up change:
- Conceptualization
- Creativity, innovation, sensitivity to change
- Handling risks
- Visionarity

on the basis of scholarship. In what kinds of situations and learning environments, and with what kinds of methods should traditional scholarship-based content be taught in order that these general abilities are formed? Or other way around: How should vocational content be taught so that these kinds of general qualifications and competences are learned? We can see that learning content derived from *theory* and *praxis* does not open up the horizon of "learning by making", i.e. the horizon of social individualization.

Deriving the content of the Lehrplan/curriculum from the starting point's *theory* or *praxis* gives us different results. But we have – as I discussed earlier – a third possibility to derive the contents of upper secondary education: production, *poiesis*. How in this case do we start to outline the contents?

A good starting point is – I think – to re-enact the classical three elements of the work process: workers, tools, and objects of work. The basic quality of the work process is heavily dependent on the relations between these three elements. Nowadays they are not outsiders to each other but mediated conceptually: no one of the three can be defined without making a reference to the other two, and at the interface there is a need for new content. We can open up seven content areas for vocational education:

## I Vocational General *Bildung*

- Questions of the economy of humankind.
- A general picture of our era, its formation and basis of production, history and main challenges.

- An analysis of the relationship between living and "dead" work, their terms, composition and limits as economic, social, natural, and human resources.
- Qualifications and competences needed in every vocation (i.e., Ruohotie's list)

## II  Vocational *Bildung*

### 1. *The Methodology of Production*

- Content which analyses how a vocation is connected to the production units as a whole, and to national and international economic development on the basis of the objective of the vocation.

### 2. *Mastering craftsmanship/profession*

- General methodology of vocations: Questions of personal view and attitude to work; questions of epistemology, ethics, and aesthetics in vocational *praxis*.

### 3. *Methods of work*

- An analysis using tools/working methods; conceptual or/and technical.

### 4. *Objective*

- An analysis of the objects of work independently of work, i.e. research-based picture and analysis of the features of the objects of work.

### 5. *Gestaltung*

- Learning to master tools/working methods in work situations, and in the service and development of work.

### 6. *Specific vocational skills*

- Methods of sweetening/handling/producing the objects of the vocation. Traditionally the central part of vocational education.

The three main approaches to forming the content of education – Beings, Doings, Makings – lead us to different results. It should be noticed, however, that the *Bildung* is not the monopoly of any one approach. Vocational and general *Bildung* are sisters, not step-sisters. The question is how to incorporate the two kinds of *halb-Bildung*, not melting them into a single mass: What is the place and function of the three approaches: Learning by being, by doing and by making? This is the key question.

When the icon of the modern era – the *machine* – turns into – as we say in Finland – the *knowledge* machine – we also have a new order of production: machines have learned to use language, languages have learned to use machines and language itself is a very basic element of production. Work can proceed neither without languages nor languages function without machines. When languages and machineries are combined in a single work process, we have a network of networks, work as *poeta faber* (Röder, 1989), poetry and work, or better still, poetic work. In this situation, we need a new *gestalt* beside the production process. The modern cultured experts have to be able to generate a social situation through which all the three questions of *philotekhne* can be posed and solved.

This means that the division of labour established in the early days of the modern era is fundamentally over. This does not mean – of course – the collapse of the division of labour but a transformation of its principles. The fundamental elements of traditional craft work, i.e. verifying (Being), valuing (Doing), and enhancing (Making) are now the fundamental aspects of all work.

To be able to handle this situation, the education of cultured experts is not only a synthesis of heads and hands. To use a traditional, even romantic expression: the development of experts and citizens with "a bright head, hot heart and golden hands" (Shuhomilinski, 1977) is to be formed and informed according the rules of Beauty, by making the sensefullness of touch a fusion of all three, the bright head, hot heart and golden hands under the government of beauty. Question is not only how to learn a set of specific skills and knowledges, but how to learn a set of virtues (Volanen, 2007; adapted from Kirkeby, 2000):

| | |
|---|---|
| *Euboulia* | • Broadminded prudence |
| *Euphoria* | • Enthusiastic sense of reality |
| *Hyponomé* | • Brave patience |
| *Prolépsis* | • Competence for anticipatory visualization |
| *Epibolé* | • Practical intuition |
| *Maieutike tekhne* | • Craft of giving birth to Goodness, Faithfulness and Beauty |

It is a long journey from being a master in a medieval guild, from the "nobility of the common man", to modern-day professions. Neither will society any longer represent itself as an organic whole nor a machine in which each individual can work for the good of all as a differentiated cell or cog. Vocation has increasingly become a job. All individual bonds with the whole have been transferred outside the work of any given profession, to be mediated in public, in a public domain. This public domain is not our own creation either, but, rather, packaged publicity.

It need not be so. We can see that *Bildung* is currently being measured in a new way. Alongside the measure of traditional national *Bildung* comes a time-related qualifier. The yardstick of *Bildung* is linked to an ability to define and solve the basic problems of our age. Let it be added – for the sake of clarity – that, of course, in order to illuminate our own age also requires knowledge of other ages. Ultimately the question is one of how we should implement practical humanism and a fully mature *Bildung*. The goals, significance, and meaning of human activity on the one hand and the tools for carrying out that activity on the other should neither be separated from one another, nor should people be cut off from each other on this basis.

As professionals we all find ourselves confronted with a conflict between our own work and the basic problems of our era: How would I solve the problems I face in my own work if I look at them, for instance, as a parent, a citizen, or a human being, and not just as an employee? What solutions emerge for my examination when I consider my professional problems from all these various angles?

The motives involved in our work clearly transcend the boundaries of our various occupations.

The reality of *Bildung*, its link with life on earth is in the last analysis decided in actual work in an occupation. The era-relatedness of a *Bildung* is apparent in its ability provide us with the means to live in the global village, to see a period and its problems here and now. Working in an occupation is one area of *Bildung* where those problems are settled for us all if only we have the ability and the freedom to perceive and read them in our everyday life. This in turn requires a fully matured *Bildung* and fully empowered citizenship – also at work.

# References

Agamben, G. (1993). *The coming community*. Minneapolis: University of Minnesota Press.
Agamben, G. (1999). *The man without content*. Standford: Standford University Press.
Bartels, K. (1965). Der Begriff *Techne* bei Aristoteles [The concept *Techne* by Aristotles]. In H. Flashar & K. Gaiser (Eds.), *Synusia. Festgabe für Wolfgang Schadewaldt zum 15. März 1965* (pp. 275–287). Pfüllingen: Neske.
Blumenberg, H. (1957). *Nachahmung der Natur*. Zur Vorgeschichte der Idee des schöpferischen Menschen [*The imitation of nature*. On the prehistory of the idea of creative man]. *Studium Generale, 10*, 266–283.
Brown, A., & Manning, S. (Eds.). (1998). *Qualifications for employment and higher education: a collaborative investigation across Europe*. Hämeenlinna: Tampereen yliopiston opettajankoulutuslaitos.
Bsirske, F., Mönig-Raane, M., Sterkel, G., & Wiedemuth, J. (Eds.). (2004). *Es ist Zeit: Das Logbuch für die ver.di – Arbeitszeitinitiative* [It's time, the logbook for work time initiative of ver.di]. Hamburg: VSA-Verlag.
Cahoone, L. E. (1995). The plurality of philosophical ends: Episteme, praxis, poiesis. *Metaphilosophy, 26*(3), 220–229.
Dabrowski, A. (1990). The academic fields of knowledge. *Science Studies, 2*, 3–21.
Engeström, Y. (1995). *Kehittävä työntutkimus. Perusteita, tuloksia ja haasteita* [Developmental work research]. Helsinki: Hallinnon kehittämiskeskus.
Engeström, Y. (1999). Activity theory and individual and social transformation. In R. Miettinen, Y. Engeström, & R.-L. Punamäki (Eds.), *Perspectives on activity theory* (pp. 19–38). Cambridge: Cambridge University Press.
Engeström, Y. (1990). *Learning, working and imagining*. Helsinki: Orienta-konsultit Oy.
Glissmann, W., & Peters, K. (2001). *Mehr Druck durch mehr Freiheit* [More pressure with more freedom]. Hamburg: VSA-Verlag.
Haug, W. F. (2003). *High -Tech-Kapitalismus* [High-tech-capitalism]. Hamburg: Argument-Verlag.
Keiler, P. (1999). *Feuerbach, Wygotski & Co. Studein zur Grundlegung einer Psychologie des gesellschaflichen Menschen* [Feuerbach, Wygotski & Co. A study to found the psychology of social man]. Hamburg: Argument-Verlag.
Kirkeby, O. F. (2000). *Management philosophy, a radical normative perspective*. Berlin: Springer.
Konttinen, E. (1991). *Perinteisesti moderniin. Professioiden yhteiskunnallinen synty Suomessa* [Achieving modernity in a traditional manner. The social emergence of professions in Finland]. Tampere: Vastapaino.
Kuutti, K. (1999). Activity theory, transformation of work, and information systems design. In R. Miettinen, Y. Engeström & R.-L. Punamäki (Eds.), *Perspectives on activity theory* (pp. 360–376). Cambridge: Cambridge University Press.
Lasonen, J., & Young, M. (Eds.). (1998). *Strategies for achieveing parity of esteem in European upper secondary education*. European Comission, Leonardo da Vinci Programme:

Surveys and Analysis: Post-16 Strategies Project. Jyväskylä: Institute for Educational Research.

Leontjev, A. N. (1978). Activity, consciousness, personality. Englewood Cliffs, NJ, Prentice Hall.

Riedel, M. (1973). Arbeit [Work]. In H. Krings, H. M. Baumgartner, & C. Wild (Eds.), *Handbuch Philosopischer Grundberiffe* (pp. 125–141). München: Kösel-Verlag.

Riedel, R. (1976). *Theorie und Praxis in Denken Hegels Interpretationen zu den Grundstellungen der neuzeitlichen Subjectivität* [Theory and practice in Hegels' thinking, Interpretations of the foundings of the modern subjectivity]. Frankfurt/M: Ullstein-Verlag.

Rubinstein, S. L. (1977). *Grundlagen der Allgemeine Psychologie* [Basics of the general psychology]. Berlin: Volk und Wissen.

Rückriem, G. (2003). *Tool or medium the meaning of information and telecommunication technology to human practice. A quest for systemic understanding of activity theory.* Toiminta03 – Toiminnan teorian ja sosiokulttuurisen tutkimuksen päivät, ISCAR Finnish section, Kauniainen, Finland. Retrieved March 15, 2004, from http://iscar.org/fi/ruckriem.pdf

Ruohotie, P. (1999). Työelämä muuttuu, muuttuuko opetus? [Working life is changing – Does the instruction change?]. *Ammattikasvatuksen aikakauskirja, 1*(2), 4–7.

Röder, P. (1989). Poeta Faber. Der frühromantische poiesis-Gedanke und die Idee der 'freien bewussten Tätigkeit' bei Karl Marx [Poeta faber. The early romantic concept of poiesis and the idea of 'the free conscious activity' according to Karl Marx]. *Deutsche vierteljahrsschift für Literaturwissenschaft und Geistesgeschichte, 63*(3), 521–546.

Schmitthenner, H., & Peters, J. (2003). *Gute arbeit . . .Menschengerechte Arbeitgestaltung als gewerkschaftliche Zukunftsaufgabe* [Good work]. Hamburg: VSA-Verlag.

Shuhomilinski, V. (1977). *Sydämeni lapsille annan* [I give my heart to children]. Moscow: Progress.

Schumann, M. (2003). *Metamorphosen von Industriearbeit und Arbeiterbewusstsein* [Metamorphosis of industrial work and worker's consiousness]. Hamburg: VSA-Verlag.

Sfard, A. (1998). On the metaphors for learning and dangers of choosing just one. *Educational Researcher, 27*(2), 4–13.

Siegrist, H. (1990). Professionalization as a process: patterns, progression and discontinuity. In M. Burrage, & R. Torstendahl (Eds.), *Professions in theory and history* (pp. 177–202). London: SAGE publications.

Solmsen, F. (1963). Nature as crafsman in Creek thought. *Journal of the History of Ideas, 24*, 473–496.

Stenström, M.-L., & Lasonen, J. (Eds.). (2000). *Strategies for reforming initial vocational education and training in Europe.* Jyväskylä: University of Jyväskylä. Institute for Educational Research.

Taminiaux, J. (1987). Poiesis and praxis in fundamental ontology. *Research in Phenomenology, 17*(2), 137–169.

Thomsen, D. (1990). *Techne als Metapher and als Begriff der sittlichen Einsicht* [*Techne* as metaphor and as concept of ethical insight]. Freiburg/München: Karl Alber Verlag.

Toikka, K. 1982. *Kvalifikaatio ja työn vaatimukset koulutuksen suunnnittelun lähtökohtana* [Qualification and the demands of work as a startings point to educational design]. Helsinki: Valtion painatuskeskus.

Toikka, K. (1984). *Kehittävä kvalifikaatiotutkimus* [Developmental qualification research]. Helsinki: Valtion koulutuskeskus.

Turner, S. T. (1993). *Citizenship and social theory.* London: SAGE publications.

Ulmer, K. (1953). *Wahrheit, Kunst und Natur bei Aristoteles* [Truth, art and nature according to Aristotle]. Tübingen: Max Niemeyer Verlag.

Veresov, N. (1999). *Undiscovered Vygotsky.* Frankfurt am Mein: Peter Lang Verlag.

Volanen, M. V. (2005). Craft work as a methodological mirror for labour development, learning the skills. *Special edition of the Finnish Journal of Vocational and Professional Education*, 11–23.

Volanen, M. V. (2006). *Filoteknia ja kysymys sivistävästä työstä* [Philotechne and the question of educative work]. Koulutuksen tutkimuslaitos, Jyväskylä: Yliopistopaino.

Volanen, M. V. (2007). Craft and art in engineering. Philotechne as an ideal of *Bildung* in engineering education. In S.H. Christensen, M. Meganck, & B. Dalahousse (Eds.), *Philosophy in engineering* (pp. 65–81). Copenhagen: Academica.

Volanen, M. V. (1992, October). Open structures and open options in education. Paper presented in OECD VOTEC -seminar: *Assessment, certification and recognition of occupational skills and competences*, Oporto, Portugal.

Whalley, P., & Barley, S. (1997). Technical work in the division of labor: Stalking the wile anomaly. In S.B. Barley, & E.J. Orr (Eds.), *Between craft and science* (pp. 23–52). Ithaca: Cornell University press.

Wolf, H. (1999). *Arbeit und Autonomie – Eine Versuch über Widersprüche und Metamorphosen kapitalistische Production* [Work and autonomy – An attempt to analyse the tensions and metamorphoses in capitalistic production]. Münster: Verlag Westfälisches Dampfboot.

Vygotsky, L. S. (1986). Thought and language. Cambridge, MA: MIT Press.

# Part II
# Integrating Work and Learning in Individual Experiences

# Chapter 4
# Connecting Work and Learning in Industrial Design and Development

Kaija Collin

## Introduction

This chapter discusses individual learning in the workplace in the light of a study of Finnish design engineers' and product developers' learning through their work. The designers' work practices and their learning in the course of these activities are described as perceived by the designers themselves. The chapter also examines their learning through the various individual and social processes ongoing in the workplace.

The chapter proceeds as follows: first, phenomenon of workplace learning or learning through work is described. Second, the work of product designers and development engineers is conceptualised on the basis on the recent literature and studies in the field. Third, the methodological choices made in the course of the research process are briefly described and evaluated and the main findings obtained from the different phases of the research process are summarised. Finally, the findings of the study are drawn together. Further ideas for researching designers' learning through their work and how the formal education of designers could be developed in connection with these ideas are offered. In addition, more general suggestions concerning the guidance of workplace learning are given, and the challenges presented by guiding and assessing workplace learning in the vocational education context are examined.

Of particular interest in the above-mentioned study is the connection at various levels between learning and work. The results indicate a need for more effective integration between education and working life. Also of interest is the connection between work and learning. The concept of connectivity here is thus approached from two perspectives. First, the need to connect the theoretical knowledge acquired at school with the practical knowledge gained from everyday work practices and, second, the need to see individual and social learning processes at work as linked.

K. Collin (✉)
Department of Educational Sciences, University of Jyväskylä, Jyväskylä, Finland
e-mail: kaija.collin@edu.jyu.fi

M.-L. Stenström, P. Tynjälä (eds.), *Towards Integration of Work and Learning*,
© Springer Science+Business Media B.V. 2009

# Characteristics of Workplace Learning and Design Work

The study, on which this chapter is based investigates design engineers' and product designers' learning at work. The main results and practical implications of the PhD study (see Collin, 2005) have previously been presented also in Collin's article (2006). The reasons for the growing interest that has been shown in workplace learning over the last decade are diverse. For instance, the concepts of the knowledge society and the learning society (see e.g. Heiskanen, 2004), which are being increasingly referred to, challenge workers and organisations to structure work in new ways. The phenomenon of workplace learning is of interest in many quarters, e.g. enterprises and organisations, vocational education personnel, human resource development practitioners, and workers themselves, but for different reasons. From the point of view of enterprises and employers, for instance, employees' learning through work contributes to the development of the vocational and professional knowledge needed for work. An equally important reason usually associated with companies and organisations is that learning is directly relevant to their specific needs which, it is hoped, will lead to better productivity and increased competitiveness (Billett, 2001). For the individual worker, constant learning may be the route to personal fulfilment and joy, progress in one's career or a way to strengthen the sense of self and identity (Lavikka, 2004). At government level goals are often focussed on making the content of vocational education programs relevant to industry and directly applicable within enterprises, whereas teachers of vocational institutions attempt to assist their students to transfer classroom experiences to other, non-formal situations (Billett, 2001). Consequently, this chapter is primarily concerned with the question of how learning in education and working life contexts may be connected so that agents at different levels (teachers, students, employers and employees) may find their learning meaningful.

*Characteristics of workplace learning*: Although studies in the complex and challenging field of workplace learning have proliferated in recent years (Billett, 2001; Engeström, 2001; Eraut, Alderton, Cole, & Senker, 1998; Gerber, Lankshear, Larsson, & Svensson, 1995; Marsick & Watkins, 1990; Wenger, 1998), they still seem to lack systematic, properly conceptualised and comprehensive theorisation (Candy & Matthews, 1998). However, despite the eclectic and pluralistic nature of the research that has been done on workplace learning and the need for appropriate conceptual and methodological tools, it is possible to discern a certain measure of agreement about what characterises this field of inquiry. First, workplace learning is described as informal, incidental and practice-bound, this is, learning and work practices are difficult to separate from each other under the rapidly changing conditions of working life (see e.g. Lave, 1993; Watkins & Marsick, 1992). This characteristic is, however, a very general one and hardly serves as a comprehensive picture of the phenomenon. So while conceptions of workplaces as informal, incidental and situated learning environments are helpful in distinguishing them from what goes on in educational institutions, they are problematic in the work context. There is a need to go beyond such characterisations and consider workplaces more broadly as learning environments. This is the reason why the characteristics of workplace learning to be described next, are seen from the perspectives of individual experiences and collective and shared practices.

Second, individual work experiences seem to have primary importance for work and learning (Beckett, 2001; Boud & Miller, 1996; Gerber, 2001). The basis of workplace learning lies largely in experience, that is, the ways in which people make sense of situations they encounter in their daily lives (Marsick & Watkins, 1990; Weick, 1995). Learning is embedded in everyday problem-solving situations (Bereiter & Scardamalia, 1993), in the accumulation of competencies, in learning through mistakes and in interactive negotiations with colleagues. The basis of learning in the workplace is thus seen as the making of practical decisions and as the application of personal experience to the solving of specific problems or the performing of specific tasks, using intuition and common sense (Gerber, 2001) and making sensible judgements (see also Beckett & Hager, 2000). Learning is perceived here as the accumulation of experience and with reflection taking place, if at all, only after (cf. Schön, 1983: reflection-on-action) the task has been completed or the problem solved (e.g. Fisher, 2002; Rasmussen, 2002; Torraco, 1999).

Third, working tasks and contexts determine what and how it is possible to learn at work (Brown, Collins, & Duguid, 1989; Karakowsky & McBey, 1999; Lave & Wenger, 1991). Competence can be neither separated from the context in which the performance is expected to occur nor transferred from one context to another (Ellström, 1997; Järvinen & Poikela, 2001; Orr, 1996; Sandberg, 2000; Torraco, 1999). It has been widely recognised (see e.g. Darrah, 1995, 1996; Eraut, 2002; Lave, 1993; Wenger, 1998) that in large part workplace learning is accomplished through participation in workplaces and is best understood by examining the relationship between practical work activities, the cultural and social relations of the workplace and the experience and social world of the participants (Evans & Rainbird, 2002).

Finally, learning is shared and it usually seems to occur together with colleagues and various networks connected individual worker's practices (Eteläpelto & Collin, 2004; Gherardi, 2001; Orr, 1996; Rainbird, Fuller, & Munro, 2004). Learning, the technical performance of work tasks and the social life of the workplace are not separate elements of the work process (see Henriksson, 2000). They are inherent and intertwined. As teamwork and networking become more widespread, more and more jobs come increasingly to involve social activities. Despite the few concrete accounts that have been published on how learning and competent occupational activity take place in everyday social work situations (Eteläpelto & Collin, 2004), the most concrete forms of learning in the workplace are argued to take place within the format of asking for and giving advice in relation to everyday work activities. Rational everyday activity is found to grow through the local logic of everyday talk, particularly in the intensity and intimacy of face-to-face interaction, for instance, with colleagues and customers (Boden, 1995).

*Characteristics of product design and development*: Technical product design and development has previously been described as an individual and linear problem-solving process. More recent studies, however, emphasise that design is a collaborative and "messy" practice rather than intentional planning or the following of a general problem-solving procedure (Gedenryd, 1998; Henderson, 1999; Schuler & Namioka, 1993). It is also a group endeavour and takes place within multi-professional teams and within larger organisational contexts (Eteläpelto, 1998; Sharrock & Button, 1997). Consequently, design work should be seen as an innovative and creative practice which requires continuous learning and development.

Apart from the study described in this chapter a few other studies have recently been conducted in the area of engineers' learning. Senker (2000) investigated the work of engineers and technicians in companies whose task was to develop engineering products and who worked in an environment of rapid technological change. Like Lave (1993) and others before him, he found that, at a general level, working and learning cannot be separated. Instead, the complexity and variability of engineers' learning processes and the extent to which most are embedded in day-to-day work is considerable. More concretely, learning seems to arise largely out of the challenge posed by work, for example, solving problems, improving quality, getting things done, coping with change, and out of interaction with colleagues and customers. Learning at work can be described as taking place through and from experiences gained from various sources and contexts, for instance, from past mistakes. Senker (2000) concludes by saying that many engineers' working lives could be described as a "continual apprenticeship" in which all learning does not necessarily take place at the initial stages of working life but throughout it. In doing so, he provides another term for thinking about a tradition which has long existed in the Nordic countries about life-long learning, and which has been popularised and embodied in various official policies (see Angervall & Thång, 2003).

An additional view of workplace learning is offered by Rasmussen (2002) who studied designers' work in Denmark. On the basis of in-depth interviews with 26 industrial designers, he emphasises, in addition to the experiential and social aspects of learning, the importance of the aspects of visuality and creativity for designers' work and learning. Design practice, as well as the learning acquired through it, requires the freedom to organise and carry out one's work. It also depends on the availability of time to rebuild, modify and reorganise one's daily work experiences through formal and informal dialogue with colleagues. He concludes, however, that the prerequisites for learning in the workplace are seriously restricted, if there is no possibility for communication between the different people within the company. A shared understanding of the various roles that people have at work and the free flow of information across the contexts of work are needed for the job to be done and learning to fully take place.

## Researching Engineers' Learning at Work

As stated above, workplace learning as a phenomenon seems to be made up of elements which concern work practices per se, how workers learn through their work experiences and how in turn these experiences simultaneously define their individual agency, and how social and communal elements affect how learning takes place and what kind of learning is possible in various environments in the first place. Following from this conclusion, the study described here adopted a multiple perspective on the practices of work, design work especially, and the ways learning can take place through those practices. Empirical interest was thus focused on how designers themselves perceived their practices and learning through those practices. Further, the social and collective elements of learning were investigated more closely.

## Aim of the Study

The aim of the research process was to capture design engineers' own conceptions and experiences of their learning in authentic work contexts as well as describe how their learning is connected to the work itself and to various social processes relating to their work practices. The study thus addressed three major questions: (1) What conceptions do design engineers have of learning at work? (2) What role does previous work experience have in on-the-job learning in the domain of design work? (3) How do engineers learn through shared practices of design and development work?

*How was the study conducted?* Ethnography was chosen as the broader methodological approach. Within the ethnographic frame a variety of complementary data collection and analytical tools were used. Designers' conceptions and experiences were mapped with the help of interviews ($n = 18$) and analytical methods applicable to the research questions, such as phenomenographic and narrative analysis. Shared practices were examined through observations (5–6 weeks in each company) and ethnographic analyses. In addition, the designers' experiences of the relation between learning in formal education and through their work practices were compared. The design and product engineers were chosen as participants for the study from two high-tech companies in central Finland. One company is an international supplier of industrial workstations and flexible production systems while the other supplies services to the electronics manufacturing industry. The educational background of the participants varied from vocational education to university degrees and their work experience varied from a few months to more than 20 years (for further details, see Collin, 2005.)

## What Is Workplace Learning Like for Designer?

This section summarises the main findings of the study on design engineers' learning at work. Table 4.1, which follows after the presentation of the results, presents a summary of the findings.

*Design engineers conceptions of learning at work*: The first phase phenomenographic analysis of this study revealed the multi-faceted nature of workplace learning. The analysis produced six different conceptions of learning at work (see Collin, 2002). The first and the second categories emphasised the importance of

**Table 4.1** Summary of the main findings

| Conceptions of learning at work | The role of experience in learning | Work and learning as shared practice | Integration of theory and practice |
|---|---|---|---|
| 1) Learning through doing the job<br>2) Learning through co-operation and interaction with colleagues<br>3) Learning through evaluating work experiences<br>4) Learning through taking on something new<br>5) Learning through formal education<br>6) Learning through extra work contexts | 1) The challenge of social interaction at work<br>2) Acquiring a holistic picture of work processes and projects<br>3) Learning from other peoples' experiences<br>4) Creating one's own view | 1) Maintenance of a sense of community and a good atmosphere<br>2) Practice is situated, interim and open-ended<br>3) Practice includes conflicts and contradictory aims<br>4) Practice involves the shared solving of work-related problems linked with networks outside workplace | A) Relationship between theory and practical action:<br><br>- as a continuum<br>- theoretical knowledge to be replaced by practical knowledge required at work<br>- as complementary and often integrated<br><br>B) Different contexts of education and work |

doing the actual job and learning through co-operation and interaction in everyday work practices. The role of prior experience for learning at work was also seen as useful although the designers stressed that their work also involves learning through doing something wholly new, that is, through acquiring new information, considering different options, experimenting, developing fresh ideas, acting creatively and producing a new product. In addition, designers were of the view that the role of previous education and various other influences outside the work (such as friends and customers, etc.) should not be overlooked as a source of learning. (See Table 4.1, first column.)

*The role of previous work experiences for designers' work and learning*: On the basis of the conceptions of learning at work obtained from the phenomenographic analysis, the role of experience for designers' work and learning emerged as a theme that merited closer scrutiny (see Collin, 2004). Experience seemed to play a major role in designers' everyday interaction with each other and co-operation in general. Co-operation and interaction are a means for learning but, at the same time, also the focus of learning, which can take place only through working with other people. The designers emphasised that learning within everyday social interaction was characterised by the important role of learning through practical experience. Another dimension that emerged from the narrative analysis was the vital role of acquiring a holistic picture of work processes and projects. This kind of work process knowledge (see Boreham, Samurçay, & Fisher, 2002) is best obtained through everyday experience of the job. The designers also reported that the experiences or mistakes of other people, for instance colleagues, may be as instructive as their own. Above all, the designers stressed that work experience accumulated during the course of one's career is a vital factor in how they create their own ways of thinking and see what is important in design. (Table 4.1, the second column from the left.)

*Engineers learn through shared problem-solving and shared practices*: The social interaction and shared practices of design work were investigated more profoundly with the help of ethnographic analysis (see Collin, 2005; Collin & Valleala, 2005). Four thematic categories characterised learning through shared practices. (Table 4.1, third column.) First, the maintenance of a sense of community and a good atmosphere were important stimuli in relation to work processes and learning in them. However, the efforts made to sustain this sense of smooth interaction were considerable. A positive atmosphere was achieved, for instance, by joking with colleagues and labelling (team) participants not physically present (see Sacks, 1992). This kind of joking and social categorisation is an example of an activity in which each worker's identity and status within the work community is constructed and defined (Billett & Somerville, 2004). Categorisation enables workers to find out how they are rated in their work environment. Second, the ethnographic analysis revealed that work practices are temporary and situational and in a state of constant flux. Working goals and plans are redefined during processes and projects. Problems and their solutions are also negotiated and constructed anew on each occasion in teams and groups. Third, shared practices were not constituted without problems but included conflicts and disagreement. Everyday practice may thus include disagreement and dissension, which may harm or at least present a challenge to social learning, but which may also assist in creating solidarity between team members in the face of external forces. Fourth, the results imply that designers' work in reality often involves, in addition to co-operation with the closer social community and team described above, collaboration with various groupings and networks outside the workplace. Accordingly, as the engineers described it, their work meant continual negotiations with the customer about their requirements and how these could be met. The designers also stressed that the successful completion of a task depends very much on having as comprehensive a grasp as possible of the relevant work processes.

*Comparing designers' learning in formal and informal contexts*: The designers' conceptions of learning in formal education and at work and the relations between those learning contexts were also examined (see Collin & Tynjälä, 2003). The analysis yielded three ways of seeing the relation between the designers' perceptions of theory and their perceptions of practice in the context of work and learning. (Table 4.1, fourth column.) Firstly, the relationship between theoretical knowledge and practical competence acquired on the job was perceived as a continuum. On this view one is aware of the distinction between knowledge gained at school and knowledge accumulated at work, but at the same time one recognises both as necessary preconditions for the successful performance of one's job. Secondly, theoretical knowledge acquired in formal education was seen as replaced by new practical knowledge required at work. Thirdly, theory and practice were seen as complementary and often integrated components of competence, both of which are needed in working life. The designers perceived the *contexts of learning* in education and at work as different as well. For instance, the two contexts differ in their aims. Work and learning at work draw their deepest motivation from "an authentic, concrete or real aim that the work activity is intended to achieve". In working life such an aim is easy to picture, while merely studying for an exam is not seen as enough of a challenge to take learning seriously.

*Individual experiences and shared practices of learning at work: are they connected?* On the basis of the results described above design work and learning through it was redefined as follows: (1) Learning and work practices cannot be separated from each other. Learning is subsumed in design practice itself. (2) The separation of theory and practice is not necessary in everyday practice. (3) Prior work experience has a major role in learning through design work. (4) Design practices are situated, shared, networked and contextualised. At a more general level it can be concluded that learning in the workplace cannot be described or explained only by means of concepts and ideas borrowed from formal education. Instead, it should be addressed using its own vocabulary and processes. Neither can the nature of workplace learning be captured by describing it simply as informal. Further, studies in the area have revealed many important processes concerning learning. The most important finding of this study is that individual aspects, for instance, the employee's accumulated previous work experience and the social life of working practices should be treated as intertwined in considering the phenomenon of workplace learning (see also Billett, 2006).

## Connecting Work and Learning?

The results of this study indicate many directions for further study and have a number of practical implications. One evident challenge for further elaboration and research that emerges is the challenge of *connecting the individual and social aspects of workplace learning both theoretically and empirically*. Empirically, the challenge is how to connect these aspects analytically and methodologically. From the perspectives of workplace practice and learning a further challenge may be how to take both aspects simultaneously into account when developing work practices and enhancing learning through these practices. Consequently, in the future, it would be important to investigate the mediating processes of individual and social learning as a learning space created during both of these processes.

Learning, then, is to be seen as a holistic and ubiquitous process that takes place through normal working practices. Hodkinson et al. (2004), among others, argue in much the same vein as Beckett & Hager (2002), that the individual and the social, agency and structure are blended, thereby losing much of their significance as separate issues. Understanding and theorising workplace learning should thus avoid either over-emphasising individual agency or to slipping into organisational (contextual) and cultural determinism. On the contrary, they are interrelated and constituted by each other in every-day work practices. Learning involves a complex and often reflexive interrelationship between the community of practice, individual dispositions to learning, inequalities of position and capital, and wider influences upon, and attributes of, the field of work in question. Therefore, workplace learning cannot be understood by the abstracting any of these elements at the cost of the others.

On the understanding that workplace learning is neither wholly socially nor individually determined, the interdependence between the two has been subjected to closer scrutiny. Billett (2004), for instance, proposes that distinct contributions to this interdependence will be found in the historical, cultural, and contextual sources of knowledge located in workplaces. In his study he showed that contextual and shared knowledge is used in many situations in which co-operation and interaction with colleagues, clients and various networks take place. As Billett also shows, such shared learning emerges and is reconstituted in various situations in which, for instance, functional relationships and a cosy atmosphere of team practice are sustained, or the experience and expertise of colleagues are called on in helping to solve everyday problems. He goes on to say that these contributions from cultural and contextual sources of knowledge are shaped and privileged by situational practices.

*Practical challenges for connecting workplace learning and school learning in work practices and vocational education practices*: In recent years the importance of integrating theoretical and practical knowing in, for instance, the area of vocational education, has been widely discussed. Recent accounts on the development of expertise, to take one example, have emphasised that the integration of formal or theoretical knowledge, practical knowledge (know-how or skills), and self-regulative knowledge, including metacognitive and reflective skills (Bereiter & Scardamalia, 1993; Eraut, 1994; Eteläpelto & Light, 1999) is of fundamental importance. For example, Leinhardt, McCarthy Young, & Merriman (1995) stated that education should involve fusing theory and practice. Recent studies have also contributed the concept of work process knowledge (Boreham et al., 2002). This is knowledge which is continuously being produced in the workplace through the work process itself and is characterised by its usefulness for work; it includes the dimensions of both practical knowledge and theoretical understanding and is held collectively as well as individually. According to Boreham (2002, p. 8) work process knowledge is generated when theoretical knowledge is integrated with experiential know-how in the course of solving problems at work.

In case of design work, especially, there seems to be a need to analyse different kinds of jobs, tasks and work processes done in the contemporary workplace. In addition, how these processes and practices are related to each other in larger entities should be analysed in greater depth. The people who are actually practising inside the organisation should do this, not people from outside the organisation or team since the workers themselves are constantly reconstituting their practices. Thus, if the target of vocational education in the case of designers, for instance, is to develop innovative, risk-taking, reflective problem-solvers, then learning tasks and larger authentic WBL projects, for instance, should be designed as open-ended and context-bound. Learning tasks should also encourage experimentation and creative information gathering, and allow open and optional outcomes. Therefore, open and flexible learning environments for the needs of design students should be developed in order to be able to take the interdependence between the individual and the social aspects of learning into account.

Another way of improving vocational practices related to learning in the workplace would be the adoption of various existing work-based learning procedures. WBL can take place in a variety of forms, such as in working life-oriented projects (see Helle, Tynjälä, & Vesterinen, 2006), excursions, and an alternating sequence of placements or part-time employment. However, in implementing this kind of learning it is important that the learning contracts and contents of the learning programme are negotiated by three partners: students, employers and vocational institutions, and that the implementation of such learning is based on real-time and work-based, authentic projects (see Tynjälä, Välimaa, & Sarja, 2003). On the basis of the present findings, a promising direction for such projects would be to analyse work done in relation to what has been learned in the school environment. Such analytical learning tasks, connected to learning diaries, may provide an opportunity to critically evaluate one's learning in an authentic working environment. Fruitful co-operation, in turn, can be ensured by further developing a functional relationship between education and working life.

Given that learning at work can be approached as a multi-faceted phenomenon, including various processes in which the social and individual aspects are interdependent, it is reasonable to conclude that these aspects should be better taken into account in vocational education in general. This is especially important because the public debate about training in general has been criticised (see Eraut, 2004) not only for neglecting informal learning but also for disregarding complexity by over-simplifying the processes and outcomes of learning and the factors that give rise to it. Working contexts, for instance, can be so varied, that individual learning may be totally impossible in one context while in another it can be a successful experience both for the student and for the organisation.

Another recent study (see Virtanen, Tynjälä, & Valkonen, 2005, pp. 77–82) shows how success in work-related learning, evaluated by the students themselves, is dependent both on elements related to the individual student and on the circumstances of the workplace. Although motivational factors, among others, were important in how far students felt that they had succeeded in their learning, positive experiences of how they were treated as equals in organisational participation also played a central role in their enjoyment of their placement and of their learning at work. Thus it seems evident that providing students with the possibility to practice in many different organisational and vocational contexts during their vocational education would be one way of encouraging successful workplace learning during this life phase.

To conclude, a better understanding of the processes and practices of workplace learning may also help in developing the guidance of workplace learning periods conducted in vocational education organisations. As indicated in this study, for workers work and education are perceived as very different learning contexts. Work and learning through work was perceived as "real" action guided by the authentic problem-solving situations. Therefore the integration of formal learning and workplace learning seems to be important. On the basis of the findings of this study of designers' perceptions, it is suggested that more supportive and participative elements should be included in formal workplace learning practices so that the communal could become as important an aspect of schools' cultures as it is a natural part of workplace practices.

# References

Angervall, P., & Thång, P. -O. (2003). Learning in working life – From theory to practice. In T. Tuomi-Gröhn & Y. Engeström (Eds.), *Between school and work: New perspectives on transfer and boundary-crossing* (pp. 257–270). Amsterdam: Elsevier.

Beckett, D. (2001). Hot action at work: a different understanding of "understanding". In T. Fenwick (Ed.), *Sociocultural perspectives on learning at work* (pp. 73–83). New York: Jossey-Bass.

Beckett, D., & Hager, P. (2000). Making judgements as the basis for workplace learning: Towards an epistemology of practice. *International Journal of Lifelong Learning, 19*(4), 300–311.

Beckett, D., & Hager, P. (2002). *Life, work and learning. Practice in postmodernity.* New York: Routledge.

Bereiter, C., & Scardamalia, M. (1993). *Surpassing ourselves: An inquiry into the nature of expertise.* Chicago: Open Court.

Billett, S. (2001). *Learning in the workplace. Strategies for effective practice.* Crows Nest: Allen & Unwin.

Billett, S. (2004). Learning through work: Workplace participatory practices. In H. Rainbird, A. Fuller, & A. Munro (Eds.), *Workplace learning in context* (pp. 109–125). London: Routledge.

Billett, S. (2006). Relational interdependence between social and individual agency in work and working life. *Mind, Culture and Activity, 13*(1), 53–69.

Billett, S., & Somerville, M. (2004). Transformations at work: Identity and learning. *Studies in Continuing Education, 26*(2), 309–326.

Boden, D. (1995). Agendas and arrangements: Everyday negotiations in meetings. In A. Firth (Ed.), *The discourse of negotiation. Studies of language in the workplace* (pp. 83–99). Oxford: Elsevier Science/Pergamon.

Boreham, N. (2002). Work process knowledge in technological and organizational development. In N. Boreham, R. Samurcay, & M. Fisher (Eds.), *Work process knowledge* (pp. 1–14). London: Routledge.

Boreham, N., Samurcay, R., & Fisher, M. (Eds.). (2002). *Work process knowledge.* London: Routledge.

Boud, D., & Miller, N. (1996). Synthesising traditions and identifying themes in learning from experience. In D. Boud, & N. Miller (Eds.), *Working with experience* (pp. 9–18). London: Routledge.

Brown, J. S., Collins, A., & Duguid, P. (1989). Situated cognition and the culture of learning. *Educational Researcher, 18*(1), 32–42.

Candy, P., & Matthews, J. (1998). Fusing learning and work: Changing conceptions of workplace learning. In D. Boud (Ed.), *Current issues and new agendas in workplace learning* (pp. 9–30). Springfield (VA.): NCVER.

Collin, K. (2002). Development engineers' conceptions of learning at work. *Studies in Continuing Education, 24*(2), 133–152.

Collin, K. (2004). The role of experience in development engineers' work and learning. *International Journal of Training and Development, 8*(2), 111–127.

Collin, K. (2005). *Experience and shared practice. Design engineers' learning at work* (Jyväskylä Studies in Education, Psychology and Social Research No. 261). Jyväskylä: Jyväskylä University Printing House.

Collin, K. (2006). Connecting work and learning: design engineers' learning at work. *The Journal of Workplace Learning, 18*(7/8), 403–413.

Collin, K. (2008). Development engineers' work and learning as shared practice. *International Journal of Lifelong Education, 127*(4), 379–397.

Collin, K., & Tynjälä, P. (2003). Integrating theory and practice? Employees' and students experiences of learning at work. *Journal of Workplace Learning, 15*(7–8), 338–344.

Collin, K., & Valleala, U. M. (2005). Interaction among employees – How does learning take place in the social communities of the workplace and how might such learning be supervised? *Journal of Education and Work, 18*(4), 401–420.

Darrah, C. (1995). Workplace training, workplace learning: A case study. *Human Organization, 54*(1), 31–41.

Darrah, C. (1996). *Learning at work: An exploration in industrial ethnography*. London: Garland Publishing.

Ellström, P.-E. (1997). The many meanings of occupational competence and qualification. In A. Brown (Ed.), *Promoting vocational education and training: European perspectives* (Ammattikasvatussarja No. 17, pp. 47–58). Hämeenlinna: Tampereen yliopiston opettajankoulutuslaitos.

Engeström, Y. (2001). Expansive learning at work: Toward an activity theoretical reconceptualization. *Journal of Education and Work, 14*(1), 133–156.

Eraut, M. (1994). *Developing professional knowledge and competence*. London: Falmer.

Eraut, M. (2002). The interaction between qualifications and work-based learning. In K. Evans, P. Hodkinson, & L. Unwin (Eds.), *Working to learn – Transforming learning in the workplace* (pp. 63–78). London: Kogan Page.

Eraut, M. (2004). Informal learning in the workplace. *Studies in Continuing Education, 26*(2), 247–274.

Eraut, M., Alderton, J., Cole, G., & Senker, P. (1998). Learning from other people at work. In F. Coffield (Ed.), *Learning at work* (pp. 37–48). Bristol: The Policy Press.

Eteläpelto, A. (1998). *The development of expertise in information systems design* (Jyväskylä Studies in Education, Psychology and Social Research No. 146). Jyväskylä: University of Jyväskylä.

Eteläpelto, A., & Collin, K. (2004). From individual cognition to communities of practice. In H. P. A. Boshuizen, R. Bromme, & H. Gruber (Eds.), *Professional learning: Gaps and transitions on the way from novice to expert* (pp. 231–250). Dordrecht: Kluwer Academic Publishers.

Eteläpelto, A., & Light, P. (1999). Contextual knowledge in the development of design expertise. In J. Bliss, P. Light, & R. Säljö (Eds.), *Learning sites: Social and technological resources for learning* (pp. 155–164). Oxford: Pergamon/Elsevier.

Evans, K., & Rainbird, H. (2002). The significance of workplace learning for a 'learning society'. In K. Evans, P. Hodkinson, & L. Unwin (Eds.), *Working to learn – Transforming learning in the workplace* (pp. 7–28). London: Kogan Page.

Fisher, M. (2002). Work experience as an element of work process knowledge. In N. Boreham, R. Samurcay, & M. Fisher (Eds.), *Work process knowledge* (pp. 119–133). London: Routledge.

Gedenryd, H. (1998). *How designers work – Making sense of authentic cognitive activities* (Lund University cognitive studies No. 75). Lund: Lund University.

Gerber, R. (2001). The concept of common sense in workplace learning and experience. *Education + Training, 43*(2), 72–81.

Gerber, R., Lankshear, C., Larsson, S., & Svensson, L. (1995). Self-directed learning in a work context. *Education + Training, 37*(8), 26–32.

Gherardi, S. (2001). From organizational learning to practice-based knowing. *Human Relations, 54*(1), 131–139.

Heiskanen, T. (2004). Spaces, places and communities of practice. In T. Heiskanen, & J. Hearn (Eds.), *Information society and the workplace* (pp. 3–25). London: Routlegde.

Helle, L., Tynjälä, P., & Vesterinen, P. (2006). Work-related project as a learning environment. In P. Tynjälä, J. Välimaa, & G. Boulton-Lewis (Eds.), *Higher education and working life. Collaborations, confrontations and challenges* (pp. 195–208). Amsterdam: Elsevier.

Henderson, K. (1999). *On line and on paper. Visual representations, visual culture, and computer graphics in design engineering*. London: The MIT Press.

Henriksson, K. (2000). *When communities of practice came to town. On culture and contradiction in emerging theories of organizational learning* (Working Paper Series No. 3). Lund: Lund University, Lund Institute of Economic Research.

Hodkinson, P., Hodkinson, H., Evans, K., Kersh, N., Fuller, A., Unwin, L., et al. (2004). The significance of individual biography in workplace learning. *Studies in the Education of Adults, 36*(1), 6–25.

Järvinen, A., & Poikela, E. (2001). Modelling reflective and contextual learning at work. *Journal of Workplace Learning, 13*(7/8), 282–289.

Karakowsky, L., & McBey, K. (1999). The lessons of work: Toward an understanding of the implications of the workplace for adult learning and development. *Journal of Workplace Learning, 11*(6), 192–201.

Lave, J. (1993). The practice of learning. In S. Chaiklin & J. Lave (Eds.), *Understanding practice. Perspectives on activity and context* (pp. 3–34). Cambridge: Cambridge University Press.

Lave, J., & Wenger, E. (1991). *Situated learning. Legitimate peripheral participation.* Cambridge: Cambridge University Press.

Lavikka, R. (2004). Fulfilment or slavery? The changing sense of self at work. In T. Heiskanen & J. Hearn (Eds.), *Information society and the workplace* (pp. 143–177). London: Routledge.

Leinhardt, G., McCarthy Young, K., & Merriman, J. (1995). Integrating professional knowledge: The theory of practice and the practice of theory. *Learning and Instruction, 5*(4), 401–408.

Marsick, V. J., & Watkins, K. E. (1990). *Informal and incidental learning in the workplace.* London: Routledge.

Orr, J. E. (1996). *Talking about machines. An ethnography of a modern job.* Ithaca, NY: IRL Press/Cornell University Press.

Rainbird, H., Fuller, A., & Munro, A. (Eds.). (2004). *Workplace learning in context.* London: Routledge.

Rasmussen, L. B. (2002). Work process knowledge and creativity in industrial design. In N. Boreham, R. Samurcay, & M. Fisher (Eds.), *Work process knowledge* (pp. 74–93). London: Routledge.

Sacks, H. (1992). *Lectures on conversation* (Vol. 1). Oxford: Blackwell.

Sandberg, J. (2000). Understanding human competence at work: An interpretative approach. *Academy of Management Journal, 43*(1), 9–25.

Schuler, D., & Namioka, A. (1993). *Participatory design. Principles and practices.* New Jersey: Lawrence Erlbaum Associates.

Schön, D. A. (1983). *The Reflective practitioner.* London: Temple Smith.

Senker, P. (2000). What and how do engineers learn? In H. Rainbird (Ed.), *Training in the workplace* (pp. 227–243). Houndmills: Macmillan Press Ltd.

Sharrock, W., & Button, G. (1997). Engineering investigations: practical sociological reasoning in the work of engineers. In G. C. Bowker, S. Leigh Star, W. Turner, & L. Gasser (Eds.), *Social science, technical systems and cooperative work. Beyond the great divide* (pp. 79–104). London: LEA.

Torraco, R. J. (1999). Integrating learning with working: A reconception of the role of workplace learning. *Human Recourse Development Quarterly, 10*(3), 249–265.

Tynjälä, P., Välimaa, J., & Sarja, A. (2003). Pedagogical perspectives on the relationship between higher education and working life. *Higher Education, 46*(2), 147–166.

Virtanen, A., Tynjälä, P., & Valkonen, S. (2005). *Työssä oppiminen opiskelijoiden arvioimana Helsingin kaupungin ammatillisissa oppilaitoksissa* [Work-related learning assessed by students in vocational schools in the city of Helsinki]. (Helsingin kaupungin opetusviraston julkaisuja No. A1). Helsinki: Helsingin kaupunki.

Watkins, K. E., & Marsick, V. J. (1992). Towards a theory of informal and incidental learning in organizations. *International Journal of Lifelong Education, 11*(4), 287–300.

Weick, K. E. (1995). *Sensemaking in organizations.* London: SAGE.

Wenger, E. (1998). *Communities of practice. Learning, meaning and identity.* Cambridge: CUP.

# Chapter 5
# Work Integration in Social Enterprises: Employment for the Sake of Learning

Fernando Marhuenda

## Introduction

Work integration social enterprises (WISE) are companies that have been known under different names in most European countries since approximately the end of the 1970s. They are run under very different legal formats and show a variety of features, and can thus be rather heterogeneous. Nevertheless, they all share a common aim: they are companies set up with the main purpose of providing jobs for people who, for several reasons, have not been able to find employment in an ordinary firm even if they have the capacity to be productive. The purpose of WISE, therefore, is to establish a working relationship with those individuals who have been already rejected by the labour market and to hire them to do the work precisely for the same reasons that they have not been able to find a job or hold it under ordinary circumstances.

WISEs are in fact the last in a series of measures in Western societies to facilitate the social inclusion of people through work (Fernández, Galarreta & Martínez, 2008), a step to be added on top of other measures such as rehabilitation of drug abuse, reinsertion in society after having served a custodial sentence, vocational training courses, social aid and others. WISEs are intended not only to facilitate entry into the labour market for those persons, but also to foster their employability by continuing the socio-educational process in which they have been involved throughout their journey out of social exclusion. It is in this sense that WISEs have been established as learning organizations in which the productive activity that they foster plays an instrumental role in achieving the expected benefits: Economic survival in order to satisfy employees' educational needs until they are able to 'abandon' the organization and enter the ordinary labour market.

Despite their short history, WISEs have already been studied in several European countries and some of that research has been published (Borzaga & Defourny, 2001; Castelli, 2005; Nyssens, 2006;). Several approaches have been taken in these

F. Marhuenda (✉)
Department of Didactics and School Organization, Faculty of Philosophy and Sciences
of Education, University of Valencia, Valencia, Spain
e-mail: Fernando.Marhuenda@uv.es

studies, mainly economic and sociological. In this chapter I attempt to provide a pedagogical perspective, considering WISEs as learning environments in which people may experience employment relations in such a manner that they will be well equipped subsequently to experience everyday life in a positive and constructive manner. WISEs are therefore intended to act as 'schools of citizenship' for individuals with a record of failure in their lives. Also, WISEs are learning environments for those who are in charge of supporting their less fortunate workmates in companies.

First, I will point to the main results of the research done on WISEs and which provide us with a background of assumptions enabling us to approach them from an educational perspective. Second, I will introduce the case of Novaterra and Iuna, two organizations which promote WISEs and which have been networking since the early 1990s, paying particular attention to the work processes they use in order to achieve their goal of social integration and to perform their related tasks. Third, I will examine the work of Iuna from different perspectives of work-based learning, work-related learning, in-company training and others that, even if produced and developed in ordinary working environments, provide us with good elements to address educational processes in WISEs.

## Work Integration Social Enterprises (WISE): Previous Research

WISEs are a type of business or company that, despite existing in different forms since the early 1980s, are limited in scope and have not been subject to research until recently (Borzaga & Defourny, 2001; Carmona, 2001; Claver, 2004; Claver & Vidal, 2003; Coque & Pérez, 2000; FEEDEI, 2003; Martínez, 2004; Nyssens, 2006; Vidal, 2005; Vidal & Claver, 2004).

Their aims are not only those typical of any company (to obtain gains through productivity and investment) but, equally as important as, to achieve the social integration of people employed in the company who would otherwise encounter so many difficulties entering the labour market that they would most probably end up living on welfare.

Companies with such objectives are spread throughout Europe (López-Aranguren, 2002), where they take different forms. In Italy and Luxembourg, they are often ordinary companies that provide just a few jobs for such individuals, whose costs are then supported within the larger structure of the company itself. But also in Italy, together with Germany and France (where they started in the late 1980s, mainly promoted by social workers in that country) they have often developed often as new entrepreneurial structures, where 'ordinary' workers, 'accompanying' those who are the objects of integration, play a key role in the management of the company (Castelli, 2005).

Many of WISEs in Germany, and also in Denmark and Austria, have been set up by NGOs or other civil associations and by trusts which have either been involved in the integration of vulnerable people or work directly with official bodies responsible for other reintegration processes (ex-drug addicts, ex-prisoners, HIV carriers, the homeless, ethnic minorities, ex-prostitutes), and they have often chosen as market activities those related to goods and services such as recycling, fair-trade or environ-mental activities. All make intensive use of a low qualified labour force and demand low or minor investment in machinery, therefore relying upon human resources both for success in the market and personal development. Despite these features being widespread across Europe, we may also identify country differences: Germany, as well as Finland and the Netherlands, is also pushing for ordinary companies to hire workers under the above mentioned conditions. This is happening, though with less success, in other European countries, where the legislation exists but largely ignored in practice.

Germany also has work integration social companies promoted by local com-munities (*Integrationsbetriebe* or *Sozialebetriebe*), and supported by money raised from the penalties imposed on companies which do not conform with the legal re-quirements to hire people with disabilities of various kinds. The Netherlands and Denmark also have a system of sheltered employment supported by the public ad-ministration.[1] In Spain, there is no state regulation with regard to such companies, although up to three parliamentary attempts have been made to pass a specific law and, therefore, each federal region has the right to institute its own regulations. This has allowed for a variety of forms under which these companies exist; currently there are more than 160 such companies registered in the whole of the country.

There are several types of WISE companies, varying from those which provide employment for a large number of vulnerable workers to those whose main goal is to serve as a further stage in the reintegration process and who, therefore, attempt to find work for them in the ordinary labour market and thus make room in the integration company for new vulnerable workers. Whether a company is of one type or another is sometimes the choice of the owners of the company, sometimes a result of the abilities of the workers employed in the company and how they progress over time.

WISEs, like any other companies, are part of networks: social networks, cus-tomers, suppliers, but also support networks often rooted in civil society. They seek also support from public authorities, often financial support or fiscal measures, to help them survive in a competitive market; ultimately, they are providing society with two services in one: the goods they make and the social inclusion of otherwise excluded people on the other.

Underlying the different WISE models we find across Europe, is a shared un-derstanding of the relations between employment, citizenship and local sustainable development in which learning, adult learning and lifelong learning play an impor-tant role. I can state, therefore, that 'WISE' are a labour context at the forefront of which is a pedagogical aim that usually takes into account elements from various ed-ucational perspectives, including theories of supervision, organizational knowledge

---

[1] At the time of writing the chapter, though a state law was approved in December 2007 (Ley 4/2007).

and learning processes, learning at work and personal and career development. I will describe the case of Iuna first and then examine it in the light of these pedagogical elements.

## The Novaterra Trust and Iuna, a Social Promoter of WISEs

The Novaterrra Trust[2] is a social entrepreneur that has been actively providing training and employment opportunities for marginalized people in the suburbs of Valencia, Spain, since the early 1990s. First conceived as a civil association closely linked to civil action on the outskirts of town, and firmly involved in developing training programs in several occupations (gardening, cook and construction among others), it has also been lobbying the regional government, together with other organizations, to achieve a comprehensive plan for the social integration of people living in highly marginal conditions. One impressive and recent result of this lobbying activity was the approval, in January 2007, of a regional law regulating WISEs in Valencia (Ley 1/2007).

Mission and actions of the Novaterra Trust are the following:

1. Novaterra is a non-profit organization with the aim fostering the social inclusion of disadvantaged social groups through the means of employment.
2. It develops its mission through the following areas of action:

   - training for employment: working habits, occupational values, working culture, specific skills for certain occupations and trades
   - employment intermediation: welcoming people, providing career guidance, helping in the process of searching for employment, managing the supply and demand for employment, promoting employment and entrepreneurship
   - raising consciousness in the wider society
   - research and development of tools, skills, measures, models and programs in order to facilitate successful entry into the labour market
   - political action, lobbying, negotiation and criticism of policies
   - networking and fostering the development of civil society, promotion of voluntary action, devising joint action with other organizations sharing similar aims

It was in the late 1990s that the members of the association decided to move a step further and to start their own business as a social promoter of WISE. This movement owed to the evidence, amassed after more than 10 years experience of training and guidance provision, that these measures were not enough to overcome the social stigmatization surrounding some individuals such as former alcoholics or drug addicts, ex-prisoners, the mental ill, homeless adults, and ethnic minorities. These were people who were unable to gain access to the labour market even when

---

[2] http://www.novaterra.org.es

adequately trained and of proven skill in their occupations. Therefore, the association established a company and managed to attract a large group of investors. They named it Iuna.[3] It was to be a social promoter consisting basically of a small team of creative people whose mission would be to set up several integration businesses able to compete and survive in the market as well as to employ sufficiently skilled people who otherwise had no chance whatsoever of entering the labour market.

The result of this process has been the setting up of four different companies thus far, one of them a courier company, employing over 20 people, another a gardening company, which now employs half a dozen individuals, the third a fair-trade and biological food company, and the fourth a firm renovating apartments. The social promoter currently has a team of four people: a project manager, a HRD manager, an administrator and a promoter. Their responsibilities include the following: searching for new business opportunities, monitoring the development of those already set up, allocating employees under processes of social insertion to those occupations which best suit them for integration purposes, and organizing the businesses in educational environments while at the same time ensuring that they prove productive enough.

As is the case with so many 'WISE', the sort of businesses most likely to be run by them are those regaining low capital investment and high intensity of labour force. These are enterprises which allow as many vulnerable people as possible to be employed, removing them from social care and providing them with the right to work. This often means opening the gate to other forms of social integration.

However, as opposed to what often happens in such companies, there is no type of marginalization among those employed by Iuna's companies. It is often the case in Europe that such businesses employ people with the same handicaps or disabilities, whether social, physical or mental. However, those employed by Novaterra have multiple problems and do not fall in the same category. Nonetheless, most of them share a specific feature: due to various social problems, they have developed illnesses that in the long term force them frequently to seek health assistance. This implies a considerable rate of absenteeism, up to 20%, compared to the national average 3% and, among civil servants, close to 10%. This is obviously something that has an impact on the productivity of the companies. Nevertheless, it does not imply that they do not perform satisfactorily; only that work has to be adapted to their particular conditions. This is an important element in the organization's mission.

Alongside these companies, the organization also has other activities that centre around the reintegration process of these adults into employment and society. It currently runs a 2-year scheme where approximately 100 people are being assisted into the labour market, with contacts with over 130 companies. It is also running temporary workshops in different occupational areas, usually others than those represented by the companies, so as to reach other people as well. It also represents more than 15 such companies in the region within the national federation of WISEs. Furthermore, it has contributed to the introduction in Spain of the two 'ethical banks' currently operating in the country: through these, it is attempting to raise

---

[3] http://www.iuna.org

funding for its activities in other ways. The ethical bank is an attempt to escape from the way of proceeding of traditional banks which often fail to recognize the particular conditions under which such companies work. These conditions render them less competitive in terms of profits which, furthermore, are always reinvested in the companies' activities and expansion. Novaterra, therefore, also plays an important role with regard to the social responsibility of entrepreneurship, particularly through the introduction of social balances in evaluating the effectiveness and productivity of a company. As a whole, it attempts to transform society through introducing the principles of equal opportunity and social justice within the labour market and it does so by enhancing networking and relying upon social capital in order to improve the quality of human capital.

## Learning Environments in WISE

The impact of WISEs upon individuals has been assessed in a few studies. Such evaluations have shown that the abilities of workers in WISEs develop significantly in comparison to level on entry. When measured on a seven-point scale, mean improvements of two points have been found in almost every area. Improvements have been noted in areas related to social competences (Lindgren & Heikkinen, 2004), such as the following: occupational skills, relational skills with colleagues, relational skills with managers, socio-cultural skills, the ability to fully accomplish the tasks allocated, the ability to work in an autonomous manner, knowledge of professional tasks and improvement of the personal overall situation (Borzaga & Loos, 2006; Vidal & Claver, 2004).

Taking these results into account, our research context is in two of the companies owned by Iuna. These are the courier and the gardening companies, both of which employ an individual whose main duty is to mentor the workers who are being reintegrated, and who therefore acts both as a manager and colleague. They give weekly and daily instructions, allocate incentives and sanctions within the framework set by the company and the collective agreement in the sector, keep a weekly record of the workers' performance and personal improvement, which serves as the basis for assigning the worker new duties and responsibilities. The mentor also takes care of the reintegration workers in areas other than those of work relations, such as ensuring medical supervision, support with housing problems and attending to personal development or even leisure opportunities. Employment is therefore the key element around which all other areas of the individual are monitored in order to assure level of development is attained that enables the autonomous normalization of her/his life. Once this point has been reached, the individual in question is encouraged to look for employment in the ordinary labour market in order to make room in the company for new people under integration processes.

I used these examples to review and reflect on the training and learning principles behind the relations established in these companies, and which usually rely on different forms of work-based training and learning, experiential learning and situated learning as well as supervision and mentoring approaches. Our focus, therefore, is the educational processes which take place in these companies, given that they prioritize an educational and social profit over an economic profit. Obviously in relation to the process of becoming an employee and reconstructing one's identity in order to overcome stigmatization and to get rid of a record of social failure, citizenship education also plays an important role.

Gardening is an activity often done as team-work, particularly when providing services to members of the public. It is an activity done in the open air, and is subject to seasonal weather conditions which in many cases determine the tasks to be performed. Gardening allows workers to establish contact with people who are neither employers nor customers, but who benefit from the skilled work by enjoying it and who often assess its aesthetic quality. You are observed while you do your work in a garden, partly because you are wearing a uniform which makes you openly visible to others. You are assessed by people according to their own knowledge of the issue, and you are also valued both for your work as well as your sympathy and attitude. It is an activity which shows its results in the mid and long term, given that flowers, bushes and trees have their own life cycles and that their appearance changes often at the hands of the workers. This means planning, often on a weekly basis, so that something that remains unfinished today may be continued tomorrow. Many people have at least a very basic notion of gardening even if very few develop that knowledge to the level of expertise required to earn one's living by it, no matter how lowly it is perceived. Most often your colleagues are also present, if not continuously then at least several times during the day, and usually you are within their line of sight as well. All of these circumstances make it easy for the mentor to obtain enough information about the worker's performance assisting not only in the occupational but also in the social and relational sense. I must add to this the fact that there are shared times when everyone assembles for a break, lunch, a cigarette and so on.

The mentor in the company is often assigned to one or more workers under an integration process. The mentor is in charge of training them in both technical skills as well as taking care of their social integration, personal development, providing support as it is needed and will have many opportunities to talk, train and correct them during the day. Even the allocation of tasks for the following day or week may be planned according to the stage the worker is in.

Courier services, on the other side, have a rather different profile. Most of the work is done on an individual basis, by motorcycle, going from one place to another. Indeed as a courier many people may see you, mainly for advertising reasons, as the name of the brand and how to access it is highly visible on your uniform and other items of equipment. But because you move fast from one place to another, no one really notices you and you receive no external assessment other than the abuse of other drivers trapped in a traffic jam. Those who assess your performance are the customers, who have demanded your services because they are in a hurry and thus want to see you there as soon as possible but also see you depart even faster. Therefore, you work under pressure, the pressure imposed either directly or indirectly by customers via the traffic manager at the courier base who assigns you your work. There is hardly any chance to plan work in the mid term, it is often hard even to make a daily plan of the workload, as it is frequently unpredictable. Each co-worker in the company is given different routes and commands, and there are seldom chances when you can meet your colleagues other than those of the lunch break, and that only happens when it can be planned or is under a shift system. The work you do as a courier remains invisible, there is no one to appreciate it as you are just a messenger delivering forms and notes, redistributing information that you do not control and that you do not know the destination. These circumstances contribute to seeing this job as a very low skilled one, even lower skilled than gardening: the main skill you need is to have a driving licence and from then on you can start working, the initial training is brief and concise and continuing training scarce unless the range of possibilities, is widened to include such skills as basic motorbike repair. Speed is the most important factor in this work. The weather has also an impact upon courier services, but you have to work no matter what the weather is like, and time remains equally important even if the weather is having a very bad effect upon traffic.

The mentor in the courier company is based at headquarters, assisting with telephone calls and distributing tasks among the couriers who are already working elsewhere. Under pressure of time and demands from customers, the mentor must take also into account who has done what already during the day, who is closer to the new customer, but also other factors such as what the customer is like in order to select a courier who is able to handle the pressure of time in an appropriate social manner. These decisions are taken very rapidly and their effectiveness, particularly in terms of the integration processes, can only be assessed at the end of the day. Workers bring those day's problems together with them to work the next day: how much more I had to do than someone else, how pleasant or understanding that customer was, whether my motorbike is in better shape than someone else's, etc. Chances for the mentor to assess and train the worker under process of integration are rare, often communication is via the radiophone, and therefore meetings with these workers must be planned and space reserved for them, something that cannot always happen during the working day unless someone else takes charge of manning the phone and distributing commands. When such meetings take place, they are perceived by both participants as *ad hoc* structures, often seen moments of assessment rather than as educational or training ones.

The HRD manager in Iuna has devised a series of documents and management tools in order to facilitate the appropriate development of the work of mentors and of her own work, as she is the one responsible for hiring new workers and finalizing their contracts. The documents and management tools used in the companies as tools to foster the integration process and improve the employability of their workers are as follows:

- a welcome handbook on Novaterra, Iuna and its companies
- a code of rules for each company, within the framework of the collective agreement of the sector, where such exists
- job descriptions clarifying the duties of company mentors as well as profiling those employed in each job
- yearly planning for each company, stating aims and the procedures to be employed to achieve them

- monthly meetings with each of the workers under the integration process in order to assess their improvement
- weekly meetings with the mentors in order to improve everyday working conditions and to assess the development of the workers in the company
- employability diagnosis of the integration workers, during their trial period
- individualized integration plans or personal development plans for each of the workers under process of social insertion in the company, specifying their stage of development as well as the aims, measures, guidelines and assessment procedures to be used to help them in their personal and working development up to a maximum term of 3 years
- a handbook to aid the decision-taking processes of mentors in various everyday situations
- the contract with the worker herself or himself, including the integration and normalization process among the tasks to be accomplished by the worker

Novaterra is also seeking to learn and develop from management tools devised by other WISEs elsewhere in Spain, such as the employability assessment handbook devised by Martínez (2004), Fernández, Galarreta & Martínez (2008), the guidelines for developing a personal insertion plan (Carmona, 2001) or the overall management handbook for WISEs (Coque & Pérez, 2000).

## Mentors and What their Job Involves

In every 'work integration social enterprise' we find at least two sorts of workers. On the one side, those undergoing a process of reintegration in society and for whom the job they have in the company implies a further step in that process. These are all adults who have experienced damage of different kinds, often mixed (both mental and physical), and who have undergone processes of social exclusion and, in consequence, processes of social reintegration. On top of these, they often hold limited educational qualifications as well as a lack of higher order cognitive processes. Boud & Griffin (1994, p. 211) have identified the important features involved in adult learning processes: "Maintaining self-esteem, becoming increasingly responsible for own learning, finding own direction for learning, investing energy, involving and committing oneself, dealing with personal energy ebb and flow, relating to others, finding personal meaning in content and experiences, noticing, clarifying, consolidating and synthesizing new learning, testing new ideas, skills, behaviours and ways of being, asking for and using feedback, planning the uses of new learning in other situations or finding and accepting satisfactions, joys and excitement in learning".

All of these have here a very particular meaning: Self-esteem is subject to the influence of external factors like colleagues, behaviours – a greeting – or customers' reactions – taking into account the tone of voice used or the look in others' eyes. Becoming responsible may imply being punctual, being able to carry on working even if you feel tired, or telling the truth about a problem or mistake at work. Integration workers in WISEs are finding their own way for their lives, not just for learning; taking control over one's life when one has survived rather than lived may for a while become risky business. Involving and committing to the company are often double-edged swords, when the company becomes your key reference in life and it is through the company (your boss or the HRD manager) that you search for new accommodation or look to for psychological support or even for a loan to repay debts. Under circumstances such as these, awareness of learning is very hard to achieve. One often tends to think that learning is something that one is able to do and therefore something which one is competent at. In such cases the mentor is not always readily perceived as a trainer but rather as merely an 'information point', whereas it is precisely they who are committed to providing the integration work with support as they are already aware of those individuals' situations.

And then there are those whose role is both to contribute to the productivity goals of the company as well as to train, mentor, mediate or educate the other responsible workers. This consists of a number of roles which often come together in the same person, and which make it hard to define this position in the company: it includes several management features – and indeed these individuals have several responsibilities as well as a number of people in the charge – while at the same time they are work-mates alongside the rest, and in order to fulfil their role and to satisfy their colleagues' needs in the process of reintegration, they have to be close to them. It is workers of this type that we are going to deal with.

Between 2005 and 2006, the HRD manager together with the mentoring workers from these two companies started a process of action-research in Novaterra. Researchers joined them in this process, which had several aims: to establish common criteria for handling the integration processes, to provide further training for these mentoring workers, and to assign a new mentor, who joined the company in late 2004, in learning the job. Hence, we worked with the HRD manager and three other employees in the two different companies described above.

The first is a middle-age woman who has long experience of work as an administrator and chief-administrator in large companies; and also a record of training delivery, both initial and continuing, with severely marginalized populations. She has worked for the courier firm for 4 years as chief of traffic, in charge of receiving all the requests from customers and assigning tasks to the approximately 20 workers in the company. This position allows her to establish a pedagogical relation with all of the workers, and her duties have been established according to the demands of the customers as well as to the needs, stages, conditions and possibilities of the workers, some of which change daily. Therefore, she usually takes time to talk to the workers and help them cope with their difficulties. In order to do this she receives the help of an assistant who takes charge while she is dealing with the workers on an individual basis.

The two other people work for the gardening company. One of them, a young man with MSc in Biology who has long work experience as a gardener, has been within this company for almost 5 years. The other is a very young woman, a gardener herself, and new in the company. Both of them work in the open air, and most of their work consists of assigning teams to perform tasks for their customers (ranging from municipalities to private clients). Most of their pedagogical work takes place in the course of everyday work.

These three people, together with the HRD manager and the researcher established a group meeting on a monthly basis, with assignments set for each meeting and a professional development plan (see Table 5.1). Furthermore, a weekly meeting was held between the HRD manager and each of the other three employees in order to boost progress with the assignments and to solve everyday problems at work.

All three mentors are well aware of their roles and duties. In the context of their company, they help design the insertion pathways of their workmates, they have to apply and assess the implementation of the measures included in those insertion plans, they have to hold regular meetings with their workmates, motivate them, help them cope with problems, and get in touch with institutions supporting the integration process. Above all, they have to foster certain habits in workers that contribute to their successful integration in society. In order to achieve this, they need good communication and observation skills, and pedagogical tact (Van Manen, 1991) in order to negotiate educational situations such as the following two cases.

**Case 1**. Personal development in the gardening company.

This worker had been addicted to drugs in the past and has been attending a rehabilitation program with some success. During the first four months in the company he made progress, but since then he has been coming to work in a bad mood, he gets angry easily and has quarreled with his colleagues on minor issues. He always calms down and acknowledges after a while, but there have already been too many serious incidents. The last took place not just with his colleagues but with the mentor herself, and she and the manager are now clear that something must be done about this, like applying a penalty in order to avoid such situations in the future. In any other company such behaviour would not be allowed and he might risk his job; therefore some external aid must be provided to help him control his temper. But they are afraid that he may feel treated like a child if a system of sanction is established for such a purpose and particularly for his behaviour.

**Case 2**. Working conditions and equipment in the courier company.

A worker is complaining about the state of the common room: rubbish is left lying around, no one takes care of it and some people have even stolen others' refreshments from the fridge. In order to avoid conflict with the other workers, she is demanding that the mentor intervene, as the common room is part of the premises of the company. But that same worker is not taking good care of the motorbike allocated to her and, therefore, the mentor thinks this is a good opportunity to draw attention to this problem as well. The worker claims that the motorbike was already in a bad state when she received it, and that is indeed true. In fact, some of the motorbikes need either good restoration or even replacement, although the company cannot allow for such costs in the coming months.

The above cases are just a couple of examples of particular situations which, despite resembling any other job situation, come up under specific circumstances: Those of retaining and training workers to allow them to progress towards social reintegration. These situations then become valuable pedagogical events that can be utilized, if not to improve the professionalism of workers, at least to facilitate their personal and social development. I turn now in the concluding section of the paper to some of the principles, discussed in the course of our own practice, according to which situations like those described above may be managed in just such a pedagogical manner.

**Table 5.1** Different areas for the professional development of mentors

1. The pedagogical relation, 'being accompanied and accompanying': Noticing, accepting and complying with these roles and their evolution as the process continues. Planning and timing of educational moments and learning processes. Responsibilities for the definition, planning and assessment of the itineraries for insertion into social and work life. Involvement of other institutions in supporting workers into reintegration into social life. How to turn work into a purposeful learning environment.[a] How to cope with specific working conditions, particularly the space and time arrangements of the workplace.

2. The content of the learning process: what specific learning is needed in the reintegration process that is absent in existing vocational training. Knowledge about:

– Labour: What is the ordinary structure of a company? How do companies in the relevant sector (courier, gardening) organize themselves? The workplace as work: pay, involvement, personal bargaining, social hierarchies, relations of exchange, affection and disaffection processes at different moments. The mission of the company. Motivation, involvement, risks, effort. Basic habits (timetable, cleanliness, presence). Safety and health issues at work, care of tools and machinery, personal hygiene. The will to work. The joy of work well done. Quality, productivity, attitude. Self demand and self assessment.

– Social relations: To differentiate context, moments and persons. To respect everyone. Fostering positive relations among people, collaboration and teamwork, participation in different activities and decision-making. Fostering communication skills: listening to someone else, expressing oneself, asking for something, thanking someone, requesting someone.

– Personal growth: Fostering self-initiative, desirable behaviours and positive attitudes: Accepting demands, acknowledging one's mistakes, assuming responsibilities, patience, looking for positive elements in everyday situations, avoiding blaming others, avoiding prejudice. Fostering healthy life habits and simplifying everyday life. Dealing with issues always present in their lives: death, violence, gender-orientated violence, lack of trust.

3. Elaboration and use of tools for the mentors (Carmona, 2001; Martínez, 2004). Modelling, assessment of work performance (contrasting, mirroring situations, correcting). Establishing and applying norms. Asking for any information needed and to providing all the necessary information. The context is that of a company, not a course or a workshop. To allocate to each an appropriate workload. Fostering activity. Keeping a record of progress, tracking it and giving feedback to the worker.

4. Roles and styles of the mentor.

With regard to personal relations: Facing unexpected problems. Facing changes in mood. Taking care of medication, its consumption and its effects. Giving workers appropriate care and affection.

With regard to the company: Giving instructions, giving assignments. Working with workers and with customers, who are often not aware of the particularities of these workers.

To develop confidence, both as a co-worker in the company as well as from the hierarchical viewpoint.

[a]In everyday working life, situations arise which are not specific to this integration processes but which serve as educational moments in order to develop certain skills: when someone gets nervous at work (be it me, my boss, the customer); the attempts we make to show that we are competent in front of the others; when someone takes someone else's drink at lunchtime; harmony is not always present in the everyday relations at work.

# Balance of Education and Learning Processes in WISEs

Norros & Nuutinen (2002) have defined uncertainty as the epistemic key features of action in which emotion plays an important role. This brings them to define the notion of 'core tasks': "By core task we mean the result-critical content of a particular work activity on which the achievement of the goal of the work depends" (p. 29). In order for WISEs to achieve their ambitious aims, they have to identify core tasks in the environments that they provide, in order to facilitate the necessary motivation, cognitive and social processes necessary to turn as many situations as possible into educational and development contexts where people are able to develop appropriate everyday habits. This must be done in such a manner that even situations which are stressful or socially demanding can be handled from an educational perspective: The mission is not to select the best skilled workers, but to identify the learning possibilities of those who have been stigmatized for whatever reasons so that they may become skilled enough in order to satisfactorily perform in working life. Success then becomes then a collective issue in which the interests of the company and the worker can only be achieved if they meet each other. In the previous section I have tried to identify some of these core tasks as perceived by those managing them.

Equity and justice in education, as Connell (1997) has claimed, become key elements of the definition of the work environments in such companies as those we have examined, and they become principles for HRD practices in order to overcome the disadvantage that these workers bring with them when entering the company. Such HRD practices may be observed in these companies, hence showing that they are working hard to bring together work, knowledge and learning. No matter how low the skill requirements of the occupations they offer are, it would be reasonable to claim that professional knowledge (Eraut, 1994) is being fostered in them and that in their organization the companies are making an effort to become a powerful learning environment (De Corte, Verschaffel, Entwistle, & Merriënboer, 2003). Work experience in these companies becomes a form of apprenticeship which involves specialized as well as cognitive and social elements.

Possessing information of different kinds is crucial for mentors fostering the abilities of the integration workers. Their task is to give instructions and assess performance in trying to develop the ability of those in their charge to perform the kinds of routine tasks common in courier work and gardening and also facilitate the ability to take decisions that, even if minor, sometimes enhance the autonomy and knowledge of these workers. In the end, it is the purpose of these companies to utilize courier and gardening services in order that the integration workers may develop new schemas about social life, life in society, living with others, what work involves, and different ways of understanding the demand-supply relation through involvement in the provision of such services. And this is achieved in these WISEs by allowing people to face real problems, which sometimes prove to be open and complex as well, while others remain routine. The collaborative involvement of the mentors is also crucial, as they are able to plan and regulate the progress of their integration colleagues as well as cope with their sometimes inefficient input.

HRD practices and assisting processes in these companies have to be so transparent that there is not much room for a hidden curriculum (Garrick, 1998), nor for tacit knowledge nor on the parts of those acting as mentors. This is because the latter have to plan the personal development of their colleagues even if it is not always possible to plan tomorrow's workload, as we have seen. All their experiences, contexts, and different situations are learning opportunities not only for the target group, but also for the mentors themselves as well as other colleagues who may well benefit from sharing what has happened to others. Informal learning becomes deliberate mentoring in WISEs; this the mentors understand, and their commitment to the aims of the company is beyond doubt. Indeed, support of the HRD and networks in which both Novaterra and Iuna take part is a key element in coming to grips with the many intangible elements that are encountered in the always difficult process of social integration in adults who have suffered throughout their lives. These networks also promote new chances for personal development through connections with either customers or suppliers.

The full potential of work relations has to be reaped, and WISEs aim to become sites where, however low the level of qualifications required, the acquisition of work process knowledge (Boreham, Samurçay, & Fischer, 2002; Fischer, Boreham, & Nyhan, 2004) is fostered. They not only guarantee the right to work but also the right to education, and from this perspective they may also be considered as part of educational policy (Bailey, Hughes, & Moore, 2004). This is possible only by turning the hardness, lack of trust and hand-to-mouth survival that these workers have experienced and become habituated to over the years into care, trust, and decent level of living. Indeed, these are not just learned, but the role of their mentors in assessing them in a climate of trust and care is another key to the success of WISEs.

# References

Bailey, T., Hughes, K., & Moore, D. (2004). *Working knowledge. Work-based learning and education reform*. London: Routledge.

Boreham, N., Samurçay, M., & Fischer, M. (2002). *Work process knowledge*. London: Routledge.

Borzaga, C., & Defourny, J. (Eds.). (2001). *The emergence of social enterprise*. London: Routledge.

Borzaga, C., & Loos, (2006). Profiles and trajectories of participants in European WISEs. In M. Nyssens (Ed.), *Social enterprise. At the crossroads of market, public policies and civil society* (pp. 169–194). London: Routledge.

Boud, D., & Griffin, V. (1994). *Appreciating adults learning: From the learners' perspective*. London: Kogan Page.

Carmona, G. (2001). *El plan personal para la inserción socio-laboral: teoría y práctica en la empresa para la inserción laboral* [The personal individualized plan for social integration through work: Theory and practice in Work Integration Social Enterprises]. Huelva: Universidad de Huelva – Observatorio Local de Empleo.

Castelli, L. (2005). *European Social Entrepreneurs looking for a better way to produce and to live*. Ancona: LeMat.

Claver, N. (2004). *Efectos de las empresas de inserción sobre los trabajadores: un análisis evolutivo* [Effects of work integration social enterprises upon workers: A developmental analysis]. REDSI, No 3. Retrieved May 17, 2007, from http://redsirevista.cebs-es.org/index.asp?IdArt=69

Claver, N., & Vidal, I. (2003). *Las empresas sociales en el ámbito de la integración por el trabajo* [Work integration social enterprises in the field of social inclusion through work]. CIRIEC, *46*, 39–62.

Connell, R. W. (1997). *Escuelas y justicia social* [Schools and social justice. Temple Uni Press, 1993]. Madrid: Morata.

Coque, J., & Pérez, E. (Eds.) (2000). *Manual de creación y gestión de empresas de inserción social* [Handbook for the creation and management of work integration social enterprises]. Oviedo: Publicaciónes de la Universidad de Oviedo.

De Corte, E., Verschaffel, L., Entwistle, N., & Merriënboer, J. V. (Eds.). (2003). *Powerful learning environments. Unravelling basic components and dimensions.* Amsterdam: EARLI-Pergamon.

Eraut, M. (1994). *Developing professional knowledge and competence.* London: Falmer Press.

FEEDEI (2003). *Identificación y diagnóstico integral de las empresas de inserción en España* [Identification and integral diagnosis of work integration social enterprises in Spain]. Madrid: Popular.

Fernández, A., Galarreta, J., & Martínez, N. (coords.) (2008). Manual de acompañamiento en las empresas de inserción. Proceso y herramientas. Bilbao, Equal Lamegi. English translation: Handbook for accompanying processes in Work Integration Social Enterprises. Procedures and tools.

Fischer, M., Boreham, N., & Nyhan, B. (Eds.). (2004). *European perspectives on learning at work. The acquisition of work process knowledge.* Luxembourg: CEDEFOP.

Garrick, J. (1998). *Informal learning in the workplace. Unmasking human resource development.* London: Routledge.

Ley 4/2007, de 13 de diciembre, para la ragulación del régimen de las empresas de inserción. BOE n° 229, viernes 14 de diciembre de 2007.

Ley 1/2007, de 5 de febrero, de la Generalitat, por la que se regulan las empresas de inserción para fomentar la inclusión social en la Comunitat Valenciana (2007/1587). (DOGV no. 5447, de 9 de febrero de 2007, pp. 6653–6660). [Law 1/2007 by which work integration social enterprises are regulated in the Comunidad Valenciana].

Lindgren, A., & Heikkinen, A. (2004). *Social competences in vocational and continuing education.* Bern: Peter Lang.

López-Aranguren, L. M. (2002). *Las empresas de inserción en España. Un marco de aprendizaje para la insercion laboral* [Work integration social enterprises in Spain. A framework for learning for social inclusion through work]. Madrid: CES.

Martínez, N. (Ed.). (2004). *Herramientas profesionales en las empresas de inserción* [Professional tools in work integration social enterprises]. Bilbao: Universidad de Deusto – Departamento de Psicopedagogía.

Norros, L., & Nuutinen, M. (2002). The concept of the core task and the analysis of working practices. In N. Boreham, R. Samurçay, & M. Fischer (Eds.), *Work process knowledge* (pp. 25–39). London: Routledge.

Nyssens, M. (Ed.). (2006). *Social enterprise. At the crossroads of market, public policies and civil society.* London: Routledge.

Van Manen, M. (1991). *The tact of teaching: The meaning of pedagogical thoughtfulness.* Alberta: Althouse Press.

Vidal, I. (2005). *The socio-economic performance of Spanish Social Enterprises in the field of integration by work.* Paper presented at the 1st European Conference of the International Society for the Third Sector Research. CNAM, Paris, France.

Vidal, I., & Claver, N. (2004, June). *Las empresas de inserción social por el trabajo en España. Síntesis resultados del proyecto PERSE* [Work integration social enterprises in Spain. Synthesis of project results]. CIES. Retrieved May 17, 2007, from http://www.mes-d.net/Doc/PERSE%20espanol.pdf

# Chapter 6
# Educating Novices at the Workplace: Transformation of Conceptions and Skills of Students on a Metal Industry Course

Mari Murtonen, Sari Sahlström and Päivi Tynjälä

## Introduction

Traditional formal education has often been accused of being disconnected from the learning of real working life competencies. Recent studies have shown that students may feel that formal education is 'too theoretical', and graduates often claim that they do not possess the competencies needed to do their jobs (e.g., Mora, García-Aracil, & Vilas, 2007; Stenström, 2006; Tynjälä, Slotte, Nieminen, Lonka, & Olkinuora, 2006; van der Velden, 2006;). A similar criticism often levelled by entrepreneurs and employers is that the slow process of formal education hinders it from responding to the acute needs of working life (e.g. Billett, 2007). The content and pedagogical practices of formal education programmes may not serve the needs of current jobs. To overcome these problems, some employers have adopted an old – but until recently largely forgotten – practice of educating workers in the workplace. This 'education on demand' may be realised through different models, varying from close co-operation between formal education and industry to the traditional dual system of vocational education and training, as in Germany, or to specialised training programmes organised wholly by companies themselves (for more on corporate universities see, e.g. Andresen & Lichtenberger, 2007; Rademakers, 2005). The goal in all these models is to bridge the gap between education and work, and to provide students with real life experience so as to better equip them with the skills and knowledge needed in productive working. The aim of this chapter is to examine a specific example; the company-based training of shipyard workers. Our assumption is that training carried out in an authentic work environment, and its close vicinity in the company school, could provide a promising starting point for realising the connective model of work experience (Griffiths & Guile, 2003; Guile & Griffiths, 2001) described in Chapter 2 of this volume. Thus, we examine whether features of the connective model are present in a shipyard metal industry course run by the company in the workplace. We also examine company-based training from the expertise development point of view and analyse how the transition from novice towards

M. Murtonen (✉)
Department of Education, Assistentinkatu 5, 20014 University of Turku, Finland
e-mail: mari.murtonen@utu.fi

*expert* begins and proceeds in a workplace-based training programme carried out in a combined classroom and authentic work environment. In our analyses we draw on ideas from two different directions of research: classical studies of expertise and studies of conceptual change. This is a novel approach to vocational development.

We start by discussing the theoretical viewpoints and previous empirical findings of expertise research that supports the idea of providing education and training in the workplace. We also discuss possible problems related to workplace training. We examine the development of expertise from different complementary perspectives and describe expertise as a complex phenomenon composed of cognitive, social, and bodily aspects. In the second part of this chapter we present empirical findings from a study conducted in the shipbuilding industry where future employees are trained in the company's own school and in an authentic production environment.

## *The Place of Novices: At School or at Work?*

In the course of history, the question of how to create a competent workforce has been answered, broadly, in two opposite ways. At one pole of the continuum are the kinds of practices that Lave and Wenger (1991) have described as legitimate peripheral participation. Here, *novices* participate in authentic work from the very beginning – first in peripheral, less critical tasks, gradually advancing to more demanding responsibilities. The medieval guild system and present-day craft workers' training often represent this model. At the other pole of the continuum are school-based education and training systems in which novices are taught the theory of the field at school and provided with practical training in separate training areas or through authentic work placements. According to the study by Dubs (2006) both school-based and work-related training have their own benefits. For example, students in school-based education generally develop a better understanding of the theoretical bases of a profession and have a higher level of readiness for further education, whereas students with work experience in a dual system are initially much better in dealing with demanding job situations and have fewer problems with work rhythm and job-related stress. (However, these differences even out over time). In adapting to a new workplace and in satisfaction with choice of profession after completing their basic education, the two groups seem to be more or less equal. Thus, it can be assumed that the connective model of work experience (Guile & Griffiths, 2001), which combines the strengths of school-based and work-based learning may provide an ideal solution for raising the quality of the workforce development. In this chapter we examine whether the ideas of the connective model are found in the case of company-based training in the metal industry.

The possible benefits of company-based training in the workplace can be viewed from many theoretical angles. Below, we examine this question, first, from the cognitive viewpoint, as a matter of developing expertise. We also draw on the situated learning theories and ideas about learning as a *bodily process*. Studies on student motivation also provide interesting perspectives on work-related learning.

## *The Role of Practical Experience in the Development of Expertise*

Classic studies of expertise, such as the model by Dreyfus & Dreyfus (1986), have described the pathway from novice to expert in terms of specific steps or stages. In the first stage, novices have to devote almost all of their attention to performing procedures in the way they have been taught. For example, a *novice* automobile driver needs to focus on in which order to press the pedals to change gear. For the experienced driver these procedures are automated, leaving the driver free to concentrate on more important things such as the traffic situation. *Novices* are very dependent on the rules which they have been taught and judge their performance mainly by how well they follow those rules. They do not yet have the ability to take into account situational factors which sometimes may make following the rules unnecessary or even harmful. At the second stage of development the *advanced beginner* starts to learn not only by remembering rules but also by experience and situational factors. A driver at this stage is able to incorporate the situational sound of the engine into his gear-shifting rules, and the student nurse learns from experience how to distinguish the breathing sounds that indicate a pulmonary edema from those suggesting pneumonia. Thus, in this phase, experience is more important for learning than any form of verbal description. The next stage of development is the *competent performer*. It is typical of competent performers that they no longer merely follow the rules but have a goal in mind and plan their actions. One important difference between the competent performer on the one hand and the advanced beginner and novices on the other is that while the latter feels little responsibility for the outcome of their acts the former – after wrestling with the question of the choice of a plan – feels responsible for the product of his or her choice. The development of expertise then proceeds towards *proficiency*. At this stage the usual procedures have become automated and no deliberate concentration on them is needed. Instead the performer is able to act 'intuitively'. On the basis of her experience she is able to fast and holistically recognise familiar patterns and act flexibly in familiar situations. Proficient performers, while intuitively organising and understanding their tasks, will still find themselves thinking analytically what to do. Thus, on the basis of prior experience, the proficient driver, approaching a curve on a rainy day may intuitively realise that she is driving too fast. She then consciously decides whether to apply the brakes, remove her foot from the accelerator altogether, or merely reduce pressure. In the last stage, the *expert* generally knows what to do on the basis of her mature and practised understanding. She automatically adapts her actions to the situation and behaves in the most appropriate way. When things are proceeding normally, experts do not solve problems or make decisions but they automatically do what normally works. They also become one with their equipment, making the most benefit of the tools available. However, in problem situations where they face totally new problems they need to critically reflect on their actions.

The stage model by Dreyfus & Dreyfus (1986) depicts the development of expertise after schooling. Thus, the starting point is that when students graduate or obtain qualifications they are novices and the actual growth towards expertise takes place only through practical experience. An interesting question is whether the development of expertise can be accelerated by organising education and training in the workplace as early as possible. In this way students can acquire the practical experience necessary to move from novicehood to a more advanced level of expertise. The dual model of vocational education and training (VET) and company-based training aim at this target.

Classic studies of expertise have also found that experts' knowledge structures and problem-solving methods differ from those of novices (e.g. Chase & Simon, 1973; Newell & Simon, 1972). Experts tend to cluster knowledge in larger chunks that help them to perform better than novices in problem-solving situations. Experts thus do not just know more than novices, they also have a different way of structuring their domain-specific knowledge (Boshuizen, Bromme, & Gruber, 2004). In problem-solving situations, experts use proportionally more time than novices building up a basic representation of the problem situation before searching for a solution. In this way they can form a more profound picture of the task and what it requires. Despite spending more time on the initial phases of problem-solving, experts usually end up with a solution faster than novices. This is a result of automated operations developed by experts during their long experience. (Chi, Glaser, & Rees, 1982; Feltovich, Prietula, & Ericsson, 2006; Lesgold et al., 1988). Thus, an important prerequisite for the development of knowledge structures is both repetition of similar situations and variation between the situations the individual encounters.

## *Multiple Perspectives, Complex Problems and Authentic Situations in Expertise Development*

According to the recent cognitive learning theories, a learner benefits from obtaining multiple representations and perspectives on the subject (van Someren, Reimann, Boshuizen, & de Jong, 1998). In traditional formal education institutes instruction is usually organised by one teacher at a time. In this way, students normally form only one representation of, or perspective on, the subject. The number of repetitions may also be low and restricted to similar situations, thereby decreasing the possibility of variation in representations. According to the study by Stark, Gruber, Hinkofer, & Mandl (2004, p. 59), learners with multiple perspectives were able to apply their knowledge more flexibly to complex tasks than learners who analysed business cases from only one perspective. By varying work situations and workmates, education and training organised in the workplace may offer a bigger number of representations and possibly more teachers or facilitators instead of only one model for learning.

While formal education may still often apply the ideas of behaviourism, such as breaking the topic to be learnt into smaller pieces and introducing them one by one, education in the workplace offers complex problems to students. Lehtinen (2002; see also Jacobson & Spiro, 1995) studied the learning of research methods in a university and concluded that facing complexity from the very beginning helps students to understand the domain better. In addition to concrete and procedural knowledge, complex domains usually consist of abstract and multifaceted knowledge that is hard for students to understand because they are not yet able to form links between their prior knowledge structures and the new knowledge. According to Leech (2007, see also Lakoff & Johnson, 1999), abstract knowledge has its roots in concrete metaphors; however, the chain of abstractions is so long that it cannot be tracked backwards. Thus, there is a link missing between the abstract knowledge offered to students and their own abstract knowledge that is based on concrete understanding. Facing the complexity of the domain from the very beginning helps students to situate the problem better into the 'environment', even if they are not able to understand all instances of the complex domain at the outset. Dealing with complex situations also helps students to cope with idealised models, i.e. models that are abstract, crystallised and beautiful, that have been developed perhaps over hundreds of years, forming a kind of compressed knowledge and body of theory, but that are incomprehensible to students because of the missing links to concrete metaphors (see also Leech, Onwuegbuzie, Murtonen, Mikkilä-Erdmann, & Tähtinen, 2007). Teachers often present idealised models as they think that internally coherent and logical models or theories should be easy for students to understand. However, these models are abstractions of reality and students have difficulty in understanding them, especially if they have no connections with concrete applications or analogies.

As regards to the question of multiple perspectives and complexity, understanding of so called negative knowledge is also important. According to Minsky (1997, p. 515), "In order to think effectively, we must 'know' a good deal about what not to think!" It is not enough, or maybe not even possible, to understand what something is without understanding what it is not. To think and act efficiently we must know, what is the core of the issue, what are the central things and what not so central things, and also what are the irrelevant or even harmful instances. An example of this kind of negative knowledge could be learning to use a computer. If you were to ask a computer expert what you must not do if do not want to mess up the machine, the expert would probably answer that there is nothing you could do which would mess it up totally. When, however, the machine ends a total mess, the expert then tells you that you were allowed to press anything apart from just that particular combination of keys. You could not know that beforehand because you did not have a basic understanding of what are normal commands and what are not. In the development of expertise, the learner goes through a transformation where he or she begins to understand the central issues in relation to the most peripheral and negative issues. Negative knowledge is not so much knowledge about what one does not know, i.e. metacognitive negative knowledge, but just knowledge about what something is not and what does not belong or connect with it. Authentic work situations provide more opportunities than school-based learning for encountering situations where negative knowledge is needed.

The recent rapid development of situational and social learning theories (e.g. Eteläpelto & Collin, 2004; Gruber, Law, Mandl, & Renkl, 1995; Lave & Wenger, 1991; Wenger, 1998), means that learning is no longer seen only as an individual effort but rather as a social and context-bound process. Learning takes place not only at the cognitive level in individual students but also on other levels, such as those of the emotions and the body, and on the level of social groups and networks. At the workplace, learning occurs in an authentic social and physical environment and thus the path from novice to expert is influenced by the whole reality of the work to be done. Learning can thus also be seen as a bodily process, a process where we understand something by using our body that further transforms our thoughts and emotions about the subject (e.g. Lakoff & Johnson, 1999). Learning is based on the body also in recent neuropsychological theories (e.g. Spitzer, 1999), according to which when we are watching someone performing a task, our nervous system activates the same areas in the brain as would be activated were we doing the task ourselves. Thus, these studies suggest that learning from an expert in an authentic context may be an effective way to learn.

Motivational arguments have also been presented for moving education and training to the workplace. According to Boshuizen (2004, p. 92), "For many students practical experience is what makes them tick. Keeping them in school will lead to loss of motivation, learning for exams instead of learning for competence, all other kinds of dysfunctional study behaviour and a knowledge base that does not match practical requirements." Empirical studies support this statement. For example in recent Finnish studies on workplace learning in VET, students reported high levels of intrinsic motivation when learning at work (Tynjälä, Virtanen, & Valkonen, 2005; Virtanen, Tynjälä, & Valkonen, 2005). Similarly, Helle and her colleagues (Helle, Tynjälä, & Olkinuora, 2006a; Helle, Tynjälä, Olkinuora, & Lonka, 2007; Helle, Tynjälä, & Vesterinen, 2006b) found that among university students participating in a work-related project-based course, the most important motivational benefits were experienced by those students who at the outset had learning-related problems in motivation and self-regulation.

## *The Promise of the Connective Model*

Although workplace training clearly has many positive effects, it may not be without problems and disadvantages compared to school learning. For example, Hughes (1998) has reminded us about the different interests and aims of workplaces and schools. While the priority of the school is to support learning, the main purpose of the work organisation is to make a profit or to provide services for customers. Learning is thus subsidiary to the other goals of the workplace and therefore it may be far from an ideal learning environment. The most well-known conceptualisation of workplace learning, the model of legitimate peripheral participation (Lave & Wenger, 1991) has also been criticised for the idea of transmitting existing practices instead of transforming knowledge and creating new practices (Fuller & Unwin, 2002). One critical aspect is related to the modes of knowledge included in the model. As shown in Chapter 2 of this book, expertise can be depicted as an integrated whole combining conceptual, practical and regulative knowledge. What distinguishes legitimate peripheral participation and workplace learning in general from school-based learning is its highly practical and experiential nature (e.g. Collin 2004). This may lead to neglect of the development of conceptual knowledge in learning at work.

The connective model of work experience and integrative pedagogy aims to bridge the gap between conceptual and practical knowledge by emphasising the unity of theory and practice and the integration of conceptual and practical knowledge as the key to the development of expertise (Guile & Griffiths, 2001; Tynjälä, Välimaa, & Sarja, 2003, Tynjälä et al., 2006). Studies on Finnish VET have shown that in those fields which have adopted the connective model (social and health care), students' self-evaluated learning outcomes have been on a higher level than those of students in fields where workplace learning practices follow the traditional model (Tynjälä & Virtanen, 2005; Virtanen & Tynjälä, 2006, in press). Furthermore, the benefits of the connective model seem not to be limited to students. Since the model emphasises the development of work rather than merely reproducing existing practices, the collaborative building of learning environments may also contribute to organisational learning (see Chapter 7).

## The Development of Vocational Expertise During a Company-Based Training Course

The purpose of the case study we describe here was to analyse student learning and the development of expertise during a course in metal work given in a shipbuilding company's own school and in an authentic work environment. We were interested in whether the connective model of work experience would describe this instance of workplace-based learning, and how students' development towards expertise proceeds in such a learning environment. Our assumption was that the transformation in students' knowledge and skills would be seen on both the verbal and task-performance levels. According to the theories of conceptual change, learning can be described as change in students' thinking and conceptions, whereas according to the theories of expertise, performance in conducting a task changes along with the level of expertise. Since the conceptual and practical (or experiential/bodily) levels are intertwined in high-level expertise (see Chapter 2), we aimed at observing students' development at both levels of learning. More specifically, we addressed the following two research questions: (1) How far were different features of the connective model experienced by students during their course? (2) What transformations occurred in students' competencies and expertise during training?

While the outcomes of workplace learning are often hard to measure (Hager, 1998), the outcomes of school learning have usually been examined by measures of the development of theoretical knowledge or conceptual understanding. In recent decades studies of conceptual change, in particular, have shown that the way people conceptualise their knowledge reflects their holistic understanding of the topic as a whole (e.g. Chi, 1992; Vosniadou, 1994). So far, studies on conceptual change have focussed merely on school learning and on specific, strictly defined academic concepts. In our study we applied some of the ideas that have come out of conceptual change research to workplace learning, with the aim of exploring how learning can be seen not only on the level of performance but also on the conceptual level.

The case study was conducted at the Aker Yards Ship Industry School in Turku, Finland, which annually gives many different types of courses varying in length from a few days to half a year. To answer our questions, we needed the participation of students enrolled on a longer course to be able to track changes in their conceptions and competencies. Thus, we selected a course for ship plate maker-welders that lasted for a half year in 2005. Altogether18 students attended the course and participated in the study. Nine students were selected for further observations on the basis of their low prior experience in the field. All 18 students were men, and they were 21–46 years old, (mean 26.6 years). The students selected for observations represented the age distribution of the whole sample.

The basic principle of the course was to integrate the students as soon as possible into the authentic work environment of the shipyard. After the first orientation week, spent mostly in the classroom, the students moved to a large shop floor where they practised the basic procedures of their job in a special training area and were able to participate in the social community of the experienced workers. After 1 or 2 months of training the students were given positions as production assistants, and after 3 months they were given more demanding responsibilities. In this way the idea of legitimate peripheral participation (Lave and Wenger, 1991) was realised in the training. The course instructors were all involved in the production process as well, thereby ensuring a close relationship between teaching and authentic practice.

The data were collected with questionnaires administered to all 18 students at the beginning and at the end of the course, and with a stimulated recall interview methodology with observations and interviews to nine students. The questionnaire included items on the connection between classroom learning and work-based learning and about students' expectations and experiences concerning their learning on the course. Observation data and interviews were collected on the practical training environment, that is, the particular part of the shop floor that was used for teaching purposes. The nine students that were selected for observation and interviews were grouped in smaller three-person groups. Each group first observed a demonstration by the instructor of a flame-cutting task, after which each student attempted the same task. The students did not observe each other's performance, but were instructed to wait in the cafeteria. They were also instructed not to talk about the task so as to avoid giving each other tips. The first observation was conducted at the very beginning of the course. As the majority of the students had never done flame-cutting before this observation situation, they were true novices. The observations were videotaped. Because of the high level of noise on the shop floor, no interviews were conducted during the observations. Only the instructor was briefly interviewed after each student's turn on the student's performance in general. Next, the researcher moved the camera to a quieter meeting room in the same building where the digital recording of each student's performance was instantly loaded into a laptop computer. After this, the students were invited to the room one at a time. The student was asked to sit by the laptop and watch himself while simultaneously telling what he thought at each point, what he was doing and how he thought it went. In other words, an interview with stimulated recall was conducted. The researcher sat next to student throughout and encouraged him to continue his thinking aloud and asked questions if needed. This stimulated recall interview was videotaped with the camera behind the student so that the laptop screen and the student's pointing at the screen were visible.

The 'think aloud' protocol was used early in the history of psychological research to attempt to access the thoughts of subjects engaged in a task. Stimulated recall procedures were developed as an on-line cognition-capturing device to use in situations where think aloud protocols were not possible or where a think aloud protocol would interfere with the performance of the task being examined (Stough, 2001). In this study, evaluation of his performance by the student himself was impossible while the task was being done, and thus a stimulated recall interview was appropriate for our purposes.

A similar observation and stimulated interview was conducted at the end of the course, but in addition to showing students their end-of-course performance on the computer, we also showed them their video from the beginning of the course and asked them to say what they think they did differently and how they think they had progressed. Students thus analysed their two videoed performances using the think aloud method at the end of the course. Their thinking aloud process was supported by encouragement from the researchers to continue thoughts they begun, and the interviewer also asked additional questions to prompt the students to elaborate on their descriptions. No specific questions were asked, but when a student spontaneously expressed an idea, for example, on the connectivity between teaching and work, he was asked to elaborate it. The same flame-cutting task was done at the end as at the beginning of the course, and the working environment and interviewing room were the same. All the students were very cooperative and showed good oral skills in giving their views on their working and thinking. The same researcher conducted all the videotaping and interviewing, while a second researcher was present on some occasions.

Because of the relatively small sample statistical analyses were confined to the distributions of specific variables extracted from the multiple-choice questions. The stimulated recall interview data was transcribed by the same researcher. Two researchers watched the videos. After watching the videos and discussing them, one researcher read the transcriptions. Qualitative analyses of the data were conducted to compare students' performances and their verbal descriptions of them at the beginning and at the end of the course and to identify what kinds of changes had taken place during the training. Thus, conceptual understanding of the topic and practical demonstration of the skills in question were combined in the data collection and analysis. Important points of transformation and conceptual change were sought and their nature and features discussed in detail among all three researchers in this study.

## Connectivity Between Classroom Learning and Work

In order to investigate the actualisation of connectivity between classroom learning and learning at work, we asked the students to answer questions relating to different features of the connective model of work experience. Students' ratings on the different indicators of connectivity are presented in Fig. 6.1. Generally, the students thought that the features of the connective model were present in the actualisation of their education. The low ratings given to the negative statements "There was little relation between classroom instruction and actual practices at work" and "Instructors do not seem to be very clear about what goes on in actual work" indicate that the relationship between classroom instruction and work practice was considered by the students to be rather close. This was supported by the relatively high agreement with the statements "Situations that arise at work were also discussed during lessons" and "Situations that arise at work were handled in practical training sessions in the training workshop". These results suggest that students were encouraged to make reflective connections between formal classroom instruction and more informal learning in work situations, which is a central pillar of the connective model of work experience. Students also highly agreed that they needed both manual and thinking skills at work and that they could perform similar tasks in another workplace. These findings are in line with the connective model, which emphasises boundary crossing between different contexts as well as equality between thinking and practical skills. Although the students rated the specific features of the connective model highly, the mean value of the general statement on the connection between classroom lessons and learning at work (item 7) was not very high. This suggests that there is room for improvement in the relations between classroom lessons and learning at work.

Figure 6.2 shows how much students expected to learn in different ways at the outset and their ratings of that learning at the end of the training. The students' ratings indicate that some changes had occurred in their views. Generally, they gave lower ratings at the end of the course than at the beginning. There are several possible reasons for this. For example, it may be that the students were enthusiastic at the beginning and on this account gave very high ratings. All the ratings, however, were positive (= mean over 3.5 on scale 1–7) both at the beginning and at the end, indicating that the students' expectations were high and that they were satisfied with their education. At the beginning of the course, they expected to learn most by doing themselves, from guidance and tips from the more experienced workers in the shipyard, from course instructors in the classroom and from their superiors in the shipyard. At the end of the course, they agreed that they had learned a lot by doing themselves, as well as from guidance and tips from their experienced workmates and demonstrations by their instructors. Thus, in these respects the students' expectations were realised.

In contrast, the students reported that they did not learn from the course instructors in the classroom or from the course materials as much as they had expected. This finding indicates that although the education was organised in the workplace, the theoretical classroom lessons suffered at some level from the same problems as traditional school learning, that is, understanding of the teaching and course

## Please evaluate the following claims:

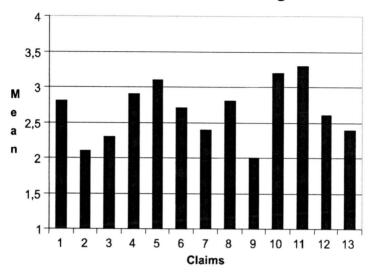

1. Classroom instruction covered topics that were useful at work
   (*M* = 2,8; *SD* = 0,7)
2. There was little relation between classroom instruction and actual
   practices at work   (*M* = 2,1; *SD* = 0,9)
3. The tasks were similar in lessons and at work   (*M* = 2,3; *SD* = 1,0)
4. Situations that arise at work were also discussed during lessons
   (*M* = 2,9; *SD* = 0,5)
5. Situations that arise at work were also handled in practical training
   sessions in the training workshop   (*M* = 3,1; *SD* = 0,9)
6. At work, we had to apply theoretical knowledge learned at school
   (*M* = 2,7; *SD* = 0,9)
7. Learning at work and classroom lessons were well connected with each
   other   (*M* = 2,4; *SD* = 0,8)
8. It seemed that the school and the shipyard production cooperated
   well   (*M* = 2,8; *SD* = 0,8)
9. Instructors do not seem to be very clear about what goes on in actual
   work   (*M* = 2,0; *SD* = 0,7)
10. On the shipyard I noticed that I need both manual and thinking skill
    at work   (*M* = 3,2; *SD* = 0,9)
11. I would be able to perform the same tasks at another workplace
    (*M* = 3,3; *SD* = 0,9)
12. In classroom lessons instructors encouraged students to consider things
    critically at work   (*M* = 2,6; *SD* = 0,7)
13. Workplace learning has given me a critical perspective into classroom
    lessons.   (*M* = 2,4; *SD* = 1,0)

Scale : 1 = totally disagree, … 4 = totally agree

**Fig. 6.1** Students' ratings of the different indicators of connectivity at the end of the course

## How much have you learned from...

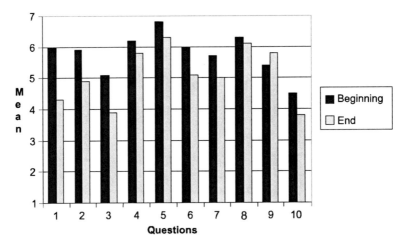

1. ...course instructors in the classroom   (I: *M* = 6,0; *SD* = 0,8) (II: *M* = 4,3; *SD* = 1,3)
2. ...co-operating and discussing with other students   (I: *M* = 5,6; *SD* = 0,9) (II: *M* = 4,9; *SD* = 0,9)
3. ...course materials, e.g., books   (I: *M* = 5,1; *SD* = 1,5) (II: *M* = 3,9; *SD* = 1,1)
4. ...demonstrations by the instructors   (I: *M* = 6,2; *SD* = 0,7) (II: *M* = 5,8; *SD* = 0,8)
5. ...by doing the job yourself   (I: *M* = 6,8; *SD* = 0,4) (II: *M* = 6,3; *SD* = 0,7)
6. ...guidance and tips from superiors at the shipyard   (I: *M* = 6,0; *SD* = 1,0) (II: *M* = 5,1; *SD* = 1,0)
7. ...discussion with other students when working at the shipyard   (I: *M* = 5,7; *SD* = 0,9) (II: *M* = 5,0; *SD* = 1,1)
8. ...guidance and tips from the more experienced workers   (I: *M* = 6,3; *SD* = 0,6) (II: *M* = 6,1; *SD* = 0,7)
9. ...watching the more experienced workers at work   (I: *M* = 5,4; *SD* = 1,7) (II: *M* = 5,8; *SD* = 1,2)
10. ...unofficial caféteria and lunch discussions   (I: *M* = 4,5; *SD* = 1,3) (II: *M* = 3,8; *SD* = 1,8)

Scale : 1 = totally disagree, ... 7 = totally agree

**Fig. 6.2** Students' expectations of their learning in different ways at the beginning of the course and their ratings of their actual learning at the end of the course

materials did not reach levels that the students considered useful or important. Thus, theory seems to be detached from practice. This interpretation was supported by the stimulated recall interviews, where some students spontaneously asserted that some of the classroom teaching was 'too theoretical'. For example, these students reported that classroom lessons about interpreting blueprints were hard to understand and were not yet useful to them. The amount of abstract knowledge and new knowledge was felt by students to be high in these lessons and had no connection to their prior knowledge (see e.g. Leech et al., 2007). Blueprints were also introduced to them without any need for their use in production at that moment; in other words, no concrete procedural knowledge was needed at that time. This is a good example of 'unconnective' teaching.

According to the results, the students also thought that neither co-operation and discussion with other students nor guidance and tips from their superiors in the shipyard nor the course material had played as important role as they expected in the beginning. In professional work, discussions with workmates are usually experienced as an important source of learning (e.g. Hakkarainen, Palonen, Paavola, & Lehtinen, 2004). In our data the students did not seem to place much value on discussions with their peers as a factor supporting learning. It is possible that in manual work it is not so easy for people to recognise the role of reflection and discussion in learning. The only form of learning that the students found more beneficial than they had expected at the beginning was watching the more experienced workers at work. As described earlier according to recent neuropsychological studies (e.g. Spitzer, 1999), when we observe someone performing a task, our nervous system activates the same areas in the brain that would be activated were we to do the same task ourselves. This study suggests that watching the performance of more experienced peers is conducive to the learning of skills, and our findings show that a company training model in which providing students with access to following and participating in authentic practices is experienced useful by the students.

## Transformation of Skills and Competencies During a Course

To analyse how students' skills had developed during the half-year period of their education we analysed both the observation data (videos) and the stimulated recall interview data. On the basis of this combined data we identified the following types of changes in students' knowledge and competences:

1) Changes in agency
2) Changes in understanding the critical instances/aspects of the task
3) Changes in understanding the goal of the task
4) Changes in performance
5) Changes in bodily performance
6) Changes in use of concepts
7) Changes in self-confidence.

These changes involve both conceptual changes and performance changes and they seem to have taken place integratively. Below, we describe in more detail how these changes were evident in the data.

A notable difference in students' descriptions of their task between the beginning and the end of the course was in the *agency ascribed to decisions*. At the beginning, all the students used expressions such as "it should be done in this way" or "the instructor told us to do it like this". Their descriptions usually included the same terms and examples that the instructor had used. At the end of the course, the actor had changed into the student himself. For example, the instructor told all the students to use a drawing stick to draw a line on the steel plate to be cut. At the end of the course most (seven of nine) students drew the line with chalk, against the instructor's original instruction. The students usually commented that it was their personal choice. For example, one student said "I think it's easier to do with chalk" [than with a drawing stick] (S3). When asked about chalk, one student said that he usually used chalk in production tasks, but used a drawing stick for this particular task when performed for research purposes.

Inteviewer: "You drew with a drawing stick. You also have chalk. Do you ever use chalk?"

Student (S4): "Yes, it depends what you are burning. In this case I did it with drawing stick because, in principle, it makes a sharper mark." . . .

Student (S4) continues: "In ordinary production I usually draw with chalk. It can be seen more easily and it is not so precise in there. Or just by sketching — it is not always necessary to mark."

The student thus used a drawing stick in the formal observation situation, but did not do so normally when at work. Thus, he might have assumed that he was expected behave in a specific way in this research situation, regardless of his normal behaviour.

One student commented on why he did not use a ruler, although the instructor had told them to use one at the beginning of the course: "I didn't think I needed a ruler anymore. I was able to do it without the ruler." (S3) This indicates that the student thought he was able to manage the given task using his own methods, that is, he knew already where he could violate a rule. In the classic description by Dreyfus and Dreyfus (1986) of the development of expertise, violating the rules is an indicator of moving from the novice phase to that of the advanced beginner. Thus, our data show that the workplace-based training was effective in supporting this development.

The feeling of they were managing to accomplish the task was connected to the students' views about the end product and to their belief in the success of their actions. This indicates changes in students' *understanding of the critical aspects of the task* and also changes their *understanding of the goals* of the work. Evidence of such changes was seen in the observation data in terms both of change in students' performance and of change in the expressions they used in their talk. One student commented about not using a ruler and about being sure he could manage the task as follows: "I know how to look at it, I have seen and made so many blocks. I can figure out what it should be like." (S4) Thus, knowing what the final product should look like and understanding critical and non-critical aspects of the task, gives students the confidence to perform the task in a way they find suit them best. The same phenomenon was also observed in another student. The interviewer mentioned to him at the end of the course that on his first attempt the student checked the result every now and then by looking at the steel plate to see whether the flame really did cut the steel. At the end of the course the student did not check the result while working. The student replied: "Now [second time] I did not have to check, I knew when the plate was cut." (S3) The finding that students had the end product in their mind indicates that they had moved from the level of the advanced beginner to the next phase of expertise development, that is, to the level of the competent performer.

The chief characteristic of competent workers is that they have a goal in mind and plan their actions according to this goal. In the present study, the development from novicehood to competency seemed to be much faster than is suggested in the original Dreyfus model. The explanation for this may be nature of the work: the flame-cutting tasks described here are simpler than the tasks the original model was based on.

Violating the rules was not limited only to students' performance. The instructor also seemed to tolerate more freedom in performance in certain situations. At the beginning of the course, the instructor gave the students strict instructions about how to do the given task. He told students always to flame-cut towards oneself, not away from oneself or sideways. At the beginning of the course he spontaneously commented to the researcher, when he was present at the observation, that a student who was not following this instruction was doing the task the wrong way. In the end of the course in cases where the task was poorly done, he also commented that the direction of flame-cutting was a problem. However, if the student succeeded well, the instructor did not pay attention to the direction of flame-cutting. For example, one of the students had clearly learned to flame-cut well. He did not flame-cut towards himself at all, but the instructor did not mention this, but said the job was well done. Taking into account the fact that in the interviews the students said that it is often not possible to flame-cut towards oneself in real working situations, we assume that instructors tolerate breaking this rule if they notice that a student has understood the main idea of the task. A rule is often used in the beginning with novices as a starting point and to help students to understand the main idea of the task; but since a student has grasped the idea, the rule is no longer useful, except possibly in theory. Rules of this type could be termed as "scaffolding rules", as they are needed as aid in the construction of knowledge or a skill, and can be jettisoned once the skill has been learned.

Pedagogically, giving a novice a clear rule may be helpful in terms of not confusing the student, but at the same time it distorts reality. When entering real work situations, they notice that the rule is not used in practice and, as some interviewees reported, teaching seems to be separated off from real practice. Students may not understand why they are taught something that is not valid in real work situations. In other words, they are not able to see the pedagogical benefit of the rule. Thus, it might be worth trying to introduce students to the task in all its complexity from the very beginning (Lehtinen, 2002) to help them to understand that the job can be done in many ways, but that for a novice, certain methods, such as, scaffolding rules, are best at the beginning.

Our claim that learning and the development of competence is also a *bodily process* seemed to be confirmed by our data. The videos showed that changes occurred in students' bodily performance between the beginning and the end of the course. When conducting the flame-cutting task at the beginning, the students had difficulties in finding a comfortable position for their body by the flame-cutting table. In the end, none of the students seemed to have any trouble in finding a good stance. For example, one student who had his particular difficulty at the beginning of the course moved his weight from leg to another leg seeking to find a comfortable stance. In the end he had no such difficulties. He went to the flame-cutting table and went to work without paying attention to or spending any time on finding a position. Although he had not done much flame-cutting during the work training period, he seemed to be more confident and fluent in this particular task than at the beginning of the course. He had mainly been working as a welder. He reported that finding a good position to work in is essential, as jobs were mostly done in difficult positions. He said he had learned to "...find as comfortable a position as possible, where it feels good. Then you just keep it." (S2) He assumed sometimes a job may last for days and that the worker would have to work in the same space in a difficult position throughout his shift. Learning to cope with ones' body by finding a good working position seems to be a particular skill that develops during education on the shop floor. This skill also seems to be transferable to different jobs, for example, from welding to flame-cutting.

In addition to finding a comfortable working position, finding the right position for the metal plate on the workbench was difficult for the students at the beginning of the course, but at its end the lie of the plate was selected fast. Most students were turning the about 30 × 40 cm steel plate many times before selecting the position for cutting in the beginning, but in the end they just laid the plate down to the desk and started to work with it. This problem was partially connected to the teachers' guidelines about always flame-cutting towards oneself and not sideways or away from oneself.

The *concepts* that the students use varied between the first and the second observation. In general, the changes in concepts use resembled those seen in the case of agency. At the time of the second observation, the students were more confident about the concepts they used. At the first observation, they mainly tried to copy the teacher's language and if they did not remember the right words, they got stuck like one student (S9) who tried to explain what he was doing but did not remember the words used to explain the angle at which flame cutter was supposed to be held. At the second observation, the students seemed to find the right terms to explain phenomena. One student (S7), for example, used concepts referring to the size of the flame and to the effect of the length of the tube on cutting when explaining why he succeeded the second time but not the first time. Thus, transformation in behaviour was connected also to the use of concepts.

A notable and quite general finding was that the students generally seemed to have progressed in the flame-cutting task on many levels, whether or not they had done any flame-cutting during the half-year period. All the students performed the task on the second measurement with *increased confidence* and decreased novice-like actions, such as trying to find the right position for the steel plate and the right bodily position. They also talked about the task in a more expert-like manner at the second observation, by giving their own opinions about the best way of conducting the task and by using more of the correct terms when referring to the tools and the task. This finding suggests that the students' knowledge and expertise developed on a general level during their education in the workplace. All these changes seemed to be also connected to the students' self-confidence, as their behaviour at the end of the course was based on their own beliefs about how things should be done, not on some others' instructions. They had grown into reliable workers who trusted themselves to be able to do the job in the best possible way.

## Discussion

The results of this study showed that the students were very satisfied with their education in the workplace. In their assessments of the different forms of learning, they reported they had learned most from watching the more experienced workers doing the same job. This type of learning by following an expert model is well in line with the idea of legitimate peripheral participation (Lave & Wenger, 1991), which emphasises the importance of involving novices in authentic practices from the very beginning. Also, recent theories of neuropsychology (e.g. Spitzer, 1999) seem to explain this kind of learning. These theories have indicated that when we are looking at someone performing a task, the same areas are activated in our brains as be activated were we to do the task ourselves. Thus, the idea of learning from the model of an expert seems to obtain both theoretical and empirical support.

Although students rated their education in the workplace quite high in terms of the connective model of work experience, it also seemed to suffer from problems similar to those encountered in traditional school learning. The students were not very convinced at the end of the course that they had learned much from the teachers in the classroom or from the course material. Some very abstract domains especially, were considered hard to understand. The problem of 'idealised models', i.e. models that are compressed theories of abstract knowledge, seems to be present in this type of education as well. Instructors may present idealised models as they think that internally coherent and logical models or theories are easy for students to understand. However, these models are abstractions of reality and thus students have trouble understanding them, especially if practical applications or procedural knowledge related to these models is missing. Therefore developing an integrative pedagogy which is based on the uniting of theoretical, practical, and self-regulatory knowledge (see Chapter 2) is highly recommended for company-based training as well as for school-based education.

It was also found in this study that rules of the kind we called 'scaffolding rules' were used in teaching. Scaffolding rules were rules that were taught to students but that were not really used in the authentic work situation. When students had learned a given task well, they no longer respected the rule in question. Even the instructors no longer expected students to follow such scaffolding rules after the student had attained a certain level of expertise.

Development and transformation in the students' skills and competencies during the course occurred on the levels of agency, understanding the critical instances/aspects of the task, understanding the goal of the work, in performance, in bodily performance, in the use of concepts and in self-confidence. The students' development was not always attached to specific tasks that they had performed or to the amount of experience they had acquired in certain jobs, but was more general and transferable in nature. We assume that this is due to the connection between learning in the course of real work with formal learning in the classroom. In other words, a real working environment and the related classroom learning seemed to support all aspects of learning, namely, the cognitive, social and bodily aspects. Growing into a fully fledged member of the whole socio-physical working environment seems to help students to develop skills and competencies in handling many kinds of jobs and also to transfer their skills to managing tasks that they have not in fact greatly practised. This skill probably also includes negative knowledge about what kinds of tasks they cannot manage or what should not be done (see e.g. Minsky, 1997). A simple flame-cutting job is the kind of job students could trust themselves to manage even if they had not done a similar job many times. The students thus seemed to develop the identity of a shipyard worker that included ideas of responsibility and competence in basic jobs, during their education in the workplace.

The transformation in students' competences was seen, for example, on the level of coping with given tasks and talking about their behaviour. At the beginning of the course the students were insecure about all their actions – cognitive, bodily, and verbal. In the end, all these areas had gone through a positive change. Even if a student had not had much experience of the task in question during the course, he was more competent to conduct it at the end than at the beginning. The finding that students have the end product in mind indicates that they have moved from the level of the advanced beginner to the next phase of expertise development, that is, to the level of the competent performer. A competent worker has a goal in mind and plans his actions according to this goal. The development from novice to competency in the current study seems to be much faster than in the original model by Dreyfus and Dreyfus (1986). The explanation for this may be nature of the task: The flame-cutting tasks described here are simpler than the tasks which the original model was based on. In addition to better task performance, the students were using more professional and sophisticated concepts at the end of the course. Their whole system of concepts had gone through a change and they felt more comfortable in speaking about the job than they had at the beginning.

Also of note in this study was change on the level of agency in terms of the violation of rules. In the classic description of the development of expertise by Dreyfus and Dreyfus (1986), violating the rules is an indicator of moving from the novice phase to a more advanced level. At the end of the course the students in this study no longer respected all rules that had been given to them at the outset. This is partly due to the nature of some rules being what we called scaffolding rules, i.e. they were no longer needed, but also as a result of the students' learning in the context of real production that they can decide what is important and what is not (cf. negative knowledge; see Minsky, 1997), and how a job can be best done. The development of this kind of expertise was not necessarily connected with the amount of experience that a student had had on the specific task, but was more general in nature. Education in the metal industry, at least in the case of the workplace studied here would then seem to promote the development of general skills in managing basic jobs in the domain independent of the amount of actual experience in a particular task. At first glance, this finding seems to contradict the earlier research the results of which have emphasised strong domain specificity and a low level of transfer of different skills in the development of expertise (e.g. Feltovich, Prietula, & Ericsson, 2006). However, our finding on the transfer of skills can be explained by the fact that in the shipyard and metal industry domains different tasks often have some features in common (e.g. adapting body positions while working), a factor which may promote transfer between tasks.

In sum, our study of workplace-based education in the metal (shipbuilding) industry shows that among the education providers features of the connective model, integrating conceptual and experiential learning, were evident. However, the findings also indicated that fully realising the connective model is a challenging task and there remains room for improvement.

**Acknowledgments**  We would like to thank the Academy of Finland and the Aker Yards shipyards in Turku, Finland for supporting this research. We especially thank the Rector of the Aker Yards Ship Industry School, Raimo Oksanen, for making this research possible and the Ship Industry School instructors, Leevi Weman, Pentti Pohjola, and Elmo Laine, for their helpful co-operation. Finally, we wish to thank the students who took part in the study.

# References

Andresen, M., & Lichtenberger, B. (2007). The corporate university landscape in Germany. *Journal of Workplace Learning, 19*(2).109–123.
Billett, S. (2007). *The pedagogic practices of small business operators*. Paper presented at the AERA 2007 Annual Meeting, Chicago, USA.
Boshuizen, H. P. A. (2004). Does practice make perfect? A slow and discontinuous process. In H. P. A. Boshuizen, R. Bromme, & H. Gruber (Eds.), *Professional learning: Gaps and transitions on the way from novice to expert* (pp. 73–95). Dordrecht: Kluwer Academic Publishers.
Boshuizen, H. P. A., Bromme, R., & Gruber, H. (2004). On the long way from novice to expert and how traveling changes the traveler. In H. P. A. Boshuizen, R. Bromme, & H. Gruber (Eds.), *Professional learning: Gaps and transitions on the way from novice to expert* (pp. 3–8). Dordrecht: Kluwer Academic Publishers.
Chase, W. G., & Simon, H. A. (1973). Perception in chess. *Cognitive Psychology, 4*, 55–81.
Chi, M. T. H. (1992). Conceptual change within and across ontological categories: Examples from learning and discovery in science. In R. N. Giere (Ed.), *Cognitive models of science. Minnesota studies in the philosophy of science* (pp. 129–186). Minneapolis, MN: University of Minnesota Press.
Chi, M. T. H., Glaser, R., & Rees, E. (1982). Expertise in problem solving. In R. J. Sternberg (Ed.), *Advances in the psychology of human intelligence* (pp. 7–75). Hillsdale, NJ: Lawrence Erlbaum Associates.
Collin, K. (2004). The role of experience in work and learning among design engineers. *International Journal of Training and Development, 8*(2), 11–127.
Dreyfus, H. L., & Dreyfus, S. E. (1986). *Mind over machine. The power of human intuition and expertise in the era of the computer*. Oxford: Basic Blackwell.
Dubs, R. (2006). An appraisal of the Swiss vocational education and trainng system. *Swiss research on vocational education and training, Vol. 4*. Bern: h.e.p. Verlag.
Eteläpelto, A., & Collin, K. (2004). From individual cognition to communities of practice. Theoretical underpinnings in analyzing professional design expertise. In H. P. A. Boshuizen,

R. Bromme, & H. Gruber (Eds.), *Professional learning: Gaps and transitions on the way from novice to expert* (pp. 231–249). Dordrecht: Kluwer Academic Publishers.

Feltovich, P. J., Prietula, M. J., & Ericsson, K. A. (2006). Studies of expertise from psychological perspectives. In K. A. Ericsson, N. Charness, P. J. Feltovich, & R. R. Hoffman (Eds.), *The Cambridge handbook of expertise and expert performance* (pp. 41–67). Cambridge: Cambridge University Press.

Fuller, A., & Unwin, L. (2002). Developing pedagogies for the contemporary workplace. In K. Evans, P. Hodkinson, & L. Unwin (Eds.), *Working to learn* (pp. 95–111). London: Kogan Page.

Griffitths, T., & Guile, D. (2003). A connective model of learning: The implication for work process knowledge. *European Educational Research Journal, 2*(1), 56–73.

Gruber, H., Law, L.-C., Mandl, H., & Renkl, A. (1995). Situated learning and transfer. In P. Reimann & H. Spada (Eds.), *Learning in humans and machines: Towards an interdisciplinary learning science* (pp. 168–188). Oxford: Pergamon.

Guile, D., & Griffiths, T. (2001). Learning through work experience. *Journal of Education and Work, 14*(1), 113–131.

Hager, P. (1998). Understanding workplace learning: General perspectives. In D. Boud (Ed.), *Current issues and new agendas in workplace learning* (pp. 31–46). Springfield (Va.): NCVER.

Hakkarainen, K., Palonen, T., Paavola, S., & Lehtinen, E. (2004). *Communities of networked expertise: Professional and educational perspectives.* Amsterdam: Elsevier.

Helle, L., Tynjälä, P., & Olkinuora, E. (2006a). Project-based learning in post-secondary education – theory, practice and rubber sling shots. *Higher Education, 51*(2), 287–314.

Helle, L., Tynjälä, P., & Vesterinen, P. (2006b). Work-related project as a learning environment. In P. Tynjälä, J. Välimaa, & G. Boulton-Lewis (Eds.), *Higher education and working life: Collaborations, confrontations and challenges* (pp. 195–208). Amsterdam: Elsevier.

Helle, L., Tynjälä, P., Olkinuora, E. & Lonka, K. (2007). "Ain't nothin' like the real thing." Motivation and study processes in university-level project studies. *British Journal of Educational Psychology, 77*(2), 397–411.

Hughes, C. (1998). Practicum learning: perils of the authentic workplace. *Higher Education Research & Development, 17*(2), 207–227.

Jacobson, M. J., & Spiro, R. J. (1995). Hypertext learning environments, cognitive flexibility, and the transfer of complex knowledge: An empirical investigation. *Journal of Computing Research, 12*, 301–333.

Lakoff, G., & Johnson, M. (1999). *Philosophy in the flesh. The embodied mind and its challenge to western thought.* New York: Basic Books.

Lave, J., & Wenger, E. (1991). *Situated learning. Legitimate peripheral participation.* Cambridge: Cambridge University Press.

Leech, N. L., Onwuegbuzie, A. J., Murtonen, M., Mikkilä-Erdmann, M., & Tähtinen, J. (2007). Researcher workshop for student teachers – An example of a mixed methods learning environment. In M. Murtonen, J. Rautopuro, & P. Väisänen (Eds.) *Learning and teaching of research methods at university* (pp. 205–226). Research in Educational Sciences, 30. Turku: Finnish Educational Research Association.

Lehtinen, E. (2002). Developing models for distributed problem-based learning: Theoretical and methodological reflection. *Distance Education, 23*, 109–117.

Lesgold, A., Rubinson, H., Feltovich, P., Glaser, R., Klopfer, D., & Wang, Y. (1988). Expertise in a complex skill: Diagnosing x-ray pictures. In M. T. H. Chi, R. Glaser, & M. J. Farr (Eds.), *The nature of expertise* (pp. 311–342). Hillsdale, NJ: Lawrence Erlbaum Associates.

Minsky, M. (1997). Negative expertise. In P. J. Feltovich, K. M. Ford, & R. R. Hoffman (Eds.), *Expertise in context* (pp. 515–521). Menlo Park: The MIT Press.

Mora, J.-G., García-Aracil, A. & Vilas, L. E. (2007). Job satisfaction among young European higher education graduates. *Higher Education, 53*(1), 29–59.

Newell, A., & Simon, H. A. (1972). *Human problem solving.* Englewood Cliffs: Prentice-Hall.

Rademakers, M. (2005). Corporate universities: driving force of knowledge innovation. *Journal of Workplace Learning, 17*(1/2), 130–136.

van Someren, M. W., Reimann, P., Boshuizen, H. P. A., & de Jong, T. (Eds.) (1998). *Learning with multiple representations*. Amsterdam: Pergamon.

Spitzer, M. (1999). *The mind within the net. Models of learning, thinking and acting*. Massachusetts: The MIT Press.

Stark, R., Gruber, H., Hinkofer, L., & Mandl, H. (2004). Overcoming problems of knowledge application and transfer. Development, implementation and evaluation of an example-based instructional approach in the context of vocational school training in business administration. In H. P. A. Boshuizen, R. Bromme, & H. Gruber (Eds.), *Professional learning: Gaps and transitions on the way from novice to expert* (pp. 49–70). Dordrecht: Kluwer Academic Publishers.

Stenström, M.-L. (2006). Polytechnic graduates' working life skills and expertise. In P. Tynjälä, J. Välimaa & G. Boulton-Lewis (Eds.), *Higher education and working life: Collaborations, confrontations and challenges* (pp. 89–102). Amsterdam: Elsevier.

Stough, L. M. (2001, April). *Using stimulated recall in classroom observation and professional development*. Paper presented at the annual meeting of AERA, Seattle, Washington. Full text available from ERIC.

Tynjälä, P., Välimaa, J., & Sarja, A. (2003). Pedagogical perspectives into the relationship between higher education and working life. *Higher Education, 46*, 147–166.

Tynjälä, P., Slotte, V., Nieminen, J., Lonka, K., & Olkinuora, E. (2006). From university to working life: Graduates' workplace skills in practice. In P. Tynjälä, J. Välimaa & G. Boulton-Lewis (Eds.), *Higher education and working life: Collaborations, confrontations and challenges* (pp. 73–88). Amsterdam: Elsevier.

Tynjälä, P., & Virtanen, A. (2005). Skill learning at work: Investigation into student experiences of on-the-job learning. *Learning the Skills: Special Edition of the Finnish Journal of Vocational and Professional Education, 7* (Special ed.), 106–116.

Tynjälä, P., Virtanen, A., & Valkonen, S. (2005). *Työssäoppiminen Keski-Suomessa. Taitava Keski-Suomi -tutkimus osaI*. [Students'workplace learning in Central Finland. "Skilled Central Finland" research report. Part II]. Jyväskylä: University of Jyväskylä. Institute for Educational Research.

van der Velden, R. (2006, October). *The flexible professional in the knowledge society. New demands on higher education in Europe*. Keynote lecture presented at the EARLI SIG Learning and Professional Development, Heerlen, the Netherlands.

Virtanen, A., Tynjälä, P., & Valkonen, S. (2005). *Työssäoppiminen opiskelijoiden arvioimana Helsingin kaupungin ammatillisissa oppilaitoksissa*. (Helsingin kaupungin opetusviraston julkaisusarja A1). [Students'evaluation of worklearning in vocational institutes of Helsinki.] Helsinki: Helsingin kaupungin opetusvirasto.

Virtanen, A., & Tynjälä, P. (2006, October). *Workplace learning in Finnish VET*. Students', teachers' and workplace trainers' perspectives. Paper presented at the EARLI Learning and Professional Development SIG Conference, Heerlen, the Netherlands.

Virtanen, A., & Tynjälä, P. (2008). Students' experiences of workplace learning in Finnish VET. *European Journal of Vocational Training*, 2008/2(44), 199–213.

Vosniadou, S. (1994). Capturing and modelling the process of conceptual change. *Learning and Instruction, 4*, 45–69.

Wenger, E. (1998). *Communities of practice. Learning, meaning and identity*. Cambridge: Cambridge University Press.

# Part III
# From Individual Learning
# to Organisational Development

# Chapter 7
# Transformation of Individual Learning into Organisational and Networked Learning in Vocational Education

Päivi Tynjälä and Pentti Nikkanen

## Introduction

The Finnish vocational education and training system has traditionally been largely school-based with the inclusion of only short practice periods in students' study programmes. In 2001 the system was reformed, new 3-year study programmes were introduced in all fields of study, and workplace learning (WPL; at least 6 months) became a compulsory part of all vocational study programmes. WPL is defined as systematically guided and assessed learning that takes place in authentic work environments. Thus, workplaces have to provide guidance and support for student learning and to participate in a tripartite assessment. At the beginning of the workplace learning period the student, the teacher and the workplace trainer together define the learning aims. The achievement of the aims is assessed, ideally, both during the learning period and at the end of it. Altogether, the role of the workplace as a learning environment has become much more important than it was before the reform. The implementation of workplace learning has challenged vocational schools and workplaces to develop new kinds of relationships and networks with each other. Networking and collaboration with workplaces has become part of the daily activity of vocational teachers and institutions.

Recent research on workplace learning has emphasised the importance of networking and other forms of social exchange for both individual and organisational learning. Concepts such as the 'learning organisation', the 'learning community' (e.g. Pedler, Burgoyne, & Boydell, 1991; Senge, 1990), 'innovative knowledge communities' (Hakkarainen, Palonen, Paavola, & Lehtinen, 2004) and 'ba' – a space for learning – (Nonaka & Konno, 1998) have been developed to describe the collaborative nature of learning. Learning is seen as an interactive process of knowledge creation where explicit and tacit knowledge embedded in organisations meet each other. One important feature of both learning organisations and innovative knowledge communities is that people and organisations form and utilise social networks in their work. Thus, the study of networked learning has emerged as a

P. Tynjälä (✉)
Institute for Educational Research, University of Jyväskylä, Jyväskylä, Finland
e-mail: paivi.tynjala@ktl.jyu.fi

M.-L. Stenström, P. Tynjälä (eds.), *Towards Integration of Work and Learning,*
© Springer Science+Business Media B.V. 2009

new branch of learning research (e.g. Holmqvist, 2005; Hytönen & Tynjälä, 2005; Knight, 2002; Palonen, 2003; Vesalainen & Strömmer, 1999). Many studies have suggested that innovations emerge via interactive networks (Camagni, 1991; Miles, Miles, & Snow, 2005; Nelson, 1993).

The aim of the present study was to investigate networking and networked learning between VET institutions and working-life organisations. We were interested in whether such cooperation between education and work generates innovative practices and leads to functioning networks with knowledge-creation capacity. Can these networks be characterised as 'learning organisations' or 'innovative knowledge communities' (Hakkarainen et al., 2004)? The study was carried out in Central Finland where the local vocational education administration has invested in promoting cooperation between education and working life with the aim of developing Central Finland as a learning region.

In this chapter, we first present an overview of the theoretical background of the study. We describe the main features of networks and the notions of learning organisations, innovative knowledge communities and a space for learning, *ba*, which we use as conceptual devices to examine learning in the networks of vocational schools and workplaces. After this we specify our research problems and present our findings. Finally, we discuss the significance of the findings from the viewpoint of the development of vocational education and training and working life.

## Learning Organisation and Organisational Learning

A learning organisation, also known as a learning work community or a learning company, has been defined in terms of continuous learning, transformation, adaptation, participating in management, delegation, questioning the organisation's strategy, reflective working and collaboration amongst its members, learning by experience and history, continuous experimentation, participation, system thinking, a shared vision, awareness of its core competencies, commitment to work and responsibility, teamwork, diversified group working, problem solving, creativity and innovativeness, approval and appreciation of dissimilarities, self-directivity and self-assessment, effective information flow, continuous giving, getting and helping each other, freedom, and an encouraging atmosphere (see e.g. Burgoyne, 1995; Coopey, 1996; Garvin, 1993; Nikkanen, 2001; Pedler et al., 1991; Senge, 1990). The level of generality and points of emphasis do, of course, vary in the definitions of a learning organisation. However, the main feature of a learning organisation is that people learn to share knowledge and to learn from each other. Most definitions focus on learning that takes place at the system level rather than at the individual level. The above-mentioned characteristics of a learning organisation describe the learning context in which the process of transforming learning from the individual onto the collective level (organisational) and vice versa can take place successfully.

As with the notion of the learning organisation, the field of organisational learning (OL) has also been the object of a wide diversity of opinions, definitions, and conceptualisations (Nicolini & Meznar, 1995; see also Dixon, 1994, pp. 135–136; Nikkanen, 2001). According to Dixon (1994), some of the more significant differences between the various definitions of organisational learning are (a) a focus on the organisation's relationship to the external environment versus a more internal focus, (b) a focus on adaptation versus a proactive stance of creating a desired future, (c) the learning of individuals versus a focus on the learning of larger organisational units, such as the team or total system, (d) management as the major player in OL versus a broader view that includes members at all levels of the organisation, and (e) a focus on taking action versus a focus on the organisation's underlying assumptions.

Organisational learning takes place in a learning organisation. The level of complexity increases hugely when we move from a single individual to a collection of diverse individuals. It is said that nowadays individual learning in different organisations is not enough. Although individual learning is and will always be very important, "individual learning does not guarantee organisational learning. But – without it no organisational learning occurs" (see Argyris & Schön 1978, p. 20; Pedler et al. 1991; Senge 1990, p. 139).

The descriptions of learning organisations in the literature (e.g. Pedler et al., 1991; Senge, 1990) and the more recent definitions of an innovative knowledge community (Hakkarainen et al., 2004) are in many respects similar, if not synonymous. They are distinguished mainly by the minor shifts of emphasis. Both stress continuous learning and innovation, collectiveness and the sharing of knowledge. In this chapter the terms 'learning organisation' and 'innovative knowledge community' are seen as synonyms.

## Networked Learning and Innovative Knowledge Communities

Networks are formed with independent participants; these can be either individuals or organisations. A network can be described as a loose organisation, and learning in and of networks as a form of organisational learning (e.g. Kekäle & Viitala, 2003; Knight, 2002; Van Laere & Heene, 2003; Vesalainen & Strömmer, 1999). The general aim of a network is usually to provide a forum for the exchange, transformation and creation of knowledge. Thus, a feature typical of networks is the exchange of knowledge, which takes place mutually but not necessarily symmetrically. Networks may be either competitive or cooperative. By participating in networks people are able to cross boundaries between different organisations and fields of expertise. Engeström and his colleagues (Engeström, Engeström, & Kärkkäinen, 1995; Engeström, Engeström, & Vähäaho, 1999) have called activities of this kind polycontextual work or knotworking. Networking between organisations and people has become an important element of their success strategies because of the potential that networking provides for innovative learning (Engeström, 2004; Hakkarainen et al., 2004; Miles et al., 2005). Learners in network learning can be described on four levels: individuals, groups of individuals, organisations, and whole interorganisational networks (Knight, 2002).

The potential that networks have for creating innovations can be explained by reference to the fact that in dialogical relationships between people with different kinds of expertise, participants acquire new ideas which they then develop further from their own starting points, frameworks and context. Theoretically, this potential can be described, for example, by the notion of the Zone of Proximal Development (Vygotsky, 1978) and its applications. The central tenet is that by interacting with other people one can achieve more than by working alone. Below we review how this principle has been presented in recent theories of expertise and collective and collaborative workplace learning.

In their recent book *"Communities of networked expertise"* Hakkarainen and his colleagues (2004) coined the term 'innovative knowledge communities' to describe different forms of collaborative knowledge creation. As models of innovative knowledge communities they cite Engeström's (Engeström, 1987) theory of expansive learning, Bereiter's (Bereiter, 2002; Bereiter & Scardamalia, 1993) idea of knowledge building, and the model of knowledge creation by Nonaka and Takeuchi (1995). Common to these models is that they acknowledge and stress the significance of informal knowledge in the knowledge creation process and emphasise the collaborative nature of innovation.

In our study we apply in particular the notion of knowledge creation by Nonaka and his colleagues. We see a network of organisations and their people as a forum or space that can be harnessed for the purpose of innovative learning. As described in Chapter 2 of this volume, Nonaka and Konno (1998) have depicted this kind of space using the Japanese concept *ba*, a shared space for emerging relationships. *Ba* includes physical, virtual and mental spaces for the exchange, transformation and creation of knowledge. While a team can be a *ba* for the individuals who compose it, an inter-organisational network can be a *ba* for the constituent organisations and their members. Networks, in particular, may function as what Nonaka and Konno (1998) call *interacting ba*, a space for face-to-face relationships. In interactive relations people may share their experiences and in this way externalise their tacit knowledge. Through reciprocal interaction they acquire new ideas and receive feedback on their own mental models and activities. A network often also provides its members with a *cyber ba* where documented information can be saved, stored and searched for further use and in combination with other explicit knowledge.

## Characteristics of a Learning Network

Network learning is learning by a group of organisations as a group (Knight, 2002). In other words, network learning refers to processes through which the network itself – not only its individual participants – transforms its ways of thinking and acting. However, most of the previous research has focussed on the learning of individuals or organisations in networks. In our study, we examine network learning more on the organisational and network level, but we also look at how networked learning is related to individuals' learning, and how individuals' learning may contribute to the network level.

The characteristics of a learning network are the same as those of a learning organisation or an innovative knowledge community (see Chapter 2). First, *interaction* between the network's participants is essential. Learning in networks is possible only through interactive processes. In fact, without interaction the network is not a real network, that is, a forum for mutual exchange. Therefore research on learning networks focuses mainly on the different forms of interaction, communication and sense-making that take place in networks (Knight 2002). It has been suggested that organising network learning could best be served by an approach in which inter-company groups form a core mechanism of interchange (Vesalainen & Strömmer, 1999). Second, the participants of the network need to share *common objectives* for their interaction (Paavola, Lipponen, & Hakkarainen, 2004). They need to have a shared view or vision of the aim of the networked activity. It is important that the personal visions of individuals, company objectives and the goals of the network are consistent and aligned (Vesalainen & Strömmer, 1999). Third, it is important that the members of a network are aware of the knowledge and expertise that is distributed in the network (Hakkarainen et al., 2004). Fourth, in a network, *trust and a collaborative climate* (Sveiby & Simons, 2002) are as important as they are in an organisation. If there is no trust there is no willingness to share your knowledge or collaborate with others. Fifth, *progressive problem solving* (Bereiter & Scardamalia, 1993; described in more detail in Chapter 2) as a personal and organisational stance makes sure that the members of the network and the network as a whole can go beyond their existing knowledge and create new practices.

Previous studies suggest that a dedicated infrastructure is necessary to bring about learning in a network (Vesalainen & Strömmer, 1999). In other words, well-developed systems and operating models are needed for planning learning, initiating learning processes and evaluating progress. In our study, such an infrastructure was provided by the development project called "Skilled Central Finland", which was carried out by three large vocational education providers and their working life partners in the area of Central Finland. The work consists of several development projects (mainly funded by the European Social Funds, ESF) which aim to promote partnerships between vocational institutes and working life organisations in different ways. For example, a great amount of in-service training in connection with organising and supporting students' work-based learning has been arranged both for teachers and workplace trainers, and different specialised development projects were launched to enhance the quality of vocational education and cooperation between schools and workplaces.

## Purpose of the Study

The aim of this study was to investigate innovative network learning in the network Skilled Central Finland, formed by vocational institutions and their partners in working life. More specifically the following research questions were addressed:

1) Are the prerequisites for innovative knowledge communities present in the work communities of vocational schools and working life organisations in Central Finland?
2) What kinds of innovative changes have taken place as result of the network's activities?
3) How were processes of innovation started and how did they proceed?
4) How does individual learning transform into organisational learning in the innovation process?

## Methods

The above-mentioned network, Skilled Central Finland, consisted of three education providers from three areas of Central Finland. Data for the study were collected with Internet -questionnaires, traditional questionnaires and in-depth interviews from the following groups of actors: (1) teachers in the vocational schools, (2) workplace trainers and other workplace representatives, and (3) project managers responsible for organising cooperation between vocational schools and workplaces and other actors in the Skilled Central Finland – projects. The data are summarised in Table 7.1. Altogether 330 teachers (42% of all teachers) and 420 workplace trainers (52% of the random sample) answered the questionnaires. Furthermore, 30 people were interviewed on their opinions regarding the pivotal prerequisites of innovations.

The questionnaire data were analysed, first, with factor analysis to group the variables according to the pivotal prerequisites of innovations. Second, aggregated scales based on the results of the factor analysis were formed and both mean values and standard deviations were computed for each aggregated scale. These scales were utilised in analysing differences between education providers and areas within Central Finland (these differences are reported elsewhere, see Tynjälä, Nikkanen, Volanen, & Valkonen, 2005a). The interview data were analysed qualitatively, adopting principles developed in the spheres of the grounded theory (Strauss & Gorbin, 1990) and phenomenography (Marton, 1994). Accordingly, in the initial phase of the analysis, to identify preliminary themes and categories, differences and similarities were sought in the language used by the participants. After this the level of abstraction was raised and more general categories were formed. The data were coded in two phases: in the open coding, central themes were searched for, and in

Table 7.1 Data information from the project: "Skilled Central Finland"

| Subjects | N | Questionnaires | | Interviews |
|---|---|---|---|---|
| | | N (respondents) | % | n |
| Teachers | 796 | 330 | 42 | 5 |
| Workplace mentors | sample size 800 (out of 2,478) | 420 | 52 | 6 |
| Project managers and other actors | 19 | | | 19 |

the axial coding the relationships between categories and concepts were identified and a theoretical model was generated.

## Results

### Prerequisites for Innovations in the Network

The prerequisites for innovations in the network were measured by several items in the teachers' and workplace trainers' questionnaires. The sum scales, based on the factor analysis, were named *Open communication atmosphere* (Cronbach's alpha = 0.81 for the teachers' data and 0.72 for the workplace trainers' data) and *Progressive problem solving* (Cronbach's alpha = 0.83 for the teachers' data and 0.68 for the workplace trainers' data). Because the factor structures that emerged in the data provided by the teachers and that provided by the workplace trainers were somewhat different, the results are presented on the basis of individual variables and for the teachers and workplace trainers separately.

### Open Communication in the Work Communities of Schools and Workplaces

*The teachers'* answers to the questions relating to the factor *Open communication atmosphere* in their work community can be seen in Fig. 7.1. The great majority of the teachers reported that they agreed with the statements "The members of our work community discuss matters related to work a lot" (90%) and "The members of our work community share their knowledge and experiences openly for the use of

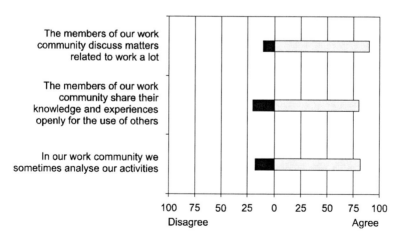

**Fig. 7.1** Teachers' answers to the questions related to an open communication atmosphere in their work community

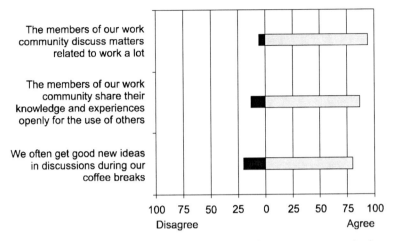

**Fig. 7.2** Workplace trainers' answers to the questions related to an open communication atmosphere in their work community

others" (80%). Also the answers to the third variable related to the aggregated scale under discussion, "In our work community we sometimes analyse our activities", showed broad unanimity (82%) among the teachers. Altogether, in the vocational schools of the region a rather open work culture and communication atmosphere for knowledge sharing seemed to prevail. Similarly, the workplace trainers' answers to the statements related to the factor *Open communication atmosphere* in their work community were also very positive (Fig. 7.2).

## Progressive Problem Solving in Work Communities of Schools and Workplaces

The variables intended to measure progressive problem solving grouped rather differently in the teachers' and workplace trainers' data. Altogether ten variables correlated with each other in the teachers' data (see Fig. 7.3), while in the workplace trainers' data only three variables loaded on the factor *Progressive problem solving* (see Fig. 7.4). Again, therefore, the results are presented for individual factors and separately for the teachers and workplace trainers.

The mean of the aggregated scale measuring *Progressive problem solving* in *the teachers'* work communities was 3.1 (max = 4). This shows that a strong positive attitude towards development prevailed among the teachers in the vocational education institutions. Most of the teachers subscribed to the idea of lifelong learning as an important principle of their work, felt it necessary to search continuously for new information, liked to develop new solutions to problems related to their work and also liked to meet new challenges in their work. The teachers (86%) also reported that their knowledge and competence are important to their educational institute. It is noteworthy that rather many of the teachers (32%) did not belong to any of the active groups in their workplace and that 41% relatively seldom worked with

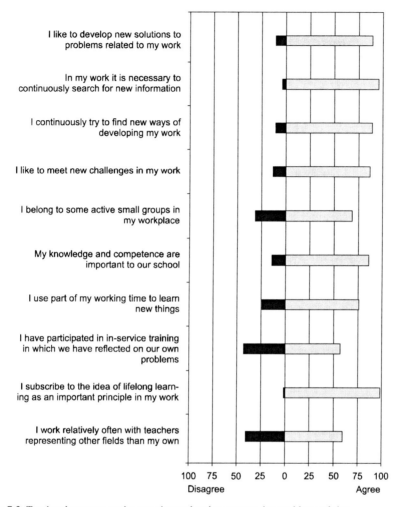

**Fig. 7.3** Teachers' answers to the questions related to progressive problem solving

colleagues from fields other than their own. Also, many teachers (43%) did not participate in in-service training where they would have the opportunity to reflect on their work-related problems and challenges.

*The workplace trainers* also quite unanimously agreed that they liked to develop new solutions to their work-related problems, to meet new challenges in their work and also continuously try to find new ways of developing their work (Fig. 7.4).

## Comparison Between Schools and Workplaces

The findings presented above show that both in the school environments and in the working life organisations the conditions for innovative knowledge communities

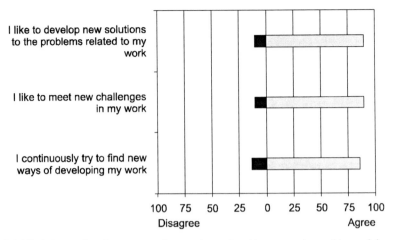

**Fig. 7.4** Workplace trainers' answers to the questions related to progressive problem solving

were propitious. Both the teachers and workplace trainers largely agreed with the statements describing the prerequisites for innovativeness. However, despite the fact that teachers and workplace trainers seemed to evaluate the conditions in their workplaces in a similar way, there were some statistically significant differences between these two sets of data.

Figure 7.5 shows the variables in which significant differences were observed. It can be seen that in several variables related to the features of innovative knowledge communities the workplace trainers gave higher ratings than the teachers of their respective work communities. These variables included: connecting work-based learning with school teaching, being given encouragement to present new ideas, decision making in teams, increased collaboration, an increase in the number of new contacts with vocational institutes, systematic planning of learning from each other, documenting and saving best practices, utilisation of people's different knowledge and skills, and utilisation of the fresh views of newcomers.

Although the mean scores of the workplace trainers were higher they were relatively high in the schools as well. Thus, the conditions for innovative knowledge communities were good in both the working life organisations and schools.

## Changes Produced by Networked Activities

On the basis of the interview data various transformations in practices, modes of actions and relationships between organisations and individuals as results of increasing networking between schools and workplaces were identified. The changes observed are summarised in Table 7.2.

The first change that was clearly visible in the ways vocational schools operate concerned competition between schools. Although competition for good students and learning results is a reality between schools working in the same district, there

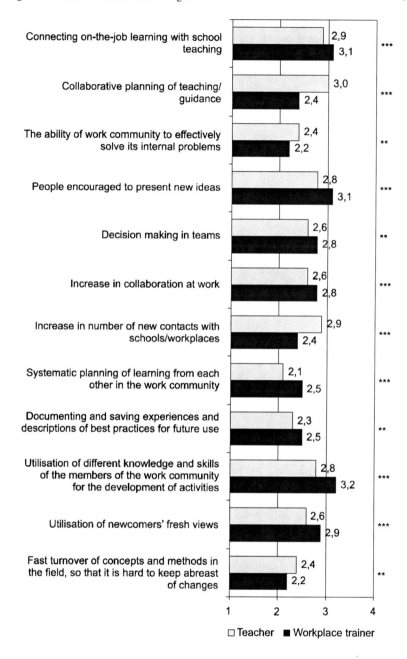

**Fig. 7.5** Differences between the views of teachers and workplace trainers in relation to the themes of networking

**Table 7.2** Changes brought about by networked activities

| Change processes | Examples of activities |
|---|---|
| From competitive networks to cooperative networks | – Starting of regional curriculum work<br>– Cooperative committees in different fields (consisting of representatives of working life and schools)<br>– Teachers' regional meetings in certain fields |
| Increase in regional cooperation and interaction | – Project Skilful Central Finland as a whole<br>– Regional meetings in different fields of study |
| Increase of interaction and cooperation between different fields of study | – Courses for workplace trainers<br>– Guidebook material for workplace trainers<br>– Standard contractual forms and directives for workplace learning<br>– Entrepreneurship training for all students in all fields<br>– Criteria for quality assurance for the workplace as a learning environment<br>– Multidisciplinary qualifications |
| Increase in projects carried out in collaboration with vocational institutes and working life organisations | – Catering: client contracts<br>– Metal work: "Learning Site" project (joint investments in machinery between schools and workplaces)<br>– Wood, paper and chemistry: adult education qualifications for employed staff<br>– Social and health care: "Team school" for entrepreneurship; "Mobile health care services" |
| Creating relationships and increasing cooperation with polytechnics, universities, comprehensive schools and informal education providers | – Regional strategic cooperation for enhancing competitiveness of economic life<br>– Cooperation related to anticipating the need for labour and skills requirements<br>– Collaboration related to recruitment fairs<br>– Common physical environments (e.g. school buildings) in some fields<br>– Cooperation related to entrepreneurship education<br>– Cooperation related to the use of e-learning |
| Changes in work-based learning (compared to former practice periods): from the traditional model towards the work process model and the connective model (for these models see Guile & Griffiths, 2001) | – More systematically organised work-based learning, improvements in guidance, extensive network of workplace trainers, tripartite assessment, etc. |
| Change in teachers' work cultures | – Teachers' work-based learning, collaboration with workplaces; increase in collaboration with different bodies |

were several signs indicating that a *transformation from competitive networks towards cooperative networks was going on*. For example, some schools working in the same field had started producing regional curricula. This way they planned to ensure the same level in the quality of teaching and learning in all schools – irrespective of whether the institute is located in the biggest city in the region or in a more peripheral area. In several fields, the schools had also established joint committees consisting of representatives from working life and schools in the region. Furthermore, in some fields teachers had started to organise meetings not only of teachers at their own school but also regional meetings where teachers from different schools could meet each other and plan common projects between their schools.

Related to the trend towards a shift from competitive networks to cooperative networks was an observed *increase in regional cooperation and interaction* in general. The aim of the development work Skilled Central Finland was to increase cooperation in the region, and the observations made in this study confirmed that this aim was being achieved. At the operational level it was realised in the many regional meetings that took place between teachers, developers, administrative staff and representatives from working life.

Third, a notable *increase in interaction and cooperation between different fields of study* was observed. In fact, school cultures in different vocational fields had hitherto tend to be very separate and interaction between fields rare. Now it was clear that schools had started to see that they can learn from each other and not only from those in the same field but also from those in different fields. For example, the schools had started to organise courses for workplace trainers where people from different fields could meet each other and share their good practices. These practices were also described in the guides produced for workplace trainers. Furthermore, schools had developed common contractual forms and directives for organising workplace learning. This was highly valued by the workplaces involved because the diverse forms and practices used by different schools had been found confusing. One major joint enterprise was the launching of entrepreneurship training for all students in all fields. Another joint venture that was under way at the time the research data were collected was the development of criteria for quality assurance for workplaces as a learning environment. In addition to these functional forms of cooperation between vocational fields there was an interesting initiative for the development of new vocational qualifications combining different disciplines such as catering and leisure time activities or agriculture and mechanics.

The fourth change that was observed in the practices of the vocational schools was *increased cooperation between schools and workplaces*. This is hardly a surprise, given that a central aim of the Skilled Central Finland project was to promote school–workplace interaction. The increased interaction took different forms in different fields of study. For example, in catering, supply contracts with clients increased and provided students with an authentic context for learning. In the field of metal work, the schools and the metal factories had made joint investments in machinery. In this way the schools and the workplaces cooperated to build 'Learning Sites' for students and teachers as well as for regular employees. Furthermore, in wood, paper, and chemistry field adult education qualifications were developed for existing employed staff, while the social and health care field organised a 'Team School' to promote entrepreneurship and 'Mobile Health Care Services' to provide new kinds of services and opportunities for work-based learning. All these practices and modes of action were new and can thus be seen as social innovations. They served not only the schools themselves but also workplaces and often the wider community.

The fifth change was that the *vocational schools had expanded their relationship not only towards working life but also towards other educational institutions* such as polytechnics, universities and comprehensive schools. They had adopted an active role in strategic cooperation for enhancing economic growth and competitiveness in the region. This cooperation included, for example, anticipating the need for labour and skill requirements, promoting entrepreneurship education, organising recruitment fairs, use of e-learning and use of common physical environments such as school buildings.

The sixth transformation in vocational education was related to *organising workplace learning*, and this was a direct consequence of the new legislation pertaining to vocational education described at the beginning of the chapter. The prescribed changes in work-based learning are not regional only but also national. In accordance with the new directives work learning periods have been transformed from traditional types of work practice towards a model which Guile and Griffiths (2001) have called the connective model of work experience. In this model schools and workplaces together create learning environments where informal and formal learning are integrated. In practice, this can be observed, for example, in systematically organised learning, explicit goals, improvements in supervision and guidance, education for workplace trainers and tripartite assessment of learning (Tynjälä et al., 2005a; Tynjälä, Virtanen, & Valkonen, 2005b; Virtanen & Tynjälä, 2008).

Last, but not least, the seventh change observed in this study was a *radical change in teachers' work cultures*. Whereas, traditionally, Finnish VET has been strongly school-based, the new legislation making workplace learning a compulsory part of education has challenged teachers to expand their expertise. Coaching students for workplace learning, educating workplace trainers and guiding learning processes in collaboration with them, developing tripartite assessment and planning development projects together with representatives from working life have all required increasing cooperation with different partners. Thus, the working culture of teachers has changed from an individual towards a collaborative culture (for more details on teacher cultures see Hargreaves, 1994). Collaborative work has increased both between the teachers and between the schools and workplaces. Effecting change in working cultures, however, is a slow process, and there were differences between educational fields in how the change process was implemented. For example, collaboration between schools and workplaces was most commonly observed in the fields of social and health care, and catering and tourism, where almost 40% of teachers reported being in contact with workplace trainers at least on a weekly basis, while in some other fields the corresponding figure was under 20%.

## Model of Innovations and Transformation of Individual Learning into Organisational learning

On the basis of the analysis of the interview and questionnaire data, a model describing innovations in the networks of vocational schools and workplaces was constructed (Fig. 7.6). The model shows how innovations originate and how the

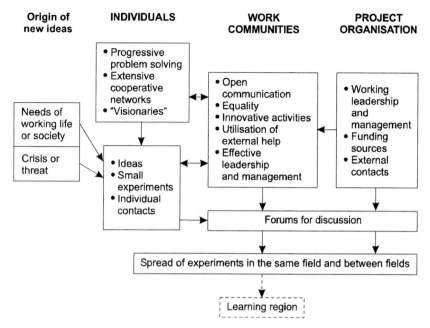

**Fig. 7.6** The origin and processes of innovations in the networks of vocational institutes and workplaces

development of ideas into working innovations proceeds in these networks. The innovations produced in the school–workplace networks can be depicted as social and functional innovations rather than concrete products. Thus, they represent new modes of action, new practices and new collaborative relationships. Examples of these kinds of innovations, as mentioned above, include joint investments between schools and workplaces, new ways of organising entrepreneurship education, new forms of adult education in the workplace and new forms of guiding students in work-based learning.

It can be seen in Fig. 7.6 that new ideas usually emerge in response to a perceived need in working life or in society or as a consequence of a visible threat or crisis. For example, the idea of joint investment between the metal industry and vocational schools was initiated in a situation where the metal industry was suffering from a lack of skilled labour and vocational schools had financial difficulties in keeping abreast of the times in terms of providing modern machinery for educational purposes. By joining forces educational institutes and workplaces were able to provide learning sites with modern machinery both for employees and for students and teachers (who also had an opportunity to update their knowledge and skills).

Figure 7.6 depicts the process of learning and innovation at three levels of actors, those of individuals, work communities and the larger project organisation which was set up precisely for the purpose of supporting innovative activities. Producing new ideas requires individuals who can be described as visionaries. Characteristic of these people is that they work in a way that Bereiter & Scardamalia (1993) have called progressive problem solving. In their work they continually set new challenges and new problems that are more complex than the problems they have already solved. When one problem is solved these people do not get into a rut but, instead, they are already setting themselves a new challenge. In this way they transcend the limits of their competence. According to Bereiter and Scardamalia, this kind of progressive problem solving is the very essence of expertise. It is also typical of such experts that they do not keep aloof from other people but rather share their knowledge and ideas with colleagues and create extensive personal networks.

Although it is individuals who get the ideas in the first place, start small experiments and share them with their personal contacts, it is their larger work communities which create the propitious circumstances for further developing the ideas and for disseminating them. For sharing ideas, it is important that there is an open communication atmosphere in the workplace, that people feel they are equal and that innovative activities are encouraged (for more see e.g. Nikkanen, 2001). Furthermore, it is important that the workplace is open to ideas coming from outside the organisation and is willing to utilise external help in developing its work. All this is promoted by effective leadership and management. Such a workplace creates the prerequisites for innovative knowledge communities (Hakkarainen et al., 2004) described earlier.

In addition to innovative individuals and work communities a further necessary condition that emerged from this study for developing ideas and disseminating good practices was the setting up of a development project organisation to systematically manage the development work in vocational schools and take care of acquiring funding for individual projects and ventures. Furthermore, the project organisation in the present case developed contacts with the local polytechnics, university and research institutes involved in creating a learning region in Central Finland. Work communities, together with their networks and project organisation arranged many forums for discussion and collaboration. Through these forums small individual experiments were presented and shared, and in this way it was ensured that new practices were disseminated not only to the schools and workplaces in the same field but also across fields. In sum, we can conclude that individual learning through progressive problem solving can be transformed into collective, organisational or networked learning in circumstances where leaders and the work community intentionally promote knowledge sharing, an open communication atmosphere and the formation of networks.

## Discussion

The results of the study indicate that the conditions for developing innovative practices for school–workplace cooperation were promising in both vocational schools and workplaces. Work communities in both contexts were characterised by open discussion, sharing of knowledge and progressive problem solving. However, in many respects the workplaces exhibited the features of *ba* or innovative knowledge communities more strongly than did the vocational schools. For example, encouragement in presenting new ideas, decision making as a team, increase in collaboration and systematic support for learning from each other, utilisation of different competences and documenting best practices were rated higher by workplace trainers than by teachers. The finding is consistent with a previous research result that knowledge creation and utilisation is slower in the field of education than in some other fields such as engineering or medicine (see OECD, 2000). The finding also supports the observation of some of our interviewees who stated that "schools lag behind workplaces in innovative practices and they are slower to change" and that "There are always individual teachers who do not follow the principles that have been agreed upon, and no penalties follow. This is not possible in workplaces other than schools." Given that in Central Finland a lot of work has been done to support innovation in the networks between schools and workplaces it can be assumed that in regions with no such great input the conditions for innovation may be weaker. Therefore it would be important to pay attention to promoting innovative work cultures in VET.

Our model of the origin and spread of innovation suggest that, at least in the context of vocational education, a separate project organisation is necessary for producing and disseminating new practices. The challenge for vocational institutes in Central Finland is how to maintain the infrastructure for innovative working if or when the externally funded project organisation is ended. How can it be ensured that the development of work practices is done as a part of normal work and not experienced as an extra burden? Perhaps in this respect there is a lesson to be learned from working-life organisations.

Our main research question was how individual learning transforms into organisational and networked learning. Our findings indicate that this requires that work communities seek to be innovative, encourage knowledge-sharing, aim at an open and equal communication climate, and provide forums for discussion and the exchange of ideas. In other words, in communities of this kind there are *ba*-spaces for learning as formulated by Nonaka and Konno (1998). Strong, visionary leadership and a special project organisation seemed also to be necessary conditions for disseminating and establishing new practices across the network.

# References

Argyris, C., & Schön, D. A. (1978). *Organizational learning: A theory of action perspective*. Reading, MA: Addison-Wesley.

Bereiter, C. (2002). *Education and mind in the knowledge age*. Mahwah, NJ: Erlbaum.

Bereiter, C., & Scardamalia, M. (1993). *Surpassing ourselves: An inquiry into the nature of expertise*. Chicago, IL: Open Court.

Burgoyne, J. (1995). Creating a learning organisation. In J. Enkenberg, M. Gustafsson, & M. Kuittinen (Eds.), *Learning organization – from theory to practice* (pp. 13–23). University of Joensuu. Research and Development Center for Information Technology in Education. Joensuu: Gummerus.

Camagni R. (1991). *Innovation networks. Spatial perspectives*. London: Belhaven Press.

Coopey, J. (1996). Crucial gaps in the learning organisation: Power, politics, and ideology. In K. Starkey (Ed.), *How organisations learn* (pp. 348–367). London: International Thomson Business Press.

Dixon, N. (1994). *The organizational learning cycle. How we can learn collectively. Developing Organizations Series.* London: McGraw-Hill Book Company.

Engeström, Y. (1987). *Learning by expanding.* Helsinki: Orienta-Konsultit Oy.

Engeström, Y. (2004). The new generation of expertise. Seven theses. In H. Rainbird, A. Fuller, & A. Munro (Eds.), *Workplace learning in context* (pp. 145–165). London: Routledge.

Engeström, Y., Engeström, R., & Kärkkäinen, R. (1995). Polycontextuality and boundary crossing in expert cognition: Learning and problem solving in complex work activities. *Learning and Instruction, 5,* 319–336.

Engeström, Y., Engeström, R., & Vähäaho, T. (1999). When the center does not hold: The importance of knotworking. In S. Chaiklin, M. Hedegaard, & U. Jensen (Eds.), *Activity theory and social practice: Cultural-historical approaches* (pp. 345–374). Aarhus: Aarhus University Press.

Garvin, D. (1993). Building a learning organisation. *Harvard Business Review, 71*(4), 76–91.

Guile, D., & Griffiths, T. (2001). Learning through work experience. *Journal of Education and Work, 14,* 113–131.

Hakkarainen, K., Palonen, T., Paavola, S., & Lehtinen, E. (2004). *Communities of networked expertise: Professional and educational perspectives.* Amsterdam: Elsevier.

Hargreaves, A. (1994). *Changing teachers, changing times. Teachers' work and culture in the postmodern age.* New York: Teachers College Press.

Holmqvist, M. (2005, December). *Collective learning in innovative networks.* Paper presented at the Researching Work and Learning Conference RWL05, Sydney, Australia.

Hytönen, T., & Tynjälä, P. (2005, December). *A learning network promoting knowledge management.* Paper presented at the Researching Work and Learning Conference RWL05, Sydney, Australia.

Kekäle, T., & Viitala, R. (2003). Do networks learn? *Journal of Workplace Learning, 15*(6), 245–247.

Knight, L. (2002). Network learning: Exploring learning by interorganizational networks. *Human Relations, 55,* 427–454.

Marton, F. (1994). Phenomenography. In T. H. T. N. Postlethwaite (Ed.), *The international encyclopaedia of education* (2 ed., Vol. 8, pp. 4424–4429). Oxford: Pergamon.

Miles, R. E., Miles, G., & Snow, C. C. (2005). *Collaborative entrepreneurship. How communities of networked firms use continuous innovation to create economic wealth.* Stanford, CA: Stanford Business Books.

Nelson, R. E. (1993). *National innovation systems: A comparative analysis.* Oxford: Oxford University Press.

Nicolini, D., & Meznar, M. (1995). The social construction of organizational learning: Conceptual and practical issues in the field. *Human Relations, 48*(7), 727–746.

Nikkanen, P. (2001). Effectiveness and improvement in a learning organization. In E. Kimonen (Ed.), *Curriculum approaches* (pp. 55–76). Jyväskylä: University of Jyväskylä, Department of Education & Institute for Educational Research.

Nonaka, I., & Konno, N. (1998). The concept of "ba": Building a foundation for knowledge creation. *California Management Review, 40,* 40–54.

Nonaka, I., & Takeuchi, H. (1995). *The knowledge-creating company. How Japanese companies create the dynamics of innovation.* New York: Oxford University Press.

OECD. (2000). *Knowledge management in the learning society. Education and skills.* Paris: OECD.

Paavola, S., Lipponen, L., & Hakkarainen, K. (2004). Models of innovative knowledge communities and three metaphors of learning. *Review of Educational Research, 74,* 557–576.

Palonen, T. (2003). *Shared knowledge and the web of relations* (Annales Universitatis Turkuensis 266). Turku: University of Turku.

Pedler, M., Burgoyne, J., & Boydell, T. (1991). *The learning company. A strategy for sustainable development*. Berkshire: McGraw-Hill.

Senge, P. (1990). *The fifth discipline. The art and practice of the learning organisation*. New York: Doubleday/Currency.

Strauss, A., & Gorbin, J. (1990). *Basics of qualitative research: Techniques and procedures for developing grounded theory*. Thousand Oaks, CA: Sage.

Sveiby, K.-S., & Simons, R. (2002). Collaborative climate and effectiveness of knowledge work – An empirical study. *Journal of Knowledge Management, 6*, 420–433.

Tynjälä, P., Nikkanen, P., Volanen, M. V., & Valkonen, S. (2005a). *Työelämäyhteistyö ammatillisessa koulutuksessa ja työyhteisöjen oppiminen. Taitava Keski-Suomi –tutkimus osa II* [Networked learning and working life cooperation in vocational education and training. "Skilled Central Finland" research report. Part II]. Jyväskylä: University of Jyväskylä, Institute for Educational Research.

Tynjälä, P., Virtanen, A., & Valkonen, S. (2005b). *Työssäoppiminen Keski-Suomessa. Taitava Keski-Suomi -tutkimus osa I* [Students' workplace learning in Central Finland. "Skilled Central Finland" research report. Part I]. Jyväskylä: University of Jyväskylä. Institute for Educational Research.

Van Laere, K., & Heene, A. (2003). Social networks as a source of competitive advantage for the firm. *Journal of Workplace Learning, 15*(6), 248–258).

Vesalainen, J., & Strömmer, R. (1999). From individual learning to network learning – networks as learners and as forums for learning. In T. Alasoini & P. Halme (Eds.), *Learning organizations, learning society. National workplace development programme yearbook 1999* (pp. 117–139). Helsinki: Ministry of Labour.

Virtanen, A., & Tynjälä, P. (2008). Students' experiences of workplace learning in Finnish VET. *European Journal of Vocational Training*, 2008/2(44), 199–213.

Vygotsky, L. S. (1978). *Mind in society*. Cambridge, MA: Harvard University Press.

# Chapter 8
# Evaluation Approaches for Workplace Learning Partnerships in VET: Investigating the Learning Dimension

Ludger Deitmer and Lars Heinemann

## Introduction

In this chapter, we analyse the role evaluation methods have typically played so far in the field of VET and argue that the adaptation of newer evaluation approaches helps to clarify the learning dimension within VET partnerships between industry and public VET schools. Ideally, these partnerships should trigger processes of mutual learning and allow an improved understanding between the different partners from industry and the VET schools. We will show that by using specific evaluation instruments, the collaboration between work and school partners can be improved in order to achieve substantial collaboration that goes beyond the mere co-existence of enterprises and schools.

First, we briefly describe the arrangements that underlie the German dual VET system, the difficulties inherent in establishing more vigorous cooperation, and how these are being addressed. In Germany, a reform was introduced in 1996 to centre learning in VET schools around *Lernfelder* (learning areas or learning arenas) that follow work processes, replacing the old idea of school subjects. New curricula were constructed to strengthen this kind of learning and foster co-operation on the local level between schools and companies. Nevertheless, the existing collaboration is often rather weak. One aim is to develop this collaboration into workplace learning partnerships (WLPs). These WLPs would then form the backbone of curricula in which learning at school and workplace is better integrated.

In this context, we discuss secondly, the role evaluation might play to sustain these partnerships. Network evaluation can become a new focus for improving the functioning and management of such co-operative activities. Typically, evaluation has been used to ensure the quality of the *products* of this kind of co-operation. But the way co-operation works needs to be investigated as well, particularly in terms of the degree of integrating theoretical and workplace-based knowledge. We will argue that new approaches are needed regarding the evaluation of these VET partnerships,

L. Deitmer (✉)
ITB: Institut Technik und Bildung; Institute of Technology and Education,
University of Bremen, Bremen, Germany
e-mail: deitmer@uni-bremen.de

M.-L. Stenström, P. Tynjälä (eds.), *Towards Integration of Work and Learning,*
© Springer Science+Business Media B.V. 2009

more specifically to determine to what extent they improve the collaborative dimension of learning. As these networks typically cross organisational boundaries and comprise many different actors, they cannot be evaluated using tools which centre on single learner/teacher frameworks.

Thirdly, in the later parts of this chapter, we present examples of new evaluation tools (EE tool and SEVALAG) that may be up to the task of getting insight into this kind of multi-actor structures. Finally, we look both at the benefits that might be obtained from these evaluation methods and the problems they face.

## Collaboration in the German Dual System: Where Is the Problem?

Together with some other Western European countries, such as Switzerland and Austria, Germany shares a long-standing tradition of apprenticeship training in a 'dual' arrangement. Dual arrangements are based on two structural elements:

- Working and learning in different workplaces and work departments in a qualified training company[1] according to collectively agreed training frameworks; and
- Systematic, technical subject-based learning at a local vocational school in a classroom situation.

Dual arrangements mean, first of all, both a public (publicly offered vocational education) and private (private in-company training) learning and working apprenticeship contract (Deissinger, 1996; Greinert, 1994). Unlike other VET systems in Europe, which are either purely state-based, like in France, or more company-based, such as the modularised training given in England (Ryan, 2001), this system forces both company and school actors to communicate and to co-operate. Organising vocational and training education in this way requires good co-ordination of workplace learning and work activities with learning at the school. This collaboration should integrate practical and theoretical learning to provide the apprentice with good professional skills.

How this collaboration between school and industry can be fostered has been a matter of debate for a long time (Sloane, 2004). The main criticism is that there is only coexistence but no co-ordination of the school-based and enterprise-based learning programmes. What is missing is active communication between trainers and teachers; without it, the development of tight integration between the practical and theoretical elements of the apprentices' learning activities will not be possible. Learning at school is not seen as being well integrated into what and how the apprentice learns at the workplace. Good practice here would mean that the learning processes undergone at school should deepen the practical learning experienced at the workplace in the industrial, service or craft company. Systematic and

---

[1] Companies have to meet certain standards to be officially recognised as a training company taking apprentices.

theory-based knowledge should enable a better understanding of the practical dimension of learning at the workplace. Improving the VET curricula was seen as a
first priority to achieve better interaction between the two partners, the enterprise
and the school.

## Learning Arenas and Learning Partnerships

This situation led to a policy debate in Germany with the outcome that the responsible state bodies (here the *Länder* Ministries for Education) wanted to improve the
collaborative dimension by changing the curriculum concept and introducing work-
based learning as a key element for both schools and enterprises. The vocational
disciplines of the occupation being trained (e.g. for the occupation 'salesperson'
(*Kaufmann*), there are business administration, book-keeping, law and correspon-
dence) are based on work and learning tasks which depart from the learning situations traditionally found in workplaces in industry or commerce. The new curricular
model should give the apprentice a more coherent and holistic understanding of
what he can learn at work and how learning at school can complement this. The
apprentice should be able to get a deeper theoretical and practical insight into his or
her occupational field.

This change in learning and teaching obviously requires the establishment of
closer interaction between workplace experiences and systematic, theory-based
learning at school. Such a reform is complex and has many implications not only for
curricula but also on other levels like the organisation of schools. What is learned
in the classroom should be in closer contact with what is learned in practice, or in
other words, learning in the classroom should enable the apprentice to better understand the relationship with the work tasks and business processes of his placement
company. Learning for and by problem solving instead of just following text books
is part of this approach (Conference of the Educational Ministries, 1999).

Not just co-existence, then, but active collaboration between schools and companies is needed. To be equipped for this, schools have to move from being traditional
vocational education schools into regional centres for initial and continuous work-
based learning. More autonomy for the regional training and development centres
which foster regional learning in networks (network learning approach) is one answer to this (Attwell & Deitmer, 2000; Deitmer, Drewing, & Heermeyer, 2000).

The intention of this reform is to strengthen the interaction between school-based
and workplace learning in such a way that the capabilities of apprentices increase
and they are better able to perform in their occupational domain. Vocational school
teachers and workplace instructors will be more directly involved in the curricula
design such as to develop a logical progression from the learning to the occupational domain in a circular process (Deitmer et al., 2003; Fischer & Bauer, 2007;
Sloane, 2004). Curricula of this kind not only have effects on the re-design of
curricular frameworks but also affect the professional development of trainers and
teachers, as the teaching and training staffs have to understand how to handle this

new method of learning and teaching. Learning situations have to be identified and developed out of the work process, i.e. one has to identify what the potential work tasks offer for learning and how these tasks can be arranged into a curriculum. The most crucial questions are:

- How can trainers and teachers collaboratively develop learning tasks out of typical work tasks?
- What kind of capabilities do teachers and trainers need to develop teaching and learning arrangements on the basis of the concept of domains of learning?
- What should be taught in the school and what should be taught in the company?
- How can these be co-ordinated in practice at the two learning sites?
- How does learning at school interact with the practical learning at the apprentice's workplace?
- How can the apprentice integrate the different learning content
- How can these processes be evaluated so that they support the co-operation between these two groups of people: teachers from the college and trainers from the enterprise?

A major challenge for the success of this reform is the creation of active, trans-institutional teams of teachers and trainers. These teams have to organise the flow of knowledge and the oscillation between theory and practice. Therefore, the reform implies not just a new pedagogical process but also an institutional and personal transformation (Deitmer & Gerds, 2002).

## Evaluation and Learning – Methods, Options, Organisations

Over the last few years, when we were carrying out various formative evaluations on networks and projects, we noticed the high potential for individual and collective learning offered, in particular, by self-evaluation methods. This led us to shift the focus of evaluation: to directly apply methods of formative evaluation to the restructuring processes of vocational schools and the development of deeper co-operation between schools and companies.

To look at evaluation from the learning point of view seems somewhat trivial at first glance – evaluation aims at analysing the strengths and weaknesses of a project or organisation and at opening up perspectives for improvements. Even a purely summative evaluation that consists in a benchmarking exercise shows the potential for change and thus aims at learning by the actors and stakeholders involved. So, we do *not* claim that certain methods of evaluation (e.g. formative ones, operating with qualitative data) will produce better learning outcomes per se. This depends heavily on what is called for by whoever is commissioning an evaluation. Moreover, there may be many unintended learning effects for the actors, including some which the commissioners of the evaluation (e.g. a control body) never had in mind. Patton's (1997) uses the term 'process value' to describe these effects – the actors' perception that by participating in evaluation, they learn to look at their own project or organisation from an evaluator's point of view and this way find out things about it that previously were (if that) tacit knowledge.

As interesting as it would be to analyse the learning potential of different evaluation methods, such a task is beyond the scope of this article. For the purpose of using evaluation to trigger learning processes, we shall instead focus on a small segment of the broad spectrum of different evaluation models and approaches, and assess their value for stimulating and supporting learning processes of the actors involved in the evaluation process (for a good overview of the different approaches, see Fahrenkrog, Polt, Rojo, Türke, & Zinöcker, 2002).

Here, we focus on evaluation approaches that – in the tradition of action research – directly aim at the processes and interactions in a project or organisation and do not concentrate on the evaluation of outcomes. Our aim here is to analyse what aspects enable and constrain learning processes, if these learning processes are an explicit evaluation aim. Obviously, for this purpose, we have to analyse two different dimensions. First, there is the evaluation method itself. It may or may not help to bring crucial actions and processes to the minds of the actors. Here, categories that are helpful in judging if an evaluation fulfils this aim are the standard ones (see DeGEval [the German evaluation society] 2002) of validity, clarity, reliability, etc.

Next, there is the context of the learning processes in question: the project, partnership or organisation itself and the actors involved. Here, a wide array of different aspects comes to mind that enable or constrain learning processes themselves or – perhaps even more importantly – foster or hinder these learning processes leading to structural change: the resources of actors and organisations as a whole to thoroughly deal with the evaluation results, time constraints, motivation and so on.

Finally, it is worth mentioning that the two dimensions evaluation method and evaluated organisation are obviously interlinked. If we look at the learning processes in a project or organisation, the 'validity' of an evaluation, for example, does not consist only in just judging performance on predefined categories. One has to ensure that the categories (and values) of the evaluation genuinely reflect the most important aspects. This can only be done by an iterative process long known to action researchers, but often not to evaluators. Here, all the problems of the involvement of the researcher, the dialectics of closeness and distance, are reflected, perhaps not in the role of the evaluator himself, but at least in the methodological approach (see e.g. Heinemann, 2005).

## Adapting Evaluation Approaches to Support the Development of More Interactive and Vital Co-operation Between Teachers and Trainers

In the German VET context, we are confronted with trainers and teachers who are expected to co-operate and to develop an integrated curriculum. This is not a trivial task, as these learning partnerships between industry and school join partners from different institutions which follow different understandings and orientations. Teachers may be orientated towards school-based knowledge and a more systematic approach to learning than their partners from industry. The latter orientate their work to the solving of practical problems and their apprentices' work tasks. The more complex the partnership, the larger the network and diversity of interests of the actors, the more easily such difficulties arise. They would like to co-operate better in their learning partnership but they lack experiences and conceptual knowledge. Formative evaluation may help them to improve their co-operation (Deitmer et al., 2003, p. 111; Manske, Moon, Ruth, & Deitmer, 2002; Smits & Kuhlmann, 2003).

Innovative partnerships between school and industrial actors therefore require tools that will assist them in improving their co-operation. The diversity of the conceptualisations and experiences of all the main actors during the process have to be elucidated and brought forward in the course of reflexive interactions. What is a method which enables the partners to self-evaluate called for their common goals, their perceptions, the partnership structure and the communication and learning processes. This type of discursive and participative evaluation can help the actors to gradually develop a clearer view of the objectives and status of their project.

At this point, we would like to give an account of the development of two self-evaluation tools that aim at analysing learning processes – the empowerment evaluation tool, that was developed in the Covoseco project[2], and the tool Sevalag, developed for the specifically German context of co-operation between schools and enterprises in the dual system. The EE tool (Empowerment Evaluation) contributes both to the evaluation and improvement of learning partnerships. The tool grew from experiences while undertaking assessments in regional and national R&D programmes (Deitmer, 2004; Deitmer et al., 2004; Manske et al., 2002). The aim of this type of evaluation is to assist the actors to access their individual and collective perceptions of co-operation, in order to find out what is working or not working well. In other words, the evaluation method tries to look into the 'black box' of the innovation process itself and the learning taking place.

## The Design of the EE Tool

The most important element of the EE tool is a criteria-based questionnaire. The criteria were selected on the basis of existing innovation research (Deitmer et al., 2003, pp. 137–170) and deal with the following five topics: goals, resources, project management, partnership development and communication/learning. These criteria are briefly expanded on below.

---

[2] The Covoseco project looked at formative evaluation tools to assist private public partnerships (PPPs). The approach was tested in 15 PPP projects in five countries (Germany, France, Sweden, Slovenia and the UK). For more details see: www.itb.uni-bremen.de/projekte/covoseco.

## Goals (1)

The goals of a network may not be completely defined at the beginning stage of the partnership, but a good mutual understanding of and agreement on goals is crucial for the success of the co-operation. The 'goals' criterion looks at the goals of the network both as a whole and at the level of individual partners.

## Resources (2)

This criterion looks at the different types of resources that are available to a partnership between schools and enterprises. It examines whether the financial and physical resources as well as the level of professional resources are sufficient.

## Project Management (3)

This criterion examines the process of managing the partnership and is broken down into three sub-criteria: clear allocation of tasks, fair distribution of work and clear rules and procedures.

## Partnership Development (4)

This criterion groups the following three sub-criteria: the development of trust; the social competences of partners; and their organisational or decision making competences. Trust is a precondition for co-operation. Social competences such as the ability to function as part of a team are also important. Persons involved in a partnership should have sufficient standing within their organisations, e.g. school or company, so that decisions made by the learning partnership can have the maximum level of impact within their organisations.

## Communication and Learning (5)

This criterion brings together the following sub criteria: effectiveness of internal and external communications; encouragement of learning; and improvement in innovation competences. Good internal communication is of crucial importance to overcome barriers and ward off uncertainties. As innovation processes are learning processes, actors in a learning partnership must be willing to share their knowledge and learn from each other.

## Overview of the Self-Evaluation Process

The moderator team formed before the evaluation starts should display a degree of independence from the specific interests of the different partners. During the first half-day workshop, the network partners weigh and score the criteria outlined above.

The evaluation approach is based on an individual and collective self-assessment by the actors – here, either teachers or trainers or both together. On the basis of criteria assessment, the actors expand the reasons for lower or higher scores in the discussions.

All learning partnership partners are encouraged to look at the current state of their learning partnership and to identify what is strong in the partnership and what is not. In other words, the evaluation tries to look into the 'black box of innovation' in a development partnership, its focus being the innovation process itself (Deitmer et al., 2003, p. 161).

After the workshop, the results are analysed. This can be done by the external moderator to ensure that a comprehensive summary of the discussion process is made and the results of the evaluation workshop are clear to everybody. These results are documented by a 'list of strengths and weaknesses', by a 'spider web', and other graphical explanations (bar and line charts). In a concluding feedback meeting, the "list of strengths and weaknesses" and the graphical explanations are discussed. The overall goal is to reflect on the results and to determine the prospects for the learning partnership.

The EE tool integrates two different value perspectives:

- *Internal evaluation of the learning partnership in order to improve co-operation.* The aim is to support co-operative learning under teachers and trainers within the partnership by identifying strengths/weaknesses in respect to aspects like goals, resources, project management, partnership development and communication & learning.
- *External evaluation.* By means of the summary, made by the external moderator, of what was said at the self-evaluation, the results of the internal evaluation session are validated from an external perspective. In some cases, this could also allow comparisons of the project with other partnerships which are engaged in a similar process.

## Case Example: Process Evaluation of the REBIZ Network by the EE Tool

Starting in May 2002 in the Bremen regional VET system, which comprises 22 VET schools, a 6-year long pilot programme on school autonomy and regional networking of work and learning partnerships began (Kurz, Schulz, & Zelger, 2007). The Bremen VET schools have been transformed into semi-autonomous vocational competence centres. This has been also the case with many other schools in line with new public management policies decided by the educational ministries in the 16 German states (Bund-Länder-Kommission, 2001). The goal is to better prepare local schools for the development of learning partnerships with local industries. The educational provision of the schools is to be improved by developing new school programmes. This programme should strengthen workplace learning and guarantee better interaction between theory and practice and work and learning. The re-organisation is being carried out by internal teams within the schools, in some cases also including trainers from industry. An evaluation of such networks, using the EE tool, was undertaken at the end of the preparatory phase. The evaluating body was the steering committee. Ten members of the steering committee participated in this (first) evaluation meeting.

## Partner Views on the Importance of the Criteria for Success

The outcome of the weighting discussion in this process evaluation was that Achievement of the Network Goals emerged as the most important success criterion for the network (21.5% of the respondents); this was followed by the criteria Communication and Learning: (19.5%), Project Management: (18%), Resources: 16.5%, and Partnership Development: (14.5%). Clearness of goals was seen as important for two reasons: Goals can be better achieved when they are clear to all partners and individual school projects can be outlined better.

*The judging process and its discussion.* The criterion 'goal', which is seen as being of striking importance received a rather low score. Deeper insights can be gained from this method of evaluation by looking at the results for the sub-criteria in more detail.

*Goal setting process.* The overall evaluation of the sub-criterion 'goals clearly defined' divided the steering committee into two groups: five persons gave scores varying from three to five and five persons score from six to eight. The discussion on these results made it clear that the group giving the higher scores believed aims of the network improved quite substantially. The other group supported their more negative scoring by judging the aim definition process as inefficient. Discussion on aims with all the actors within the network was lacking. For the schools, this led to confusion and slowed down progress.

This lack of goal setting was typically expressed as follows: "The programme does not prescribe aims precisely. Schools have many different conceptions concerning the project's aims. The ability to act depends on oneself."

*Time Resources.* The lowest score in REBIZ was for the availability of time resources. Given the relatively high weight (7.3%), this is a serious problem. In the discussion based on the quantitative figures, it emerged that the following points should receive much more attention by the partnership:

- Better division of work between the steering committee members to overcome time constraints and develop greater efficiency;
- Improving the co-operation between the Ministry of Education and school representatives by making stronger use of communication platforms which facilitate the sharing of information.

*Project management.* One critical point here was that the steering committee is not really dealing with decision making but functioning more as a platform for sharing information. Project management is being done in the individual schools, not in the network committee. Another point was that the distribution of tasks between the ministry and the schools needed to be readjusted. Distribution of work is said to function rather well between the schools but not between the programme administrator (ministry) and the schools. The contribution of the programme administration to REBIZ was evaluated as not satisfactory.

*Partnership development.* The partners gave rather positive scores to the development of the partnership within the steering committee, but not, however, on partnership with the ministry. The composition of the schools is good.

*Communication and learning.* Competencies for innovation had not improved at the time of the evaluation. Internal communication was also evaluated as rather good and it was felt that the partners are learning from each other.

*Strengths and weaknesses.* The project partners judged REBIZ as a whole as being in a rather bad state at the time of the evaluation. The scores for five main criteria (taking the median) were below 5; the score was above 5 (5,9) for only one criterion (Partnership Development).

## Feedback Meeting

Eight weeks after the evaluation meeting, a feedback meeting was held. The REBIZ partners agreed on the results of the evaluation. There was broad support for a re-design of the co-operation structure also in relation to the other network partners (e.g. public administration, trainers in industry and other school teachers). The partners became aware that a re-definition of the steering committee's role was needed and that the communication and information policy of the network was in need of improvement. According to this new understanding, the committee was able to re-organise their partnership by means of a new communication policy.

## Main Results

The evaluation dialogue triggered by the different sets of criteria enabled the members of the learning partnership to recall the history of the partnership, pointing out the effects of the partners' activities, both quantitatively (with the help of the quantitative elements of the evaluation method) and regarding content (the arguments and explanations relating to the scores and weightings given by the participants in the evaluation session).

Furthermore, in the reflection over the evaluation sessions it became clear in all cases that a major contribution of the evaluation was not just to identify strengths, weaknesses and threats but also to allow greater visibility as to the current state of the co-operative practices. The members gained a deeper understanding of their own activities in relation to others' activities. After many different evaluation sessions of that kind we found that these partnerships differ from single organisations as they represent cross-cultural organisational settings. Hence the need for assurance regarding what has been achieved by the network partners and by the specifically designed evaluation methods (Attwell & Deitmer, 2000; Deitmer et al., 2003, p. 246).

## Evaluating the Linkage Between Theoretical and Workplace Learning: SEVALAG

The evaluation tool SEVALAG (Selbstevaluation von Lern- und Arbeitsaufgaben – self-evaluation of work and learning tasks) was developed by the Institut Technik und Bildung at Bremen University (see Howe & Bauer, 2001). Its purpose is to evaluate the co-operation of workplace learning partnerships in terms of content.

This co-operation works by a process of joint development of practical tasks – *Lern- und Arbeitsaufgaben* (LAA; work and learning tasks). These practical tasks are specifically designed to integrate the more general knowledge acquired at school and the process knowledge acquired on the job. A team composed of teachers and trainers designs these tasks. The same team afterwards evaluates them using SEVALAG.

SEVALAG focuses on the content and design of learning tasks and, as a result, offers possibilities for further enhancement. It evaluates work and learning tasks with respect to eight different categories. For task content the categories are quality of the task, potential for learning, potential for shaping the work (*Gestaltung*), and co-operation between school and enterprise: For apprentices' learning, the categories are the results of learning and work, success, ability to form a holistic picture of job (*Gestaltungskompetenz*), and the apprentice's integration vis à vis school and work. These categories were derived from research on vocational learning and teaching processes. They each comprise a number of sub-categories that link concrete work and learning tasks and the more general criteria. Examples of these are degree of new knowledge acquired, quality of the final product or service, exploring possibilities of alternative design, cooperation, communication, team skills, and so on.

## Case Study: Arcelor/Mittal Steelworks Bremen

SEVALAG was further adapted by Arcelor/Mittal Steel Bremen and the vocational college Vegesack, Bremen, to strengthen co-operation between the VET school and training at the workplace (see Timmermann, 2006). One trainer and two VET teachers designed the work and learning task and afterwards jointly evaluated it. The 21 apprentices carrying out the task were asked to fill in a questionnaire comprising the same main and sub-categories as the evaluation tool.

The evaluation procedure was similar to that followed in the case of the EE tool. The participants rated the different sub-categories and discussed their ratings, giving reasons for their individual judgements and aiming at consensus. Because of the work load, the participants did not weight their criteria. The objective of the trainers' and teachers' self evaluation is to answer the central question: Does a *LAA*, (a specific work and learning task) help to develop the knowledge and competences required for participation in working life?

## *Main Results*

SEVALAG aims at structuring the development of work and learning tasks as well as monitoring the whole process in order to fully utilise the learning potential for students, trainers and teachers inherent in these tasks.

Patton's (1997) 'process value' of evaluation mentioned above, i.e. learning effects which result from the process of evaluation, no matter what concrete results the process shows, is a major element here. The very act of vocational teachers and enterprise's trainers not only designing a work and learning task, but also jointly reflecting on it afterwards was seen as highly important by all participants.

The absence of weighting criteria has been seen as a weakness of the process, although necessary for pragmatic reasons. The manpower needed for this kind of evaluation was lacking. In our case study, the participants were so absorbed by the task of developing the work and learning task, explaining it to the apprentices, monitoring its implementation in different ways and finally evaluating it, that there was simply no time left for a weighting process. To fully exploit the tool's potential, the participants would have to undergo such a process, elaborating the importance of the different criteria; what weaknesses may be neglected or should be taken seriously; whether such weaknesses are inherent in the work and learning task or are the result of external circumstances, and so on.

## Conclusion

We found both instruments to have the potential to investigate learning processes. The EE tool is directed at evaluating the co-operative process within the partnership in order to improve its management. On the basis of similar principles of evaluation, such as discourse and participation, the SEVALAG evaluation tool is directed towards the evaluation of the outcomes of the learning partnership itself. SEVALAG assesses the learning potential of the specific work and learning task (LAA) and the learning effects for the students.

One effect of the self evaluation is that the partners have judged their previous work as capable of improvement. New insights regarding the different aspects of the network process have been generated by the actors in the partnership. Thus, the big problem of non-participative evaluation activities has been avoided (see Patton's (1997) remarks on this problem). The problem that no use is made of the results of an evaluation has been avoided by directly involving the learning partners in the process of judging the evaluation and putting them as evaluators into the forefront of the assessment.

The involvement of *all* stakeholders of the learning processes has not as yet been carried out to its full potential in the development of these two tools. From an evaluation point of view (and according to newer theories of teaching and learning), it would also be important to involve the learners themselves in the process as well. There have been pragmatic reasons for not doing so, as both tools rely on focused discussions and cannot easily be expanded to large groups of users. But to include learners and empowering them to judge their own learning will certainly be a focus in the further development of these tools.

A self-assessment process with quasi-quantitative weighting and scoring helps to create a common 'performance appraisal culture' for learning partnership members, that is, it lays a foundation for common awareness of efficiency and effectiveness. The participants judged the discursive and self-assessing character of the EE and the SEVALAG tools as very useful for their project work and having a productive impact on learning. Most of the evaluated networks decided to use the method again in future to discuss the progress made. In other words, the tools deal with the most important critical success factors for work and learning partnerships.

In investigating learning potential, both tools are of an inherently qualitative nature. Using figures to describe different aspects mainly serves the purpose of focussing the discussion on complex issues such as the extent to which the learning processes can be considered successful. Thus, it is neither possible nor necessary to use these tools to directly compare different learning tasks or develop WLPs and rank them. As each complex learning task is unique, the figures do not show a general, abstract score, but reveal something about the task's adequacy in a given learning environment.

An additional benefit of both tools is that they may enable the creation of a pool of examples of good practice. Such examples can then be adapted to other situations in other learning contexts. Here, the tools have the big advantage that they already present insights into the main strengths and weaknesses of the different tasks and learning processes, thus allowing an easier process of adaptation.

This potential of the tools should also enable their use in a more general context outside that of the German dual system alone. They can be used in monitoring processes where learning and working meet and mesh, helping to identify the learning potential of work tasks as well as supporting the collaboration of actors with pedagogical and work backgrounds. As we know from the theories of situated learning as well as from practice in different countries, making use of the potentials for learning inherent in work tasks in order to integrate work and learning is a general challenge that extends beyond countries using the dual system as well as beyond initial VET.

# References

Attwell, G., & Deitmer, L. (2000). Partnership and Networks: A dynamic approach to learning in regions. In B. Nyhan, G. Attwell, & L. Deitmer (Eds.), *Towards the learning region. Education and regional innovation in the European Union and the United States* (pp. 61–70). Thessaloniki: CEDEFOP.

Bund-Länder-Kommission (2001): *Kompetenzzentren in regionalen Berufsbildungsnetzwerken – Rolle und Beitrag der beruflichen Schulen* [Competence centres for regional vocational education and training networks – role and contribution of VET schools (Heft 92)]. Bonn: Bericht der BLK.

Conference of the Educational Ministries (1999). *Guidelines for the development of new curricula by the KMK for vocational teaching in German VET schools and their relation to vocational training profiles of the Federal Government.* Conference of the educational ministries of the Länder in the Federal Republic of Germany (KMK), Bonn.

DeGEvaL (2002). *Summary of evaluation standards (DeGEval-Standards).* Gesellschaft für Evaluationsforschung [The German evaluation society]. Retrieved October 2, 2007 from http://www.degeval.de

Deissinger, T. (1996). Germany's vocational training act: Its function as an instrument of quality control within a tradition-based vocational training system. *Oxford Review of Education, 22*(3), 317–336.

Deitmer, L. (2004). *Management regionaler Innovationsnetzwerke. Evaluation als Ansatz zur Effizienzsteigerung regionaler Innovationsprozesse* [Management of regional innovation networks (Band 12)]. Baden-Baden: Nomos.

Deitmer, L., Davoine, E., Floren, H., Heinemann, L., Hofmaier, B., James, C., et al. (2003). *Improving the European knowledge base through formative and participative evaluation of science-industry liaisons and public-private partnerships (PPP) in R&D.* Final report of COVOSECO thematic network project, EU STRATA 5th framework programme. Bremen: University of Bremen.

Deitmer, L., Drewing, P., & Heermeyer, R. (2000). Qualification networks for shared learning in Lower Saxony in Northwest Germany. In B. Nyhan, L. Deitmer, & G. Attwell (Eds.), *Towards the learning region – Education and regional innovation in European Union and the United States.* Luxembourg: Office for Official Publications of the European Communities.

Deitmer, L., Fischer, M., Gerds, P., Przygodda, K., Rauner, F., Ruch, H., et al. (2004). *Neue Lernkonzepte in der dualen Berufsausbildung. Bilanz eines Modellversuchsprogramms* [New learning approaches in the German dual vocational education and training. Summary evaluation report of the German Länder VET innovation programme "New learning approaches within the German dual VET system"]. Bielefeld: W. Bertelsmann.

Deitmer, L., & Gerds, P. (2002). Developing a regional dialogue on VET and training. In P. Kämäräinen, G. Attwell, & A. Brown (Eds.), *Transformation of learning in education and training. Key qualifications revisited.* Office for Official Publications of the European Communities, European Centre for the development of Vocational Training. Luxembourg: CEDEFOP.

Fahrenkrog, G., Polt, W., Rojo, J., Türke, A., & Zinöcker, K. (Eds.) (2002). *RTD Evaluation toolbox.* Brussels: IPTS Technical Report Series.

Fischer, M., & Bauer, W. (2007). Competing approaches towards work process orientation in German curriculum development. *European Journal of Vocational Training, 1*(40), 140–154.

Greinert W. D. (1994). *The German system of vocational training. History, Organization, prospects.* Baden-Baden: Nomos.

Heinemann, L. (2005). Nähe und Distanz in der Berufsbildungsforschung [Closeness and distance in VET Research]. In F. Rauner (Ed.), *Handbuch der Berufsbildungsforschung* (pp. 568–574). Bielefeld: Bertelsmann.

Howe, F., & Bauer, W. (2001). *(Selbst-) Evaluation gestaltungsorientierter Lern- und Arbeitsaufgaben* [(Self-) evaluation of shaping oriented learning and working tasks]. In W. Petersen, F. Rauner, & F. Stuber (Eds.), *IT-gestützte Facharbeit – Gestaltungsorientierte Berufsbildung* (pp. 385–401). Baden-Baden: NOMOS.

Kurz, S., Schulz, J., & Zelger, J. (2007). *"GABEK als Methode zur kollegialen Organisationsentwicklung"* ["GABEK" – A collective method for school development in VET schools]. Retrieved October 10, 2007 from http://www.rebiz-bremen.de

Manske, F., Moon, Y. -G., Ruth, K., & Deitmer, L. (2002). Ein prozess- und akteurorientiertes Evaluationsverfahren als Reflexionsmedium und Selbststeuerungsinstrument für Innovationsprozesse [The process and actor oriented evaluation approach as a medium for reflection and decision-making in innovation processes]. *Zeitschrift für Evaluation*, Heft 2, 245–263.

Patton, M. Q. (1997). *Utilization-focused evaluation: The new century text.* Thousand Oaks: Sage.

Ryan, P. (2001). Apprenticeship in Britain: Tradition and innovation. In T. Deissinger (Ed.), *Berufliche Bildung als Orientierungs- und Anpassungsproblem. Analysen zur Berufsbildungsreform und zur Vorbildfunktion internationaler berufsbildungspolitischer Entwicklungsperspektiven.* Baden-Baden: Nomos.

Sloane, P. (2004). The application transfer between schools and enterprises in the German dual system: Putting it into practise. In R. Mulder & P. F.E. Sloane (Eds.), *New approaches to vocational education in Europe – The construction of complex learning-teaching arrangements.* Oxford: Symposium.

Smits, R., & Kuhlmann, St. (2003). Strengthening interfaces in innovation systems: Rationale, concepts and (new) instruments. In European Commission (Ed.), *Science & technology policies in Europe; new challenges and new responses proceedings of the STRATA* Consolidating Workshop (p. 306). Luxembourg: Office for Official Publications of the European Communities.

Timmermann, U. (2006). *Untersuchung eines Selbstevaluationsinstrumentes* [Reflections on a teachers' and trainers' instrument for self evaluation (SEVALAG)]. Bremen: ITB. (Unpublished manuscript).

# Chapter 9
# Developing Entrepreneurship in Small Enterprises – The Succession Process Supported by Apprenticeship Training as a Context for Learning

**Kari Itkonen**

## Introduction

The aim of this chapter is to describe the ownership change process of an operating enterprise as an example of integrating work and learning. This topic is approached both from the perspective of the theories of entrepreneurship and learning and from the viewpoint of practical experiences (Cope, 2005). In recent studies concerning the development of entrepreneurship more attention has been paid than before to the close connection between entrepreneurship and learning (e.g. Minniti & Byrgave, 2001): Learning is at the centre of the entrepreneurship process (Smilor, 1997). Successful entrepreneurs are seen as exceptional learners: they seem to learn from everything. It has even been claimed that entrepreneurship itself is a process of learning. Thus, the theory of entrepreneurship would appear to be in need of a theory of learning which makes for entrepreneurial success (Minniti & Byrgave, 2001).

Entrepreneurship can be defined as "the process of identifying opportunities for creating or realising value and of forming ventures which bring together resources to exploit those opportunities" (Rae, 2004). Thus, rather than a state, entrepreneurship is seen as a dynamic process. Some researchers have made a distinction between entrepreneurship and intrapreneurship (Pinchot, 1986; Jarillo, 1988; Kyrö, 1997). The former refers to the actual running of a business, while the latter refers to a mental state needed in any successful activity. In this chapter we look at how expertise in entrepreneurship develops especially in the context of family business. A family business is a firm where the ownership changes by generational succession (Koiranen, 1998).

Of special interest here are the factors connected with the change of ownership. An other central aim is to examine the transformation achieved through the succession process on the individual as well as group and organisation levels. The study focuses on the successor to the enterprise and the person giving it up, the process of transferring business operations and how the business develops from that point.

K. Itkonen (✉)
STAKES, National Research and Development Centre for Welfare and Health,
University of Jyväskylä, 40014 Jyväskylä, Finland
e-mail: kari.itkonen@stakes.fi

M.-L. Stenström, P. Tynjälä (eds.), *Towards Integration of Work and Learning*,
© Springer Science+Business Media B.V. 2009

The first part of the chapter presents conceptual models concerning learning and the development of expertise in entrepreneurship. The second part introduces an apprenticeship training programme which was specially designed to support successors in family firms during the transfer process.

## The Development of an Expert Entrepreneur

How, then, does one become an entrepreneur? The development of entrepreneurial preparedness (Harrison & Leitch, 2005; Politis, 2005) or entrepreneurial ability is a long process, which includes several elements. First, at the core of entrepreneurial ability is the process of creating a new business operation. Second, the growth of entrepreneurial ability can be conceptualised as a cumulative learning process that closely resembles the process of socialisation (Gibb Dyer, 1993). A third element of entrepreneurial ability concerns ways of coping with new situations. This is explained with the help of the history of the entrepreneur's earlier learning (Bereiter & Scardamalia, 1993; Mezirow, 1991).

The significance of experience and experiential learning is crucial, although a broad spectrum of learning methods is characteristic of the entrepreneur (Gibb, 2002). Growing and developing into an entrepreneur is usually a non-linear and non-continual process. Critical events generate deeper, transformative, "higher level" learning (Argyris & Schön, 1978; Mezirow, 1991). These critical phases may be followed by a stage of complementary and specialised study (Postle, 1993). Thus entrepreneur-like learning can be defined as a process through which people construct new meaning while recognising and acting on opportunities and organising and managing ventures.

Rae and Carswell (2001) presented a model of the entrepreneurial ability in which knowing, acting and making sense are interconnected (Fig. 9.1). The model is divided into two parts, that of learning and that of achieving. The purpose of this is to foreground the need for achieving ambitious goals (McClelland, 1961) which, together with the expansive processes of learning, creates the motivation for enterprising individuals to improve and educate themselves. The model emphasises the importance of career experiences (earlier life and career). The process of entrepreneurship includes both the commencement and the development of business operation.

One's personal orientation towards learning is important for the development of entrepreneurial ability. Every enterprising individual has her or his own history of learning and way of utilising both intentional and coincidental learning. Nevertheless, entrepreneurs mainly learn through "learning by doing" (Cope & Watts, 2000). In the process of learning, entrepreneurs may utilise several different means and resources such as stakeholders, customers or their own mistakes. However, the most essential thing seems to be the ability to utilise what has been learned in practice. Therefore formal training without practical applications does not seem to be effective in the domain of entrepreneurship (Rae & Carswell, 2001).

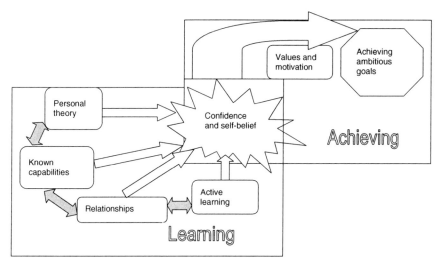

**Fig. 9.1** Development of entrepreneurial capability (adapted from Rae & Carswell 2001, p. 155)

Social relationships of an entrepreneur are created little by little and are based on earlier life and career. In the literature, an entrepreneur's career is generally divided into five periods. The elements of (1) childhood and (2) life and career preparing for entrepreneurship are present before the entrepreneurship. Entrepreneurship is thus seen differently when one is (3) young, (4) middle-aged or (5) elderly. Consequently, entrepreneurs have been classified by the timing of the beginning of entrepreneurship (Gibb & Ritchie, 1982; Gibb Dyer, 1993; Heinonen, Kovalainen, Paasio, Pukkinen, & Österberg, 2006). Experience of life shows in various ways in an entrepreneur's abilities and intentions (Gibb & Ritchie, 1982; Krueger & Brazeal, 1994; Rae, 2005).

As their careers develop each entrepreneur forms explanations and attributions often described as 'what works for me'. These components of learning have been termed personal theories (Rae, 2004). The test of these theories is pragmatic: They have been found to be valid and effective for that person in accomplishing his or her goals in the contexts in which they had been tried. These personal theories fall into four main groups: (1) vision, decision making and planning, (2) developing the business by being close to the market, (3) balancing between control and "letting go" and (4) managing through people (Rae, 2004). The development and organisation of personal theories can be highly significant in learning (Shotter, 1993) – especially in the social learning process. In the words of Baumard (1999) "practical theory is the living body of learning".

For Baumard practical theory is made up of social discourses and does not include regular, personal cognitive processes. Practitioners produce practical theories – a more general claim for their validity cannot be made because practitioners' experience is limited to their own practice, observation and social exchanges with colleagues. At the base of this "practical business wisdom" is "Aristotelian phronesis" – intuitive social knowledge and wisdom. It is practical, contextual, experiential, hard to analyse or test, and is formed and shared through social interaction (Baumard, 1999). These theories – developed out of experience – remain tacit and intuitive until they are verbalised and become a discursive resource (produced by dialogue, for example, as stories and reflective insights). In this process a practice-based theory is removed from its context and therefore the term 'practical theory' can no longer be applied (Rae, 2004).

Skills and knowledge for entrepreneurship are thus acquired through the social and contextual learning processes. But at the core of entrepreneurship there is also the powerful need to seek challenges and tackle them. The development of entrepreneurial skills can thus be summarised in the following three points (Rae, 2004):

1) Life story approach. Sense making and learning processes become available through discourse.
2) The role of personal theory.
3) Relationship between learning and achieving: learning to achieve and learning from achievements are equally vital in the process of entrepreneurial formation.

While the Rae and Carswell model shown in Fig. 9.1 presents the development of entrepreneurial capability, the more recent model by Rae (2004) describes continuous entrepreneurial learning in the longer term (Fig. 9.2). Contextual learning is central in this model as well. A novel aspect in the model is that an entrepreneurs' preceding life career is shaped into a special entrepreneur identity rather than presented as a way of life as often described in previous studies (e.g. Gibb, 2002). The

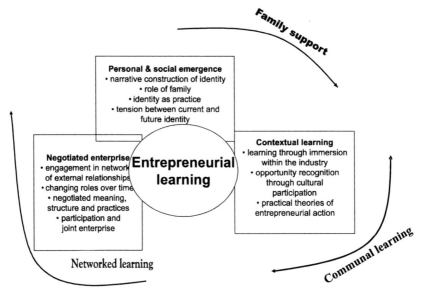

**Fig. 9.2** Model of continuous entrepreneurial learning (adapted from Rae, 2004, p. 328)

significance of interaction continues to be emphasised; Rae uses the term "negotiated enterprise". An enterprise is little by little formed into an agreement between different interest groups. In this connection it is noteworthy that rather than being a solitary activity, entrepreneurship is very often team work. The third component of the new model is personal and social emergence, which refers to the narrative construction of identity, role of family, identity as practice and fusion between current and future identity.

## Entrepreneurs Learning from the Social Perspective

The model of entrepreneurial learning described above, emphasising contextual learning, negotiated enterprise and social aspects of identity construction, suggests that special attention should be paid to the learning environments of entrepreneurs. In this respect social learning theories – especially those focusing on communal workplace learning and knowledge creation – might have something to offer the study of entrepreneurial learning. In these theories, the characteristics of ideal social learning environments have been conceptualised, for example, through the notions of communities of practice (Wenger, 1998), innovative knowledge communities (Hakkarainen, Palonen, Paavola, & Lehtinen, 2004) and *ba* (Nonaka & Konno, 1998).

Communities of practice (Wenger, 1998) are usually unofficial communities in which learning by doing is essential. Learning is based on communal as well as individual experience. In particular, in the development of identity the individual and social spheres meet when novices identify themselves with their more experienced colleagues in communities of practice. Thus, as Hakkarainen and his colleagues (2004) have pointed out, communities of practice are above all units of cultural learning.

Adopting Sfard's (1998) distinction between metaphors of learning, acquisition and participation, Hakkarainen and his colleagues (2004) have described the different perspectives on the development of expertise as follows:

- the acquisition perspective – the mental component of expertise
- the participation perspective – expertise as participation in a certain culture or community
- the creation perspective – expertise as a (networked) process of creating something new.

While the traditional studies of expertise represent the acquisition metaphor and the idea of communities of practice that of the participation metaphor, the notion of innovative knowledge communities represent the creation metaphor. Innovative knowledge communities aiming at creating new knowledge and breaking up prevailing practices (Hakkarainen et al., 2004) create the conditions for the development of dynamic expertise. They resemble cultural communities of practices, but they are also distinct from these. Dynamic innovative knowledge communities and cultural communities of practice have in common that they both provide for the supply of the implements, practices and methods of communal operation as well as shared stories and understanding. However, they also differ from each other in at least two respects. Firstly, the direction of knowledge is different. In traditional communities of practices knowledge and experience are transferred in only one direction: from experts to newcomers. In innovative knowledge communities instead the transfer of knowledge and skills inside the community is much more symmetrical. When the information intensivity and turbulence of the environment increase, leading to a corresponding increase in the stress experienced in the community, people turn to innovative knowledge communities, as their ability to solve problems new to everyone is greater than that of traditional communities of practice (Hakkarainen et al., 2004). Secondly, the core operation of innovative knowledge communities is the creation of new knowledge. In the literature such communities have been called, for example, knowledge building communities (Bereiter, 2002), communities of expansive learning (Engeström, 2004) or knowledge-creating organisations (Nonaka & Takeuchi, 1995). Innovative knowledge communities deliberately utilise the ability of human communities to construct new innovations based on earlier innovations and to use earlier intellectual achievements as a stepping stone to new achievements.

The concept *ba* is connected to the organisational creation of new knowledge, and according to Nonaka, von Krogh, and Voelpel (2006), it has several features in common with communities of practice (Wenger, 2000) or the zone of proximal development (Vygotsky, 1978; Nonaka et al., 2006; also Tynjälä, 2008). According to the definition of *ba*: *"The context of knowledge creation is ba, a Japanese concept that roughly translates into the English 'space', originally developed by the Japanese philosopher Nishida and later refined by Shimizu. Ba is shared space for emerging relationships. It can be physical, virtual or mental space, but all three have knowledge embedded in ba in common, where it is acquired through individual experiences, or reflections on others' experience"* (Nonaka et al., 2006). This *ba* learning environment is related to the model of knowledge sharing developed earlier by Nonaka and Takeuchi (1995) (Nonaka & Konno, 1998) (see Fig. 2.3 in Chapter 2). In the model primary *ba* is called *Originating ba*. The knowledge process begins in this space. It is an environment of socialization, a space where people work together and share experiences. *Interacting ba* is a place for reflecting and analyzing, and *Cyber ba* for combining new explicit knowledge with other explicit knowledge. Finally, *Exercising ba* is the space of action and utilisation of the explicit knowledge obtained before (ibid).

In their latest article Nonaka and his colleagues (2006) mention that connecting the theories of entrepreneurship to the theories of the knowledge-creating organisation could be a very profitable approach. They ask, especially in relation to the founding of a new enterprise and discovering a new possibility: Does *ba* precede the founding of an enterprise? And if so, what characterises the *ba* of entrepreneurship prior to the forming of an enterprise? What is the relationship between the origin of learning and the origin of the enterprise or organisation? It is generally assumed (e.g. Shane 2000, 2001; Shepard & DeTienne, 2005) that in the early stages of operating a business the entrepreneur's preparatory knowledge of technologies, markets and clients shapes his or her ability to notice and seize an opportunity. However, in some empirical studies it has been discovered that novice entrepreneurs do not have much knowledge – about either the market or consumer needs – before founding an enterprise (Urwyler, 2005). Although different results have been obtained in different studies, they all support the idea of the importance of a pre-existing *ba* in the starting of business.

## The Family Enterprise and Succession as the Context of the Entrepreneur's Learning Process

An enterprise today may be defined from the point of view of learning and creating new knowledge, as a combination of three parallel systems. These systems are the basic operation of the business, the projectile development function and the enterprise's own knowledge system (Nonaka et al., 2006). From the point of view of the enterprise, succession or owner change is one of the most central processes the entrepreneur goes through. It has a simultaneous effect on the operation of the enterprise and its knowledge system.

In family enterprises a major part of the everyday knowledge of how the business operates lies in the family. In several respects the competitive advantages of family enterprises differ from those of non-family enterprises (Cabera-Suárez, De Saá-Pérez, & García-Almeida, 2001). Knowledge is the main source in competitive advantage (Handler, 1994; Spender & Grant, 1996). Learning – forming knowledge – thus occupies a key position in the competitive situation of an enterprise (Fiol & Lyles, 1985; Pisano, 1994). Thus, in the succession process within the family entrepreneurs aim primarily at the cultural transfer of both knowledge and learning skills. In particular, a small enterprise may as such form a fruitful learning environment. Many of its special features explain this potential, such as the important role of learning in work and while working, concentrated decision making and the great similarity between the goals of the entrepreneur and those of the enterprise (Gibb, 2002). Creating new knowledge and finding possibilities for business is at the core of entrepreneurship. Therefore in learning, attention should be paid to the role, in particular, of innovative learning rather than reproductive learning (Holmquist, 2003; Hakkarainen et al., 2004).

The importance of tacit knowledge in entrepreneurial learning is obvious (e.g. Cabera-Suárez et al., 2001). However, more recent entrepreneurship research has also emphasised the significance of explicit personal knowledge and growth of identity (Rae, 2005). Here the importance of organisational learning also comes to the fore. In small enterprises especially, the role of knowledge that is personal and not previously distributed is great. Therefore it has been suggested that the most rewarding research object for the study of entrepreneurship is the traditional small entrepreneur ownership succession in the small family enterprise (Gibb, 2002). Succession as a particular business project is also interesting as a learning process.

The rest of this chapter describes empirical findings of a study which focussed on succession process supported by apprenticeship training. Next the apprentice training programme and the data gathering procedures are described.

## Apprenticeship Training as a Support System for Beginning Entrepreneurs

As described earlier in this chapter, the natural way for entrepreneurs to learn is by doing, and thus apprenticeship can bee seen as a promising approach to entrepreneurial learning. In Finland, apprenticeship training is used both in initial vocational upper secondary education and as a form of in-service training in many fields. Traditionally, apprenticeship has primarily been offered as an educational opportunity for adults, but in recent years this form of training has been increasingly targeted at young people as well. Apprenticeship training leads, on the one hand, to the same vocational upper secondary qualifications as the education provided by vocational institutions and, on the other, to further vocational qualifications and specialist vocational qualifications (mainly intended for adults), which require more advanced vocational skills in the field or occupation in question (Ministry of Education, 2006).

The Jyväskylä Vocational Institute has designed and organized the apprenticeship training for enterprises which are going through the succession process in Western and Central Finland. In this model firm's successors enhance their knowledge of business by taking a vocational qualification or special entrepreneurial vocational qualification. Most of the learning takes place in the workplace in the apprentice's own enterprise. All the apprentices have their own mentor, either the present owners of the firm or an outsider. In addition to workplace learning, the apprentices take theoretical classes in the vocational schools every now and then. The idea is that in the course of their work the apprentices connect theoretical and practical knowledge. Thus, apprenticeship training realised in this way may make the connective model of education and integrative pedagogy described in Chapter 2 possible (see also Guile & Griffiths, 2001; Tynjälä, 2008). In the present apprenticeship training programme the integration of theory and practice was based on the participants formulating their personal business plan and testing it in their own firm. In addition, in the classroom instruction certain aspects of practical entrepreneurship such as, the cost accounting, marketing and personnel management in the firm was dealt with. All these topics were examined in relation to the participants' business plan and their entrepreneurial practices.

## Research Questions and Data

As described above, the way of learning, the content of learning and the context of learning are dynamic elements in the learning process. In this case study we are interested in two issues:

1) How does expert entrepreneurship develop?
2) What role can apprenticeship training combined with theoretical classes play in entrepreneurs' development?

The first question concerns the content of expert entrepreneurship and the way in which that expertise is acquired. What the relation exists between the entrepreneurial creation of knowledge and the ability of an entrepreneur to notice, create and benefit from business opportunities (Grand, 2003)? The second question concerns the models of entrepreneurial and expertise learning: How well do the models presented by Rae, (2005), Rae & Carswell, (2001), and Hakkarainen et al. (2004) describe and explain this phenomenon? The knowledge creation metaphor of learning and its role of opportunity recognition is a special focus in examining the construction of entrepreneurial expertise during apprenticeship training related to the succession process.

Earlier in this chapter the three models of the social learning environment were presented. The community of practice model relates to the participation perspective, while the model of the innovative knowledge community and *ba* relate to the knowledge creation perspective. We now consider, how the family business, succession process and apprenticeship training fit into these contexts. What spaces, talk and interest groups are necessary for the creation of entrepreneurial knowledge (Steyaert & Katz, 2004)? What in particular are the roles of the family business itself and the succession process? What are the basic elements of the entrepreneurial learning of the present owner and of the successor? We discuss what kind of a learning environment the succession project forms and how its different components connect, especially in the case of succession within a family.

Our study was conducted in the context of the apprenticeship training programme described above. The entrepreneurs (the existing owner and successor) participated in a training course offered to firms in which the successor was known. Altogether 40 firms participated in the education and training programme. All of these were asked to fill in a questionnaire, and 14 were asked to participate in interviews. Most of the firms, i.e. 11 (80%), attended the interview, while the response rate to the survey was lower. All together 17 (42%) of the firms answered the questionnaire.

All the enterprises studied were small and not growing (Gibb, 2002). These are often described as handicraft entrepreneurs. They have a great amount of experience based on specialised knowledge. The next entrepreneur in these firms is known and is usually the son or daughter of the present owner. The role of the family is normally very important. Most of the enterprises in the study were already aiming at the second generation ownership (second and third entrepreneurial generation). Also among them were non-family companies.

The questionnaire data were analysed quantitatively and the interview data qualitatively. The history of learning to be an entrepreneur and the learning skills important in entrepreneurship were main themes of the interviews. In addition biographies of the present owners and their successors were collected and analysed.

# Entrepreneurial Learning: What, how and in what Context?

## *Learning and Development of an Entrepreneur: Identity and Expertise*

On the basis of our data it seems quite clear that the growth of the entrepreneurial identity starts to grow early and that identity is rather strong. Entrepreneurship as a way of life was emphasized in the owners' interviews. Similarly, successors often talked about *a pull to entrepreneurship"*. If the whole family was involved in the firm, *"it would be a shame not to try"*. A view commonly voiced by both owners and successors was: *"one must have an inborn desire to be an entrepreneur: all do not have it in them, but nevertheless one has to grow into entrepreneurship"*.

It was typical of entrepreneurs to think that entrepreneurship and intrapreneurship come from their homes and through experience. In many cases the successor had been involved since s/he was "0 years old". Often there the successor shared a common work history with the owner. The spirit of entrepreneurship seemed to be better established in the succession from the second to the third generation. Many of the owners' parents had an entrepreneurial background, for example a village shopkeeper or a blacksmith. Or the parents had "the entrepreneurial spirit", although they did not exactly own a firm. Some had a farming enterprise background.

Learning entrepreneurial drive and way of thinking seemed to be mostly informal in nature. Other studies, in turn, have suggested that many vocational and business skills are often learned in more formal educational contexts (Rae, 2004). The central skills of an entrepreneur are the ability to take risks, innovative behaviour, making a profit and leadership (van Propta, 2002, p. 20). Innovativeness was a highly characteristic feature also among the present group. It seemed to be present all the time, not in special cases alone but also in lines of action, in production and in the business idea. In our data successors seemed to be more systematically innovative than owners and they more explicitly emphasised the importance of developing new ideas. Also, tolerance of uncertainty was experienced as an essential part of entrepreneurship. It is learned mainly through experience which is why it was not mentioned by successors as yet.

The interviews with the owners revealed much experiential, practical wisdom, which was expressed in the kinds of personal theories described earlier (Rae, 2004). These personal theories were classified into five categories: a) a holistic understanding of the business, b) coordination of the different parts of business, c) networking on market, d) handling of everyday routines of the business and e) caring about the continuity and environment of the business. These categories are more general than those found by Rae (2004).

Most of the owners had begun engaging in entrepreneurial activity at an early age, either directly or after a short period of paid employment in the same field. In addition to basic education, most of the owners had vocational qualifications. Often they had had poor success at school. For some the decision to become an entrepreneur was automatic since it was the only way of making a reasonable living and in any case the previous generation was engaged in entrepreneurship. They sought a particular vocational education – not general knowledge. However, most of the interviewees reported that their learning had actually begun on the factory floor. The most important things were learned through working (in a shop floor or cooperatively with others).

Successors' careers prior to engaging in entrepreneurship were experienced less important: They were entrepreneurs either instantly or after a short period of paid employment. According to the interviewees, working elsewhere gives just enough distance – it provides possibilities for comparison. In many cases the junior entrepreneur had followed the example of the senior and had become an entrepreneur with quite a low level of entrepreneurship education. However, formal education was seen as fairly useful for the young entrepreneur: "*it gives a flying start*" for learning at work.

Our data suggest that the owner's and the successor's approaches to entrepreneurial learning are different. The owner's learning process and practices resembled those presented in the model in Fig. 9.1 (Rae & Carswell, 2001). Target-oriented and formal education played a part, but was not deemed essential in the process of entrepreneurial learning as a whole. Networks were of growing importance. The previous work career had a strong background role in the development of new business ideas. However, the most important support for owners' learning came from their own personal theories. Experienced entrepreneurs analysed life and entrepreneurship with the help of these theories. One central skill needed was that of obtaining a holistic understanding of entrepreneurial work. The learning process and its results seemed to lead to more self trust and self confidence. On the basis of the knowledge and experience already acquired the entrepreneur was equipped to meet new challenges.

The development of the successor's learning process seemed to be incomplete in the succession stage. On the basis of our findings, this process can be described by three factors: personal development, contextual learning and participation in a common enterprise — or as Lave and Wenger (1991) put it, in communities of practice.

According to our interviewees, family role models were central in personal development (cf. Handler, 1994). They were seen as powerful in all the families included this study. As mentioned before, the entrepreneurial identity starts to develop, especially in long-standing business families, during the successor's early years in the business. Our findings show, indeed, that socialisation into entrepreneurship starts at an early age.

Later, the learning of entrepreneurship is contextual in nature. It takes place in the family firm and with the help of its networks and interest groups. The work career embarked on outside the family firm had offered conditions for exploratory learning for many. Together with the knowledge needed for operating in the industry in question, this learning lays the foundation for the business idea and the ability to learn opportunity recognition.

As the succession becomes more acute, the role of the enterprise seems to become more important. The negotiated enterprise is related to early age entrepreneurship through the social context (Rae, 2004). For example, the roles of the owners and successors have to be negotiated several times all over again during the succession process. The family is constantly involved in these negotiations. Among the different interest groups, the biggest buyer, and in the case of franchises, franchising leaders have the most power and thus the most importance in the learning process. The succession process is over when the successor is the enterprise's only negotiator with these groups.

Learning in the succession process can also be depicted through the metaphors of learning described earlier – knowledge acquisition, participation and knowledge creation (Hakkarainen et al., 2004). In the case of the owner, the metaphor of knowledge acquisition was emphasized most in the history of learning. In contrast, the successors usually have more experience of cultural learning – which refers to learning described by the participation metaphor. Knowledge creation takes place in teamwork by the owner and successor. However, the successors must have enough experience and knowledge to be able to take part in the knowledge creation process.

## Support of the Learning Process

### The Succession Process

The succession process can be part of learning in the community of practice or of learning in the innovative community. As mentioned earlier, before the primary succession process there is a time for cultural and participatory learning in the community of practice. This community will also function during the actual succession process, but it is not enough for a successful change of ownership. From the knowledge creation perspective, the role of the innovative knowledge community is crucial. In our data the successors usually proved to be more dynamic than the owners. For example, attitudes towards information and communications technology differed. It was easier for the successor to come in terms with the development of ICT. Immediately there is something of their own, that they can give and to be experts on. In the best cases this helped to create "innovative communities" (Hakkarainen et al., 2004).

In many cases, the precondition of a successful succession was the reformation of the old business idea or the beginning of a new branch of the business. It seemed that succession cannot happen before an innovative community of learning has been created. First the successor must receive or take over the leadership in this community. "The old business" may function simultaneously on the side. Long-term equality of entrepreneurship leads finally to the change over: It is a long process with a number of phases.

It is also possible to look at the succession process as a knowledge-creating project by the whole organisation. Organisational learning appeared, for example, in the transformation of certain everyday practices of the firm or in a new way of dealing with customer relationships. However, the limits of the single enterprise are no longer as clear than they once were. Enterprises are nowadays networked and negotiated, and therefore organizational learning may cross the borders of organisations.

This was in fact aimed at in the apprenticeship training by encouraging participants to create interorganisational networks.

Nonaka and Konno described four different forms of learning space (Fig. 2.3, Chapter 2). Of these the originating *ba*, involving the socialising of practices was depicted as the primary *ba*. In some of the present cases this was also the only *ba*. In this learning space, however, we found an obvious danger to the making of mistakes. The tacit knowledge acquired through participating in everyday practices seemed to lead not only to functioning knowledge but also to bad habits or dysfunctional practices (see also Tynjälä, 2008). There is also a danger that the firm will not be very responsive to changes in the firm's environment. Therefore we conclude that, for the success of the succession process, instead of relying merely on practices provided by originating ba, it would be more useful to aim at developing all forms of *ba*.

## Effectiveness of the Apprenticeship Training Programme in Supporting Succession in an Enterprise

As mentioned before, the subjects in our study participated in a course of entrepreneurship organised as apprenticeship training and combined theoretical classes. The core of the entrepreneurs' apprenticeship training was the creation and elaboration of their own business plan. In other words, during the training each participant presented a business plan and modified it on the basis of theoretical and practical knowledge. This approach together with classes in economics and personal consultation relating to the participant's enterprise, seemed to give successors a good basic understanding of issues important in entrepreneurship. Table 9.1 shows the proportion of the participants in the apprenticeship training who agreed with statements about the effectiveness of the training on different aspects of entrepreneurial competence. The table shows that almost 90% of the respondents experienced the elaboration of their business plan as useful. Similarly the great majority of participants felt that the training had advanced their business change process and promoted their business skills.

In accordance with its aims the effect of the course was often felt in the development of the firm's business plan. However, this sort of training aiming at supporting the change of ownership did not seem to have any direct influence on the making of potential new business openings. Changes had often already happened earlier during the first steps of the long succession process.

The potential future entrepreneurs also reported that they had received an important grounding in the basic elements of entrepreneurship through the apprenticeship programme. They also described entrepreneurship and learning as processes that closely resemble each other. The target of the training can therefore also be supporting useful practices and contents for the successor's entrepreneurial learning.

The majority of the respondents reported that the apprenticeship training had secured the continuity of the enterprise and through this also the success of the change in ownership. The interview data indicated that, in particular, strengthening

**Table 9.1** Effectiveness of the apprenticeship programme

| Aspects of learning | At least a moderate effect; % of all $n = 17$ |
|---|---|
| *Modules of the theoretical education* | |
| – business plan | 88 |
| – business change process | 80 |
| – economic skills | 71 |
| *Support for practical knowledge* | |
| – perceiving matters holistically | 71 |
| – development of the business/business idea of the firm | 65 |
| – the common line of action (ideology) in the firm | 59 |
| – commitment to entrepreneurship | 59 |
| – the role and significance of the family | 50 |
| *Support for change of owner-manager* | |
| – securing the continuity of the firm | 81 |
| – ensuring firm choice of successor | 63 |
| *Effect on the business* | |
| – knowledge of the owner-manager | 59 |
| – development of the firm | 53 |
| – knowledge of the personnel in firm | 47 |
| – profitability of the firm | 35 |
| – productivity of the firm | 35 |
| – cooperation together with other firms | 35 |

the successor's identity was experienced as an important result from the point of view of the continuity of the change process. The decision to participate in the training and being able to perceive the whole process of change speeded up the implementation of the change in ownership.

The individual effectiveness of training was often based on how the timing of training matched the succession process. For the most participants the timing seemed to be optimal. The enterprises had sought training when the need had been perceived. Entrepreneurs felt that in relation to the resources used the training was able to have a considerable positive influence on the change of ownership in the participating enterprises.

Although the entrepreneurs were, for the most part, satisfied with the course, there were differences between the participants in how they evaluated the success of the training. The causes of these differences will be analysed in more detail in our future studies.

# Conclusions

The aim of this study was to examine the development of entrepreneurship in the succession process in the traditional family business. Entrepreneurs running a family business often emphasize that entrepreneurial behaviour is a heritable quality (Gibb Dyer, 1988). This way of thinking seems to survive across generations, and also was typical of the participants in our study. However, the entrepreneurs seemed to rely on learning as well. In business, learning by doing is often claimed to be important and, especially among the traditional entrepreneurs to be the most effective way of learning (Billet, 2007). Therefore the entrepreneurship education and training programme described in this chapter was organised through a combination of apprenticeship and theoretical classes. The basic principle was the integration of theoretical and practical knowledge in solving problems in an authentic work situation.

The education and training carried out along these lines seemed to be successful as assessed by the entrepreneurs going through the succession process or change of ownership. The majority of the participants felt that the training had helped them to develop their business ideas and improve the multiple skills needed in entrepreneurship. Thus, the idea of connecting work experience and conceptual knowledge in educating entrepreneurs seemed to function well. In addition, the principle of connectivity also found expression in other forms in the work of the novice entrepreneurs. For example, negotiated expertise can be seen as one manifestation of connectivity. The learning community of the successor constitutes several separate components, which change over time from childhood to becoming an entrepreneur. Many of the social, economic and physical factors related to family, enterprise, industry, stakeholders and other networks are connected in different ways during the development of entrepreneurship. As a result, these different connections create various spaces for learning, similar to those described as different forms of *ba*, by Nonaka & Konno (1998).

On the basis of our study, entrepreneurs' learning during the succession process seemed to be transformative rather than reproductive. The individual's tacit knowledge and the skills that are needed in entrepreneurial activity and which are acquired through cultural learning are transformed into the entrepreneur's personal theories. Triggered by the succession process and supported by negotiated expertise, these theories and their underlying assumptions may further change. Finally, the identity of the individual changes in consequence of transformative learning, and the successor becomes an entrepreneur. In addition, transformation can be connected both to learning how to be an entrepreneur and learning what constitutes the spirit of entrepreneurship.

The perceived efficiency of the apprenticeship training probably results from successors being given an opportunity in theoretical classes to attempt to solve genuine problems in the family business with the help of conceptual reflections provided by the learning community. In this way they were able to bring to the work both the expertise and knowledge, which they have gained during their career, and ideas stemming from the educational context. This gives them self-confidence, which they need to meet new challenges. The fresh know-how of the successor combined with the personal theories of the experienced incumbent and the firm's personnel often opened up new entrepreneurial possibilities.

Our study indicated that the nature of entrepreneurial learning varied across different age groups and generations. The importance of experiential learning seemed to be stronger in the older age groups and it seemed to grow with age. The nature of knowledge also varied: formal knowledge seemed to be more important for younger than for older people. Also the networks of younger people were more horizontal, while those of older entrepreneurs were more vertical. Today's stimulating growth environment offers young people broader, but at the same time, more divergent experiences. Therefore their knowledge is more incoherent than the knowledge of the older generations (see also Gibb, 2002).

Our study of traditional and small family enterprises raises many questions for future research. The family business is changing and spreading into new domains of business. Therefore more research should be conducted on the different stages of branches. What competences does the successor need in different business domains? It is also important to deal with the role of entrepreneurship in the successor's career. How is this entrepreneurship expressed? What is the process of learning opportunity recognition like and how does it vary in different business domains and regions?

It has been proposed that team entrepreneurship is often a more effective way to operate than managing the business alone. The succession process is a special – time-limited – case of team entrepreneurship. Little research has been done on changes of ownership, in samples of several existing owners and novice entrepreneurs. What are the roles of the owners and successors and how is knowledge transferred in such cases?

We also found in this study that both the ex-owner and successors of traditional family enterprises have relatively little formal education (see also Lans, Biemans, Verstegen, & Mulder, 2007). A study could be conducted on the views of the various generations about both the benefits and the disadvantages of formal education and the reasons for choices of different learning careers. This could help us to better understand which elements of formal education should be integrated into the entrepreneur's learning by doing and how this should be done. This would serve the aim of better understanding the transformation of knowledge, behaviour and identity.

# References

Argyris, C., & Schön, D. A. (1978). *Organizational learning: A theory of action perspective*. Reading (Massachusetts), Addison-Wesley.

Baumard, P. (1999). *Tacit knowledge in organizations*. London: Sage.

Bereiter, C. (2002). *Education and mind in the knowledge age*. Mahwah, NJ: Erlbaum.

Bereiter, C., & Scardamalia, M. (1993). *Surpassing ourselves: An inquiry into nature of expertise*. Chigaco: Open Court.

Billet, S. (2007, April). *The pedagogic practices of small business operators*. Paper presented at the Annual Meeting of the American Educational Research Association, Chicago, IL.

Cabera-Suárez, K., De Saá-Pérez, P., & García-Almeida, D. (2001). The succession process from a resource and knowledge-based view of the family firm. *Family Business Review, 14*(1), 37–48.

Cope, J. (2005). Toward a dynamic learning perspective of entrepreneurship. *Entrepreneurial Theory and Practice, 29*(3), 373–397.

Cope, J., & Watts, G. (2000). Learning by doing: an exploration of critical incidents and reflection in entrepreneurial learning. *International Journal of Entrepreneurial Behaviour and Research, 6*(3), 104–124.

Engeström, Y. (2004). The new generation of expertise: Seven theses. In H. Rainbird, A. Fuller, & A. Munro (Eds.), *Workpalce learning in context*, (pp. 145–165). London: Routledge.

Fiol, C., & Lyles, M. (1985). Organization learning. *Academy of Management Review, 10*(4), 803–813.

Gibb, A. (2002). In pursuit of a new 'enterprise' and 'entrepreneurship' paradigm for learning: Creative destruction, new values, new ways of doing things and new combinations of knowledge. *International Journal of Management Reviews, 4*(3), 233–269.

Gibb, A., & Ritchie, J. (1982). Understanding the process of starting small business. *European Small Business Journal, 1*(1), 26–45.

Gibb Dyer, W. Jr, (1988). Culture and continuity in family firms. *Family Business Rewiew, 1*(1), 37–50.

Gibb Dyer W. Jr (1993). Toward a theory of entrepreneurial careers. *Entrepreneurship Theory and Practice, 19*(2), 7–21.

Grand, S. (2003). Making sense of economy: Entrepreneurial strategic thinking and acting as theory building and theory testing under ambiguity. In A. Beerli & S. Falk (Eds.), *Knowledge management and networked environments: Leveraging intellectual capital in virtual business communities* (pp. 73–95). New York: Amacom.

Guile, D. & Griffiths, T. (2001). Learning through work experience. *Journal of Education and Work, 14*, 113–131.

Hakkarainen, K., Palonen T., Paavola, S. & Lehtinen, E. (2004). *Communities of networked expertise. Professional and educational perspectives.* Amsterdam: Elsevier.

Harrison, R., & Leitch, C. (2005). Entrepreneurial learning: Research in the interface between learning and the entrepreneurial context. *Entrepreneurship Theory and Practice, 29*(3), 351–371.

Handler, W. (1994). Succession in family business: A review of the research. *Family Business Review, 7*(2), 133–157.

Heinonen, J., Kovalainen, A., Paasio, K., Pukkinen, T., & Österberg, J. (2006). *Palkkatyöstä yrittäjäksi.* (Työpoliittinen tutkimus No. 297). Helsinki: Työministeriö.

Holmquist, M. (2003). A dynamic model of intra- and interorganizational learning. *Organization Studies, 24*(1), 95–123.

Jarillo, J. C. (1988) When small is not enough: How to save entrepreneurs from themselves. *European Management Journal, 6*(4), 325–329.

Koiranen, M. (1998). *Perheyrittäminen.* [Family entrepreneurship]. Tampere: Konetuumat Oy.

Krueger, N., & Brazeal, D. (1994). Entrepreneurial potential and potential entrepreneurs. *Entrepreneurship Theory & Practice, 18*(1), 91–104.

Kyrö, P. (1997). *Yrittäjyyden muodot ja tehtävä ajan murroksessa.* Jyväskylä: Jyväskylä Studies in Computer Science, Economics and Statistics No. 38. Jyväskylä: Jyväskylän yliopisto.

Lans, T., Biemans, H., Verstegen, J., & Mulder, M. (2007, April). *Learning out of business? Learning fostering the development of entrepreneurial competence of small business owners in horticulture.* Paper presented at the Annual Meeting of the American Educational Research Association, Chicago, IL.

Lave, J., & Wenger, E. (1991). *Situated learning – Legitimate peripheral participation.* Cambridge: Cambridge University Press.

McClelland, D. (1961). *The achieving society.* Princeton, NJ: Van Norstrand.

Mezirow, J. (1991). *Transformative dimensions of adult learning.* San Francisco: Jossey-Bass.

Ministry of Education (2006). *Education and science in Finland.* Ministery of Education Publications N:o 15. Helsinki: Helsinki University Press.

Minniti, M., & Byrgave, W. (2001). *A dynamic model of entrepreneurial learning.* Entrepreneurship Theory and Practice *25*(3), 5–16.

Nonaka, I., & Konno, N. (1998). The concept of "Ba": Building a foundation for knowledge creation. *California Management Review 40*(3), 40–54.

Nonaka, I., von Krogh, G., & Voelpel, S. (2006). Organizational knowledge creation theory: Evolutionary paths and future advances. Review paper. *Organization Studies, 27*(8), 1179–1208.

Nonaka, I., & Takeuchi, H. (1995). *The knowledge creating company*. New York: Oxford University Press.

Pinchot III, G. (1986).: Intraprenörerna. Entreprenörer som stannar i företaget. *Svenska Dagbladet*. Södertälje.

Pisano, G. (1994). Knowledge, integration, and the locus of learning: An empirical analysis of process development. *Strategic Management Journal 15(1)*, 85–100.

Politis, D. (2005). The process of entrepreneurial learning: A conceptual framework. *Entrepreneurship Theory and Practice, 29*(3), 399–424.

Postle, D. (1993). Putting the heart back into learning. In D. Boud, R. Cohen, & D. Walker (Eds.), *Using experience for learning*, (pp. 33–45). Buckingham: SRHE & Open University Press.

van Propta, G. (2002). *Entrepreneurial learning*. EIM Business & Policy Research, Scientific Analysis of Entrepreneurship and SMEs-paper N200216. Zoetermeer.

Rae, D. (2004). Practical theories from entrepreneur's stories: Discursive approaches to entrepreneurial learning. *Journal of Small Business and Enterprise Development, 11*(2), 195–202.

Rae, D. (2005). Entrepreneurial learning: A narrative-based conceptual model. *Journal of Small Business and Enterprise Development, 12*(3), 323–335.

Rae, D., & Carswell, M. (2001). Towards a conceptual understanding of entrepreneurial learning. *Small Business and Enterprise Development, 8*(2), 150–158.

Sfard, A. (1998). On two metaphors for learning and dangers of choosing just one. *Educational Researcher, 27*(1), 4–13.

Shane, S. (2000). Prior knowledge and the discovery of entrepreneurial opportunities. *Organization Science 11*, 448–469.

Shane, S. (2001). Technological opportunities and new firm creation. *Management Science 47*, 205–220.

Shepard, D.,. & DeTienne, D. (2005). Prior knowledge, potential financial reward, and opportunity identification. *Entrepreneurship Theory and Practice 29*(1), 91–112.

Shotter, J.. (1993). *Conversational realities: Constructing life through language*. London: Sage.

Smilor, R. (1997). Entrepreneurship: Reflections on a subversive activity. *Journal of Business Venturing, 12*(5), 341–346.

Spender, J.-C., & Grant, R. (1996). Knowledge and the firm overview. *Strategic Management Journal, 17*(Special Issue), 5–10.

Steyaert, C., & Katz, J. (2004). Reclaiming the space of entrepreneurship in society: Geographical, discursive, and social dimensions. *Entrepreneurship and Regional Development, 16*(3), 179–196.

Tynjälä, P. (2008). *Perspectives into learning at the workplace. Accepted to be published in Educational Research Review*.

Urwyler, M. (2005). *Opportunity identification and exploitation: A case study of three Swiss-based software companies*. Doctoral dissertation. University of St. Gallen.

Vygotsky, L. (1978). *Mind in society: The development of higher psychological processes*. Cambridge MA: Harvard University Press.

Wenger, E. (1998). *Communities of practice: Learning, meaning, and identity*. Cambridge: Cambridge University Press.

Wenger, E. (2000). Communities of practice and social learning systems. *Organization, 7*(2), 225–246.

# Part IV
# Transformations in Work and Education Systems

# Chapter 10
# How Workers Cope with Changes in Working Life: Adaptation Strategies

Krista Loogma

## Introduction

The ability to adapt to rapid and permanent changes and to learn is inseparable aspects of contemporary working life. In Estonia as in most Eastern and Central European countries changes in working life have been influenced by the systemic transformation of society. These changes in the economy, labour market, and in all societal institutions have been fast, conflicting and complex. In this transformation process two different, yet interconnected patterns can be detected.

On the one hand this transformation can be seen rather as 'revolutionary' change, as bifurcation, (Laszlo, 1994), accompanied by the discontinuity of most of the principles and trends in the economy and society, and not as a restructuring of the previous (communist) system. On the other hand, the changes in working life are influenced by 'evolutionary' changes, the global spread of the post-industrial/information era, driven by technological change, including the adoption of integrated and computer-based technologies, a service-orientation in production, and widespread social and cultural changes. These patterns of change have led to widespread and extremely complex changes in different aspects of working life.

From the perspective of individual employees this means having to learn and develop work-related capabilities to respond among other things, to the increasing requirements to flexibility and mobility at work. Also, employees have to consider what is needed in the present-day working environment, while looking out for opportunities to advance their own work-related development and career.

In this context the problem arises: how have employees coped with the contradictory demands of the labour market and what kind of strategies have they applied? The research interest in this article is also in the question of how the learning, development and mobility pattern of the mid-level employees are related to their identification with work. In this chapter I discuss empirically identified learning and coping strategies of mid-level employees. I argue that the meaning of work and the work identity related to it constitute a 'space of values', where the employees'

K. Loogma (✉)
Tallinn University, Institute of Educational Research, Tallinn, Estonia
e-mail: krista.loogma@tlu.ee

M.-L. Stenström, P. Tynjälä (eds.), *Towards Integration of Work and Learning*,
© Springer Science+Business Media B.V. 2009

learning, development of work-related capabilities and mobility takes place. The empirical analysis focuses on two occupational groups demanding of medium level skills in Estonia: specialists in the IT sector and skilled workers in the timber and wood processing sector.

The Estonian IT sector, being young both in terms of enterprises operating in the field and the people working in them, is expanding rapidly in terms of business volume as well as in employment figures. Generally, there is a lack of regulation as well as professional tradition in the field. The integration of technologies and the growing service component in IT products are the most important factors changing the need for competences. The wood processing sector is an industry with a long tradition in Estonia, based as it is on one of the most important natural resources in Estonia – timber. The main factors influencing the demand for competences have been far-reaching technological changes and a reorientation from Eastern to Western markets accompanied by a growing share of subcontracting work and enhanced quality standards.

In both fields many people worked without any special vocational/professional education and training. Structural reasons played an important role in this situation. In the IT sector, extremely rapid expansion caused a high demand for labour for which the education system was not prepared. The macro-context in the wood processing sector can be characterised rather by the consequences of the economic change (privatisation, reorientation from Eastern to Western markets, technological changes, rapid growth of employment in the service sector and decline in the agricultural sector, etc.). A large number of workers have had to change their occupation, moving from other industries and agriculture to the wood processing sector.

The approach to the research question is a constructivist one, with the employees' view as central. Therefore the methodology used is qualitative and based on empirical data, gathered mainly by open individual interviews with employees. The sample consisted of about 50 employees with different personal and organisational backgrounds from the two contrasting industries mentioned above: one of them was an 'old industry', the timber and furniture industry, and the second one a 'new industry', the IT industry.

## Theoretical Considerations

Proceedings from the main research task in this paper – to explain the adaptation patterns of workers in a situation characterised by a transformation in working life – I analysed the employees' concepts of learning at work, career and work identity and participation in communities of practice. A theoretical framework of this kind interrelates the above-mentioned concepts as the most significant factors in adapting to work-related change.

### *Learning at Work*

The theoretical aspects of learning in working environment or more specifically, learning at work can be studied according to the notions of experience (Dewey,

1938/1963; Ellström, 1999; Kolb, 1984) and participation (Lave & Wenger, 1991) in the process of developing occupational skills and competences. Similarly, Sfard (1998) outlines two complementary metaphors in order to explain the nature of learning – the acquisition metaphor and the participation metaphor. While the former sees learning in terms of knowledge acquisition, the latter sees learning as a process of participating in the community (Sfard, 1998). This entails, however, processes both of socialisation and identity construction. Accordingly, the learning theoretical approaches considered here are cognitive and behavioural as well as social-cultural and constructivist. The former primarily emphasise the output of learning in terms of the development of work-related skills and competence – while the latter concentrate on the various processes of socialisation from a lifelong perspective. The latter are also inseparably related to participation in various communities of practice and the development of a work identity (Brown, 1997; Lave & Wenger, 1991). The latter may, but need not, coincide with vocational/occupational identity.

Learning at work often has an informal and/or incidental character and is connected to the need to solve everyday problems on the job (Coffield, 1999, p. 5; Ellström, 1999). Thus learning at work is often a side effect of work, one which depends on circumstances/context, other people, the character of the work, including the learning potential of the work, the organisational concept of the work and other factors. The constructivist approach emphasises that learning is constructed discursively through communication processes at work, the character of learning is situated and connected with the negotiation, discussion, communication through which common understandings develop. (Billett, 2003; Brown, 1997; Lave & Wenger, 1991.)

Employees' learning at work is also observable from two closely related aspects: the organisational aspect and the employee biographical aspect. The biographical aspect is important here, since for employees, the development of skills and competences, commitment and work identity are continuous processes, changing over time, which enable the growth and accumulation of work-related experience and capabilities. The individual meaning of learning is tightly related to the biographical occupational development, expressed by the concepts of career and the closely related concept of work identity. The recent treatment of both career and work identity is based on constructivist premises, i.e. the individual's active participation in the construction of a career and work identity. (Collin, 2000; Collin & Young, 2000). The organisational meaning of learning can be expressed through a number of dynamic concepts, which describe and explain the great variety of ways of learning that exist in the working environment. The various meanings of organisational leaning are significant in this respect.

## *Career – Shift from Traditional Career to Boundaryless Professional Development Paths*

Different authors have identified several features and tendencies as characterising the principal changes that have taken place in the concept of career (Loogma,

Ümarik, & Vilu, 2004). Employees' work paths exceed the boundaries of a single firm and occupation, involving more or less in the way of career gaps and turns during an individual's professional or occupational career. This also means that career can be considered rather as an individual construction which gives meaning to the individuals' life and is more and more self-directed (Savickas, 2000; Young & Collin, 2000, p. 5). As Young and Collin (2000) claim, career means far more than just objective work paths and occupational movements; "it can involve self-identity and reflect individuals' sense of who they are, who they wish to be, and their hopes, dreams, fears and frustrations" (p. 5). The authors are thus suggesting that career should be regarded as two-sided concept involving both subjective elements, linked to self-image and identity, and objective moves, work positions, relations and style of life. Career is to be seen as an overarching construct that makes the individual's life meaningful (Collin & Young, 2000).

Sennett (1998) points to "no long term" as a central feature of contemporary working life. As traditional career paths become even rarer, so does the deployment of a single set of skills throughout the individual's working life. Watts (2000) suggests that career should be viewed as a lifelong progression in learning and in the work the individual is engaged in. According to Littleton, Arthur and Rousseau (2000) the accelerated pace of change has resulted a shift to 'boundaryless' careers. Sullivan (1999) distinguishes several features of boundaryless careers. The following features indicate the forms of boundary-crossing in different structural settings.

1. The most common of these is where the career involves a transition across organisational boundaries (Littleton, Arthur, & Rousseau, 2000). With increased job mobility and individuals' changing attitudes towards their careers, professional commitment may increasingly replace organisational commitment in the future. (Savickas, 2000, p. 58).
2. The second feature of the boundaryless career involves occupational boundary-crossing. The individual assesses his/her career opportunities and may be ready to change occupation in order to remain competitive on the labour market.
3. The third feature characterising boundaryless careers is the changing employment relationship. The new contract of employment is based on employability and employee responsibility rather than job security.
4. The importance of network relationships has been emphasised as the fourth feature of boundaryless careers. Social capital appears in a network of relationships with friends, colleagues and acquaintances that provide information and aid in the individual's career opportunities.
5. In addition, inter-role transitions (e.g. lateral promotions) that involve socialisation into new work teams and work cultures are more frequent than under the traditional career systems of the past.

## *Work Identity in the Light of Flexibility and Mobility Requirements*

Both organisations and individuals face the challenge of dealing with continuing demands for flexibility and mobility. While companies are adapting their management and organisational structures, demands on employees include continuous learning and adjusting to new technology, the work organisation and changing job profiles. The ability of employees to deal with these changes largely determines their future employability.

In all labour markets a still stronger identification with work is needed, together with a high level of work motivation and commitment, strong work ethics, good performance/high quality (Laske, 2001). The kinds of attitudes and values necessary for the commitment and identification of the individual with work are becoming more important and without that commitment, much learning cannot take place (Ashton, 1999, p. 68).

Habermas (1976) pointed to the importance of the integration of the personal and social identities. The personal identity should be persistent over the lifetime regardless of the different role systems (often with conflicting demands) people participate in during the course of their lives. At the same time, participation in different role systems leads to the formation and integration of the social identity with the personal identity (Habermas, 1976). Thus, the concept of identity refers to the connection between the personal and the social, to identification with particular social (e.g. professional) groups (us) and confrontation with other social groups (them). Work-related identity can be seen as part of an individuals' overall identity, expressed as professional/vocational identity (Kirpal, 2004).

Brown's dynamic model of occupational identity formation (Brown, 1997) points to three important considerations:

1. Continuity and change are two decisive elements that shape the processes of occupational identity formation over time. Thus, work-related identities should not be regarded as constant over time, but as dynamic. The acquisition of skills is not a simple linear process, but skills and knowledge, work roles, communities of practice and the identities they support are in a state of flux.
2. Individuals need to be acknowledged as actors in constructing their own occupational identity. Individuals do not simply take over pre-existing identities and working roles, but are actively involved in developing their identities and re-shaping communities of practice. However, identity construction process is not entirely subjective as individuals and their interactions with others are partly constrained by the structures and processes of the communities of practice in which they take place.
3. Occupational identities vary in the significance individuals ascribe to them. Developing an identity in a broader sense may carry far more relevance for a person than developing particular work-related attachments.

Lave and Wenger (1991, p. 53) emphasise the importance of regarding identities as "long-term, living relations between persons and their place and participation in communities of practice". Accordingly, identities, learning and membership in communities of practice entail each other. Furthermore, "learning and a sense of identity are inseparable: they are aspects of the same phenomenon" (p. 115). Identity development takes place along with changes in knowledge, skill and discourse as the newcomer becomes an old-timer or a real member of community of practice. Participation in communities of practice not only involves the development of knowledgeable identities, but it also entails the reproduction and transformation of communities of practice.

Multiple developments during the recent decades have contributed towards the fragmentation of the classical forms of work identities (Carruthers & Uzzi, 2000; Sennett, 1998). This trend has been accompanied by an individualisation of career paths that places greater emphasis upon the active construction of work identities by individuals themselves instead of making use of largely pre-structured identity patterns. This active construction develops through the interaction between changing structural conditions and institutional developments and personal self-definition.

The latter refers to an individual's ability "to build up new identities and integrate them with those overcome" (Habermas, 1976), or a "bricolage identity", by which is meant the decomposition of 'old' identities and their recombination into a new identity. (Carruthers & Uzzi, 2000). Individuals become reflective agents (Giddens, 1991) that are constantly re-assessing their roles and work-related identities in the light of external conditions. At the same time, they are involved in shaping those work structures and work processes.

In determining the extent to which the concept of identity includes to the connection between the 'social' and the 'personal' and a sense of sameness or difference with regard to particular communities/groups, group dynamics are of significant importance. In this context the demarcation lines drawn by employees can serve as an indicator of how conflicts that arise between work-related identity formation processes and the demands of work flexibility and mobility are personally perceived and dealt with. Despite considerable changes in work environments and growing demands for flexibility and mobility on the part of workers, identities at work are nevertheless connected with motivation and work commitment, thus making the specific socialisation processes at work very important. The primary source of identification, however, has often shifted from the occupation itself to the working team and knowledge (Casey, 1995).

## Different Patterns of Employees' Adaptation to Changes of Work

Even inside the IT sector we found different types of more institutionalised learning such as training courses, conferences, workshops, etc. The most dominant was self-directed learning while working. In many cases participation in formal learning is limited by insufficient employee learning resources, especially time for learning. In this respect the significance of all forms of informal learning, including, first of all, learning in project groups and in different informal networks like virtual networks and local communities of practice, that is, learning and consulting with other 'IT people', etc. is considerable. Among the most important were informal communication networks (club-type communities and web-based communities), which have a significant role in the self-development process. In these networks, everyone is a teacher and a student at the same time – learning from friends and acquaintances is a prominent informal way of learning, which at the same time impacts a sense of solidarity and belonging. Most of the specialists identified themselves as IT people, meaning that they feel free to move from company to company, from project to project, but remaining in the field of IT. This kind of mobility pattern is also seen as an important learning mechanism enabling the acquisition of different experience. Although the community of IT people is eager to learn using this kind of mobility pattern, they know that they have to be loyal to their current employer. The loyalty is understood here rather as confidentiality. It should be stressed that in a small country such as Estonia where 'everybody knows everybody' personal trust and reliability are essential within IT circles.

Learning was also understood as a process extremely closely connected with problem-solving in the course of everyday work, as new problems are constantly emerging. As a rule, IT specialists are free to choose their methods and tools for solving these problems. Although the changes taking place in the field were deemed inspiring and the employees considered learning as an inseparable and self-evident part of their work, some of them experienced the highly dynamic nature of working life and the 'race to keep up to date' as stressful. The cost of being an IT person is often overwork and lack of time for private life (Loogma, 2004).

For many IT specialists work is closely connected with their hobbies, as their current occupation has grown out of a strong interest in technology. The IT technology seems to be the core element of their occupational belonging while their interests are also focused around it. They feel that working with rapidly changing technologies is exciting and often this deep interest in computer-based technologies (usually originating from the early school years) is also the key to maintain a continuing motivation to learn. Many IT specialists stressed on the creative nature of their work, where every project and problem solving task is like a work of art. However, some claimed that for them work is a form of self-realisation and, consequently, if some other occupation gave them better possibilities to fulfil this need, they would be willing to change their field of activity (Loogma, 2004).

In the case of skilled workers in the wood processing sector as a whole the meaning of work is in practice highly diverse: anything from the Anglo-Saxon system of a job market for people with certain skills and sets of skills to a wider understanding of work prevalent in Germany where besides skills, work ethics, commitment, the sense of belonging to an occupational / vocational group are also important.

The skilled workers divided themselves rather narrowly into two groups with different understanding of work. One was of the joinery-kind (craftsperson) and the other was of the machinery-kind. The former were considered to be more creative while the latter were understood as doing a job based more on routine. For joiners, i.e. skilled workers with initial VET, work was a creative process, but also a way to earn a living and a source of independence and stability. They considered the core element of their occupation be the material – wood 'which is nice and warm' and has the potential to be formed into different products. They also reported that the skills utilised at work are transferable to their personal lives and homes and vice versa. On the machinery side, many of the skilled workers in wood processing sector had earlier worked in the agriculture sector and thus had had to re-define their occupational or vocational belonging. Although in these cases previous learning and working experience can have only an indirect impact on their performance of their new tasks, that experience can be an important factor helping these workers legitimise their new work activity. As one worker said: "Machines are machines. It makes no difference, whether the machine is a farming machine or a machine designed for working with wood". For workers without initial training in the timber and furniture sector, the main meaning of work seems to be more 'instrumental' – work is considered as a mean of earning a living and achieving stability of employment. The latter may partly explain their motivation to learn new skills when required. Many of those 're-defined' workers regarded their work rather as a 'job' than a 'vocation', i.e. thus referring rather to a set of specific skills than to a broader concept of competences. (Loogma, 2004.)

Generalising the empirical data, various strategies of adaptation to work-related change emerge. From the aspect of employee's learning and development, these strategies fall into two categories. The first is related to the employee's occupational identity and motivation. In this category occupational identity is based on the creative and interest-centred meaning of work which as a rule closely binds the employee to the core element of work, on which the motivation of work and learning and the work identity are also based. In turn, work motivation is based on working conditions and the economic meaning of work or other extra-work factors which need not be closely related to the core element of work. Obviously, the patterns of the meanings of work were interwoven in a specific manner in the discourse of every individual employee. In the second category, the various strategies can be differentiated according to goals related to the employee's occupational development and career/movement, which also determine the direction and scope of the employee's learning. Three principal ways/strategies of adaptation – passive, flexible and transgressive – were identified (Table 10.1) (Loogma, 2004).

*Passive adaptation*, alongside motivation, encompasses the work-related capability of employees, which is related to the minimum requirements of the employer, primarily the acquisition of relatively specific technical skills. Such adaptation was observed in the case of timber workers in relation to the redefinition of their work, both within the interest-centred and economic meanings of work. The latter was primarily related to forced movement during the restructuring of the economic system from other sectors to timber processing, where the employees were only barely able to adapt to the minimum requirements. A typical representative of this form of adaptation in the case of IT specialists is the 'geek', who is barely able to supply the requirements of the employer and is unable to adapt to the demand for social skills. Learning in this case is experiential, oriented to the acquisition of specific technical skills. The motives for learning may come from too strong relationship with the core of work or from its complete absence, the first being connected to stability seeking and the second to the phenomenon of alienation from work.

Patterns of *flexible* adaptation were found in both groups of employees. This type of adaptation represents the typical adaptation of a medium-level employee, who has a horizontal development path orientation, despite having the flexibility

| | Work identity related to interest and creation-centred meaning of work | Work motivation based on economic meaning of work |
|---|---|---|
| Passive adaptation | Aim of stability, holding on to the core elements of the work, keeping one's job and satisfaction with work. Learning mainly for development of narrowly defined technical skills. | Minimal learning to keep employability, dissatisfaction with work and alienation. |
| Flexible adaptation | Aim to become a good professional with varied experience. Mainly horizontal mobility and learning to widen professional skills profile, observing latest development in the professional field. Development of general skills. High functional flexibility, high mobility between organisations, yet holding to the core of the work and preserving independence. | Learning to widen the skills profile. Aim of stability, often putting up with forced situation like working shifts or "serfdom". |
| Transgressive adaptation | Work is a mean to achieve broader aims in life, for example self development. Learning can be conceptualised as "transgressive" when it is accompanied by integration of theoretical and practical knowledge. Mainly vertical mobility, to the management or entrepreneurial positions or movement into a different field of activity. | Aim is to keep one's job and achieve better working conditions. Transgressive learning and integrations of theoretical and practical knowledge. Putting up with unsatisfactory working conditions for economic reasons or the construction and adoption of new work identity and new pattern of skills and competences. |

to acquire the necessary general skills and competence. The primary goal in case of this adaptation strategy is to become a capable specialist, a professional in the field. This seeking in turn is related to a vocation-centred identity and unwillingness to lose contact with the core element of the work. Such an employee is generally a 'normal' employee, whose flexibility and ability to adapt, as a general rule, coincide with the employer's demands. Learning in such cases is also experiential, but in one way or another related to formal education and learning, involving both generalised and theoretical knowledge, and therefore the development of general skills and competencies. On the other hand, this pattern includes cases, where employees, having moved to the wood-processing industry from other sectors, have accepted the new situation for economic reasons and have adapted to it, displaying sufficient flexibility in the process of adaptation.

Cases of *transgressive adaptation* were also observed in both sectors. Transgression primarily means a development path, where the employee is no longer able to hold on to the core element of the work and thus retain her/his previous work identity. By transgressional adaptation is meant the transgression of a limit/boundary constructed by employees as members of certain communities of practice, combined with the demands of the employer. Transgression leads to transgressive learning, reconstruction of meanings and work-related capabilities. The transgressor, while adapting, has to dismantle his/her previous work identity and patterns of capabilities and to construct them anew. Accordingly, a former tractor driver may become a timber worker or a timber worker turn in a small entrepreneur, an IT specialist whose skills as an IT specialist have been lost in the opinion of former colleagues become a sales consultant or IT manager, (employees with mainly managerial and communicative functions). In these cases the choice made is generally explained rationally, continuity and common elements being found between the previous and current occupation/work. It is important from the flexibility aspect, that in the process of redefinition, employees find significant elements which overlap with the meaning of their previous work, on the basis of which they can construct a new identity, learning and developing their skills.

Transgressive movements can be bi-directional. In the wood-processing industry it was related to movement from other sectors to that industry, and, on rare occasions, was accompanied by the development of a new work-related self-definition and high (new) professionalism. In contrast, there were IT specialists, who were oriented to vertical movement – either to management positions, sales consultants, etc. – primarily pursuing other ambitious goals (higher position, higher salary or self-development).

## Conclusions

One of the consequences of the different structural forces and global changes in working life can be seen in the work identity – flexibility dilemma, that workers have to solve. The work identity of employees and the related sense of identification can either promote or obstruct learning and development as well as the career opportunities of employees, in as much as learning and development are related to flexibility and are oriented, in addition to specific, technical skills, towards the acquisition of general skills and competencies.

An important factor that can influence employees' motivation and work identity is the 'core of the work', which is specific to the field of activity that the employees' interests, motives and work identity are related to. In the case of IT specialists the core of the work can be considered to be information technology itself; in the case of timber and wood processing skilled workers the core of the work is the material – timber.

Where there is high mobility there is less identification with the particular company or occupation. This is especially obvious in the case of IT specialists. Specialists who identified less with technology possessed more positive attitudes towards flexibility and often connected it with work satisfaction, which is related to the readiness to broaden one's skills profile, in turn broadening one's career opportunities. If individuals can be regarded as active agents shaping their careers and develop their identities, employees themselves are involved in constructing boundaries to their careers. While for specialists with a strong technical/hacker (Himanen, 2003) identity the career paths are more restricted and identity centred around its technological core of work, a 'transgressor' serves as an excellent example of the boundaryless career as these individuals are ready to let the core of their identity go (Loogma, Ümarik, & Vilu, 2004). Moving between companies should be regarded as a manifestation of the boundaryless career, where the field of mobility constructed by individual is the IT field as a whole, transcending single companies or narrow occupational roles.

Generally, during and after the recent period of rapid transformation, coordination of the economy and education, more specifically employment and VET in Estonia, has been left mainly to market mechanisms. Although this general neo-liberal policy context has created different models of employee adaptation the central 'means' used to cope with changes in work has been informal learning. However, this kind of adaptation pattern may have consequences for the sustainability of economic development.

The contradiction between the large share and high significance of informal learning in the domain of work-related learning and the fact that it goes unrecognised or is taken for granted, together with the limited learning resources available causes a large amount of stress on the system. This situation demands that VET and labour policy must take measures to legalise informal leaning – to bring it out, recognise and certify it.

The weakness of the management became apparent in case of many organisations, although in different ways (inability to plan work, to manage a team, absence of management-related knowledge and skills, etc.). The provision of extensive learning in the working environment would certainly require a strong management and organisational culture, one which would help to orient the employees and to learn work ethics. It would therefore be necessary to significantly reinforce pedagogy and training in the working environment.

The knowledge circulating in the workplace is largely practical, acquired within the daily routine and does not usually include broader theoretical knowledge or reflection on the results of leaning from experience. This situation is unlikely to create a good foundation for an innovative leap forward in the economy.

Market mechanisms seem to be inadequate to the task of bridging the two main gaps between the economy and education: the inadequacy of general skills and competencies and work ethics. These needs have been written into the vocational guidelines, but to make them work requires measures to strengthen the professional associations and various communities of practice which play a decisive role in the formation of the work identity.

# References

Ashton, D. (1999). Skill formation: Redirecting the research agenda. In F. Coffield (Ed.), *Learning at work* (pp. 61–69). Bristol: University of Bristol, The Polity Press.

Billett, S. (2003, September). *Workplace pedagogic practices: participatory practices and individual engagement.* Paper presented at the EERA Conference, Hamburg, Germany.

Brown, A. (1997). A dynamic model of occupational identity formation. In A. Brown (Ed.), *Promoting vocational education and training: European perspectives* (pp. 59–67). Tampere: University of Tampere.

Carruthers, B., & Uzzi, B. (2000). Economic sociology in the new millenium. *Contemporary Sociology, 29*(3), 486–494.

Casey, C. (1995). *Work, self and society after industrialism.* London: Routledge.

Coffield, F. (1999). Introduction: new forms of learning in the workplace. In F. Coffield (Ed.), *Learning at work* (pp. 1–6). Bristol: The Polity Press.

Collin, A. (2000). Dancing to the music of time. In A. Collin & R. A. Young (Eds.), *The future of career* (pp. 83–100). Cambridge: Cambridge University Press.

Collin, A., & Young, R. A. (Eds.). (2000). *The future of career.* Cambridge: Cambridge University Press.

Dewey, J. (1938/1963). *Experience and education.* The Kappa Delta Pi Lecture Series. London: Collier MacMillan Publishers. (Original work published 1938)

Ellström, P.-E. (1999, November). *Integrating learning and work: Problems and prospects.* Paper presented in the TSER FORUM Workshop 'Learning in Learning Organizations' at the University of Evora, Evora, Portugal.

Giddens, A. (1991). *Modernity and self-identity: Self and society in the late modern age.* Stanford: Stanford University Press.

Habermas, J. (1976). Können komplexe Gesellschaften eine vernünftige Identität ausbilden? [Can complex societies form a reasonable identity?]. In J. Habermas (Ed.), *Zur Rekonstruktion des historischen Materialismus* (pp. 92–126 ). Frankfurt am Main: Suhrkamp.

Himanen, P. (2003). *Häkkerieetika ja informatsiooniajastu vaim* [Hacker ethics and the spirit of the information era]. Tallinn: Kunst.

Kirpal, S. (2004). Theoretical considerations. In S. Kirpal, (Ed.), *Work identities in Europe: Continuity and change.* Final Report of the 5th EU Framework Project FAME (ITB Working Paper Series No 49, pp. 6–17). Bremen: University of Bremen.

Kolb, D. A. (1984). *Experiental learning. Experience as a source of learning and development.* New Jersey: Prentice Hall.

Laske, G. (2001). Profession and occupation as medium of socialisation and identity formation. In G. Laske, (Ed.), *Project papers: Vocational identity, flexibility and mobility in the European labour market (FAME).* (ITB Working Paper Series No. 27, pp. 11–37). Bremen: University of Bremen.

Laszlo, E. (1994). *Vision 2020. Reordering chaos for global survival.* Amsterdam: Gordon and Breach.

Littleton, S. M., Arthur, M. B., & Rousseau, D. M. (2000). The future of boundaryless careers. In A. Collin & R. A. Young (Eds.), *The future of career* (pp. 101–114). Cambridge: Cambridge University Press.

Lave, J., & Wenger, E. (1991). *Situated learning: Legitimate peripheral participation.* Cambridge: Cambridge University Press.

Loogma, K. (2004). *The meaning of learning at work in the process of workers' adaptation to work changes.* (PhD Thesis, in monograph). Tallinn: Tallinn Pedagogical University Publishing.

Loogma, K., Ümarik, M., & Vilu, R. (2004). Identification – flexibility dilemma of IT specialists. *Career Development International, 9*(3), 323–348.

Savickas, M. L. (2000). Renovating the psychology of careers for the twenty-first century. In A. Collin, & R. A. Young (Eds.), *The future of career* (pp. 53–68). Cambridge: Cambridge University Press.

Sfard, A. (1998). On two metaphors for learning and the dangers of choosing just one. *Educational Researcher, 27*(2), 4–13.

Sennett, R. (1998). *The corrosion of character: The personal consequences of work in the new capitalism.* New York: Norton.

Sullivan, S. E. (1999). The changing nature of careers: A review and research agenda. *Journal of Management, 25*(3), 457–484.

Watts, A.G. (2000). The new career and public policy. In A. Collin & R. A. Young, (Eds.), *The future of career* (pp. 259–275). Cambridge: Cambridge University Press.

Young, R. A., & Collin, A. (2000). Introduction: Framing the future of career. In A. Collin & R. A. Young (Eds.), *The future of career* (pp. 1–17). Cambridge University Press.

# Chapter 11
# Connections of School- and Work-Based Learning in the Netherlands

Jeroen Onstenk

## Introduction

The Dutch VET system is under constant pressure to respond to a changing economy. It has been adapting to fundamental changes in job demands as well as to a strongly growing number of vocational students. The qualification system has been thoroughly restructured and various vocational learning paths and school types (the apprenticeship system and school-based vocational education; initial and adult vocational education) are integrated into a single vocational education and training (VET) system. New content as well as new didactics for vocational schools have been implemented to respond better to the needs of a changing economy and labour market. Regional VET Colleges are developing from industrial training centres into innovative learning centres, in order to prepare students better for working life and lifelong learning. In order to reach that objective, the challenge facing the Dutch system is making qualification structures, educational targets and new educational practices, like problem-based learning, more convergent, rather than the current state of tension or even contradiction.

In this context, apprenticeships were rediscovered in the late nineties, but with new learning and working arrangements and with new connections between school and work-based learning. Apprenticeship has become part of an elaborated system of vocational education, which includes two main pathways with different combinations of school and workplace learning. With the expansion of the objectives of vocational education to include effective problem solving on the job and work process knowledge, workplace learning has become more important. However, the quality of workplace learning remains a topic of heavy debate. There are two main issues: the quality of workplace learning and the connection between workplace and school-based learning as part of the integrated development of vocational competences. The first is tackled by updated regulation, by government as well as by national bodies and employer organisations, designed to uphold the quality of training in apprenticeship in terms of content, guidance and assessment. New content

J. Onstenk (✉)
INHOLLAND Professional University, Netherlands
e-mail: jeroen.onstenk@inholland.nl

M.-L. Stenström, P. Tynjälä (eds.), *Towards Integration of Work and Learning*,     187
© Springer Science+Business Media B.V. 2009

and didactics at school, as well as different and more intensive patterns of interaction between employers and vocational schools, are being developed to improve
the connection between learning in school and in the workplace. Working together,
employers and vocational schools strive for high-quality outcomes. The aim of this
chapter is to describe workplace learning in the Dutch VET. An additional focus is
on the quality of the connections between workplace and school-based learning.

## The Dutch VET System

Vocational education in the Netherlands consists of three layers (Cedefop, 2004).
It starts very early (at age 12) with prevocational education, the lower strand in
compulsory education, continues in senior secondary vocational education, and cul-
minates in vocational, or rather professional, higher education (in professional universities). More than 65% of all youngsters in compulsory education (age 12–16)
attend prevocational education. Most of them continue after graduation in senior
secondary vocational education. However, some 15% enter the labour market directly, most of them without a diploma, running considerable risks of becoming
unemployed within a few years (OCW, 2005).

Senior secondary vocational education (MBO) is the core of the Dutch VET
system. Recent vocational educational policies in the Netherlands show some fundamental contradictions. In the Vocational and Adult Education Reform Law (WEB)
of 1996, policy makers made an explicit choice in favour of the development of
an integrated system of vocational and adult education, rather than tearing down
system boundaries between general and vocational education at the secondary level,
as was done elsewhere in Europe. The law established secondary vocational education as an integrated national system (Onstenk, 2001, 2004). Different types of
schools, branches, curriculum designs as well as combinations of school-based and
work-based learning were integrated under a single national qualification structure.
A limited number (around 40) of large Regional VET Centres (ROC) was created,
replacing the huge number (around 400) of small vocational schools. The law gave a
great deal of autonomy and responsibility to regional colleges and national training
bodies, with the objective of building a flexible and effective VET system. This
objective, however, is still far from realised (Nijhof & van Esch, 2004).

While the 1996 law had hardly been implemented, policy priorities changed
in the new millennium. In order to fulfil European policy agreements made in
Lisbon, 2000 to answer the challenges of the global economy by becoming a competitive knowledge society, Dutch VET policies shifted from a focus on secondary
vocational education to a focus on integrating the 'vocational educational column'
from prevocational to professional higher education. Whereas the WEB was designed for the horizontal alignment of Vocational and Adult education, emphasis was now put on vertical vocational learning careers, and on crossing system
boundaries between prevocational, senior secondary vocational and higher professional education. Completion of (rather than enrolment in) vocational courses and

continuous learning in higher education became important policy topics. The first objective was to increase the number of students in higher professional education, by encouraging continuous learning after completion of the higher strands of secondary vocational education. The second objective was to effect a reduction in early school leaving. The number of students leaving secondary vocational education without a qualification remains a source of concern. Between 25 and 35% leave the system without any qualification (OCW, 2005). In order to counter this state of affairs, in 2006 the law regarding compulsory education was amended, to make sure that no one leaves the vocational educational system without at least a level 2 diploma of secondary vocational education (also called 'starting qualification').

The WEB created, for the first time in the Netherlands, an integrated system of senior secondary vocational education (MBO), bringing the formerly separate systems of school-based VET and apprenticeship into a single system (Onstenk, 2001). The national qualification structure lists all the qualifications for which vocational courses can be offered. It is designed and maintained jointly by vocational colleges and national bodies with employers' and employees' representatives. The MBO provides learning programmes to young people, starting at age 16, to develop their skills and increase their employability. Originally, students could choose between more than 700 vocational courses, offered by regional VET centres. Training programmes and qualifications are offered in four different fields: technology, commerce/administration, services/health care and agriculture. Training courses are provided within the framework of the national qualification structure for vocational education at four different levels, ranging from pre-basic and basic vocational training (1–2 years) to middle management training (3–4 years). Level IV qualifications give entry to higher professional education. Transfer of those with MBO qualifications to higher professional education (HBO) has increased sharply in the last 15 years. The levels differ in complexity, varying from assistant's training to middle management training and specialist education.

The qualification structure has, since 1999, been undergoing extensive remodelling towards competence-based descriptions (Onstenk, 2004), in order to meet society's needs for modern and flexible employees. The number of qualifications on offer has diminished, from more than 700 to around 250. New qualifications are broadly defined and robust. They indicate in general terms what knowledge, skills and attitudes are needed for the occupation, but they do not prescribe in detail the design of actual VET courses. Colleges and companies have more opportunities for tailoring education to the needs of regional companies as well as to the preferences and abilities of students.

## Workplace Learning in VET

The WEB also made workplace learning an essential part of every senior secondary vocational education and training course. There are two 'learning pathways', a school-based pathway and a work-based, apprenticeship pathway. Both pathways combine learning in school and in workplaces, but in different quantities. The school-based pathway includes workplace learning for 20–60% of the total curricular time. Before the WEB, workplace learning in school-based VET could vary between 12 weeks (in a 3-year curriculum in administrative training) to a year (in a four-year course in high level technical vocational education). Since then, the actual amount has risen: In 2005 the average over all courses in all sectors was more than 50%. The background to this is the growing value attached to workplace learning, both for the motivation of students and for the attainment of objectives with regard to problem solving and work process knowledge (Onstenk, 2003). The work-based pathway includes apprenticeship in a company for at least 60% of the time, as well as a one or two day school release. In both strands, regional VET Centres deliver the school-based component, but bear responsibility for the whole learning process as well as for awarding the qualification. Apart from quantity, these pathways differ with regard to the role and responsibilities of companies. In the school-based pathway, participants are students enrolled in college. They participate in workplace learning during a couple of shorter and longer (between 3 months and a whole year) periods in a number of different labour organisations. In the work-based pathway, apprentices are as a rule employees who combine part-time education with an apprenticeship in a company. There is, however, a growing number of apprentices, with or without an employment contract, in collective training facilities. For example, in the building industry almost all apprentices are employed by so called Regional Practice Centres, established by cooperating building companies, that can hire an apprentice for specific tasks or periods.

Since the 1950s the number of apprentices has been rising, although with fluctuations related to the economic cycle. Also, the average age of apprentices is rising. In 2004 more than 50% of apprentices – in the regular VET system – were over 27 (OCW, 2005). Since around 2002, the number of apprentices seems to have fallen (Table 11.1), partly as a result of structural changes in the Dutch economy, partly as a result of educational policies, which favour school-based education. The number of apprentices is declining, especially in the technical field, which was the traditional stronghold for apprenticeship. Nowadays, the caring and health sectors account for most apprentices, with the result that more women are taking part in apprenticeships. These are also sectors in which it has become common practice that both pathways can lead to the same qualification and job. In the technical and economic sectors apprenticeship and school-based courses train for different level jobs. Apprenticeship train for lower level jobs, with some specialist courses on a higher level. School-based education, although it, too, prepares for lower level jobs, focuses mainly on the higher levels. Participation in the school-based pathway has

**Table 11.1** Participation in the MBO courses, in thousands, 1998–2005 (OCW, 2005, p. 85)

|                                 | 1998  | 2001  | 2003  | 2005  |
|---------------------------------|-------|-------|-------|-------|
| MBO – work-based                | 131.9 | 155.9 | 152.0 | 130.5 |
| MBO – school-based (full-time)  | 255.0 | 264.5 | 281.7 | 314.9 |
| MBO – school-based (part-time)  | 23.4  | 25.5  | 20.5  | 14.8  |

shown a sharp increase during the last two decades, with a particularly high growth rate in the economic and caring sectors. Many regional VET colleges are not very interested in promoting work-based courses. They prefer increasing the amount of practical learning in companies or in simulated environments as part of school-based pathways. An important argument is the greater freedom for the school in designing these kinds of trajectories. That is, students do not need to have an employment contract with the company, as in traditional apprenticeships. Also, colleges receive greater financial support for school-based courses. One problem with this tendency is the factual absence of the school at the workplace, and the danger that commitment of the company, as well as of the student, to practical learning is lower.

## New VET Didactics

There are promising attempts to counter these dangers by establishing more connective models, which are characterised by the new practice- and competence-oriented curricular approach. Curriculum content and didactic methods in vocational education are being challenged on several levels (Onstenk, 2001). Against the background of growing demands made by business as well as by students in vocational education, schools are innovating their courses, with respect both to content, responding to the new qualification structure, and to methods, responding to the need for broad occupational competence and learning skills, while also preparing students for an accelerating rate of change and a lifetime of learning. New insights into learning and instruction are in circulation. Students ask for differentiated approaches with regard to their backgrounds, characteristics, interests and learning styles. Societal developments make new demands on (future) citizens. Content and design in vocational education are also being challenged, more directly than general basic, secondary or higher education, by change in organisations and occupations. Practitioners must be able to select and interpret knowledge and information. They must be able to solve problems, plan and co-operate. In short, they need broad professional competence.

There seems to be some synergy among these demands. Didactic and learning theoretical insights, as well as students' motivational and learning styles and new job demands, all seem to call for different didactic approaches. These could be characterised by an emphasis on self-directed learning, the development of problem-solving competences, tailor-made education and individual coaching, and guidance, rather than frontal teaching in the classroom or simply 'sitting-next-to-Nelly' in the workplace. As a result, a whole range of different forms of practice learning exist in vocational education nowadays. These can be divided into two broad categories: the 'traditional' form of workplace learning (apprentice, trainee, intern) and the recent form of assignment-driven learning. Alongside these other forms of cooperation between education and businesses have come into existence, i.e. equal partnerships between schools and companies, mostly in network relations with other stakeholders in the region. Examples are: integrated practice centres in the region, facility sharing, the exploitation of common learning facilities and the adoption of departments of companies and institutions as learning units (i.e. learning isles).

## Prevocational Education

Workplace learning has also become more important in prevocational education. In 2001, the social partners and the Ministry of Education, Culture and Science signed an agreement on learn–work trajectories to strengthen learning in the workplace in preparatory secondary vocational education (VMBO) and to serve as a firm foundation for a successful career in vocational education at senior secondary or higher level. Another aim is to reduce the drop-out rate and to increase youngsters' chances of obtaining a basic qualification by offering them an education that puts more emphasis on working and learning in practice. This development is the result of closer cooperation between regional labour market authorities and companies and schools for prevocational education. In 2003, this agreement was formalised by law. The dual training and work placement routes in VMBO will be expanded in the coming years (Onstenk, 2003).

## Organisation of Workplace Learning: Connecting Partners

Since the implementation of the WEB, which gave workplace learning a more far-reaching and important place, there have been a lot of initiatives for quality monitoring and improvement. Companies offering apprenticeships or trainee learning places have to be certified, that is, fulfil formal requirements with regard to the content of work and availability of guidance. The WEB prescribes that the apprentice, the regional VET College, and the labour organisation have to sign a training–employment contract. This contract specifies the period for learning at the workplace, the required coaching of the apprentice by the labour organisation during that period, and the learning aims for that period. In school-based courses this does *not* include a labour contract.

The WEB defines the roles and responsibilities of the parties involved. The VET colleges are responsible for the implementation of the contract as well as for assessing whether learning aims are realised. The companies have to offer a learning environment and coach the apprentice. They have to ensure that there is opportunity to do the work that the course is training for and that there is a coach with pedagogical skills. They have to agree to communicate with the school about the performance of the student. In the workplace the apprentice is trained or coached by a practical instructor. Other employees are involved in case the apprentice asks them for help or observes them. A manager facilitates that learning process by assigning a practical instructor to the apprentice and offering the apprentice the opportunity to practice and to participate in work processes (Blokhuis, 2006). The practical work supervisor (coach) also evaluates the apprentice's work experiences and progress with the apprentice. In the regional VET colleges, teachers are expected to help apprentices in acquiring the requisite knowledge and skills. There also is a teacher (mentor) responsible for guidance and monitoring progress during the workplace learning periods, although this is mainly done from a distance, and with very little actual communication and interaction. Exchanging work and learning experiences with one's fellow apprentices also takes place at the college.

The national body of vocational education has an indirect responsibility. It represents the link between education and the organised business and industrial sectors. The first task of the national bodies is to translate changes in professional practice and new and rapidly changing requirements from the labour market into educational requirements (qualifications). Monitoring and promoting the quality of learning in professional practice is their second responsibility. National bodies have to ensure that there are sufficient learning places in certified companies. They encourage and facilitate employers to thoroughly train their apprentices. Companies offering apprentice and trainee learning places are regularly supervised by the national bodies.

Within the framework of the renewal of vocational education, the objective is that companies become actual partners in the design (co-design) and implementation (co-maker) of vocational education. This objective has turned out to be rather difficult to achieve; however, when it has succeeded, it has been evaluated very positively by schools as well as companies (Onstenk & Janmaat, 2006; Inspectorate of Education, 2007). In the reverse direction, within the framework of the knowledge-based economy, it is stressed that regional VET colleges could and should play a more active role in safeguarding the employability of staff and innovation in work processes.

## Quality of Workplace Learning

Although formal requirements are established and controlled, in implementing this structure there are two serious problems: the quality of workplace learning itself (content, guidance, assessment) and the quality of the connection between workplace and school-based learning. In many cases workplace learning seems to take place separated from – rather than connected with – learning at school (Onstenk, 2003). It appears to be difficult to guarantee quality standards for work placement companies. Learning in the workplace remains problematic. The problems concern both lack of co-operation between the parties involved and lack of control and evaluation of learning in the workplace by Regional VET Colleges as well as insufficient possibilities of organisations to provide high-quality learning opportunities and high-quality coaching (Nijhof & van Esch, 2004). In order to solve these problems, attempts are being made to improve communication and the alignment of theory and practice, as well as to focus on developing the guidance competencies of workplace learning mentors at school and practice instructors in labour organisations. A large survey conducted among apprentices, commissioned by the association of students and apprentices in vocational education, revealed that, although apprentices state that learning in the workplace in most cases is very satisfying, preparation for both work experience and school assignments, and the guidance offered by the school is lacking in quality (JOB, 2005). There is often poor co-operation and interaction between the parties involved, resulting in lack of information, insufficient relevance of learning assignments, and inadequate programming and tuning of theory and practice (Blokhuis, Jellema, & Nijhof, 2002).

Workplace learning, as part of a vocational education, is expected to deliver learning outcomes, as these are specified in the qualification document referred to in the training-employment contract. These objectives are expected to direct the activities conducted by the apprentice and his practice instructors and coach and – at a distance – school mentor. However, in actual workplace learning, more and different learning processes are often involved. The connection between a specific job and the more generic qualification is not always clear. The qualification profile includes a general description of an occupation related to it, describing vocational educational attainment goals and a specific learning job (Onstenk & Janmaat, 2006). But the diversity of practices constituted under a particular occupation as social practice, be it nursing, hairdressing or metal working, has to be taken into account (Billett, 2003).

Learning takes place during the performing of activities and participating in practice. Thus, learning possibilities depend on the structures, norms, values, and practices within workplaces. There is much 'reactive learning': The learning is explicit but takes place almost spontaneously in response to recent, current, or imminent situations without any time being specifically set aside for it (Eraut, 2000). It is powerful, because it suits the needs, expectations and 'life world' of those participating in it (Cullen et al., 2002), as opposed to learning planned by the school aiming at generalised objectives. However, because the trainee or apprentice is not aware of the learning process taking place, it is sometimes hard to describe the results of learning. The occurrence of a disturbance or something unexpected can be a strong source of learning, but such an event is by nature not planned. The result is that what, and when, someone learns at a workplace is neither always predictable nor only guided by explicitly formulated learning objectives. Learning is integrated with daily routines and triggered by an internal or external jolt. As such it is often not highly conscious, but haphazard and influenced by chance. It is an inductive process of reflection and action (Marsick & Watkins, 1990).

Nevertheless individual agency always shapes what constitutes, through workplace 'affordance', an invitation to participate in learning (Billett, 2002). In instruction as well as in performing work tasks, most of the time it is the practical instructor, the practical work supervisor or the teacher who is in control. They select what to do, when to do it, and how to do it. But because learning only takes place when the apprentice is in some way involved, workplace learning opportunities are never solely dependent on processes, structures or characteristics that are the exclusive property of an organisation or workplace. A working environment structured to facilitate learning will not necessarily guarantee that employees or apprentices 'take up' the learning opportunities that are offered (Billett, 2002; Fuller & Unwin, 2003). The apprentice always has a certain amount of control and room for self-directed or self-regulated learning (Straka, 2000).

Learning, like working, is not an individual process. Apprentices learn in a social context. The apprentice is part of a social environment and a community of practice like a team, a division, a labour organisation, or professional group. Vocational learning can be seen as a process of enculturation and participation in a community of practice whose members share activities and responsibilities (Wenger, 1998). Learning in the workplace presupposes that language is a part of practice, not only because an apprentice can learn from talk, but also has to learn to talk in order to get access to the community of practice (Guile & Griffiths, 2001). Lee et al., (2004) stress that learning involves narrative work because actual learning may be 'retrospective' or 'hypothetical' learning, achieved through a series of interwoven narratives concerning the self, biographical history, and work experiences, and practices.

Blokhuis (2006) in an in-depth analysis of apprenticeships in different sectors finds that practice coaches can play a stimulating role in building these narratives, if they are available during the entire period of workplace learning, really know what is required to perform tasks and participate in daily work processes, are well prepared and are willing to search for ways of interaction instead of just using fixed routines. However, he also finds that these conditions are not always fulfilled. Sometimes the formal and trained mentor is a foreman or an employee of the personnel department, whereas actual guidance and mentoring is performed by a non-trained experienced fellow worker (Onstenk & Janmaat, 2006). This is not necessarily a bad thing. Younger, less experienced workers may even be more effective coaches, presumably because in age they are closer to the apprentice, but also because, being less experienced, they remember their own learning process better (Blokhuis, 2006).

Blokhuis developed and tested guidance guidelines, supporting the interaction between apprentice, mentor, and other colleagues. In these guidelines four phases were distinguished:

1) Orientation to the task (select a task, discuss with the student/apprentice, determine existing relevant knowledge, discuss the learning process, give instruction)
2) Preparation for the execution of the task (discuss observations, prepare together, make necessary tools, and materials available)
3) Supervision and discussion of performance and progress
4) Improvement by repetition and reflection

Using these tools made practice coaches and fellow workers more aware of their guidance practices and enhanced the chances that high-quality consistent interaction would take place. These guidelines have now been adapted for a number of VET schools and learning companies. Also, to support connecting generic objectives and concrete learning experiences, it is proposed to enrich the accreditation process for Dutch apprenticeship places by developing a data bank in which both data on content and on guidance are registered. Formal requirements are to be supplemented with more substantial ones, which take into account organisational aspects and quality of guidance, while learning opportunities and possibilities for tailor-made trajectories will be monitored much more closely than at present (Onstenk & Janmaat, 2006).

## Quality of Connections Between Workplace and School Learning

In order to obtain optimal learning outcomes in VET pathways, combining school- and work-based learning, the abstract-codified knowledge acquired in vocational school has to be connected to actual practice in a specific workplace (Guile & Griffiths, 2001). In many cases the apprentice has to adjust his knowledge, skills, and attitudes in order to perform a task in the way the workplace wants, or is used to having it done. The connection between school- and work-based learning in apprenticeships is a persistent problem (Dehnbostel, Holz, & Novak, 1992; Walden, 2005). Workplace learning in Dutch VET, through apprenticeships as well as school-based pathways, offer good opportunities for what Fuller & Unwin (2003) call expansive participation, because – and if – facilities for deeper, more investigative, and imaginative learning are provided by the vocational school through learning programmes as well as the organisation of apprenticeships through language and artefacts such as documents, tools, assignments, books or personal development plans (Blokhuis, 2006; Onstenk & Janmaat, 2006).

However, learning opportunities vary widely among apprentices and workplaces, due to a combination of structural, cultural, and pedagogical factors. Some learning environments offer apprentices good opportunities to connect on- and off-the-job learning and knowledge and skill development through participation in multiple communities of practice and through possibilities for feedback. But, especially on the lower levels, apprentices can also find themselves in restrictive working environments, characterised by narrow 'on-the-job' training, no organisational structure for progression and gaining of new skills, and little access to a relevant knowledge-base (Fuller & Unwin, 2003; Onstenk, 2003). It then becomes very difficult to establish a meaningful relationship between work experience and formal programmes of study (Guile & Griffiths, 2001). The student or apprentice, in order to cross the boundaries between school and occupation, has to translate the language of the vocational school into the language of practice and vice versa. And he should be supported in doing so. But there are many differences with respect to what are seen as close and effective connections between learning in school and in the workplace. Poortman (2007) has shown in extensive case studies how often only spurious relationships exist between assignments as commissioned by the vocational school and actual work tasks. The connective model of work experience (Guile & Griffiths, 2001, 2003) calls for support for learners in their work experience programmes to understand and use the potential of school subjects as conceptual tools. They should be enabled to see the relationship between their workplace experience and their programmes of study as part of a whole. Such connective relations and reflexive activities are often not realised. Research shows that many practice coaches are unaware of the content and subjects taught at school (Onstenk & Janmaat, 2006), or that things taught at school are experienced by practice coaches as irrelevant for solving occupational problems (Poortman, 2007). The objective of deep learning by apprentices is difficult to realise. Many school teachers do not know enough about vocational practice to help them understand the links. There is often little preparation for or effective use of workplace learning experiences in school settings

(Onstenk & Janmaat, 2006; Poortman, 2007). There is lack of opportunity to experience different instances of vocational practice in order to understand the diversity of practice. By participating in different work organisations, it would be possible to develop a better understanding of the diversity of practices constituted under a particular occupation. Also, discussing experiences with other apprentices, supported by schools or companies, could help. However, too few teachers or coaches stimulate learners to consider the particular requirements of the different practices in which they have participated, in order to understand how vocational practice differs across workplaces (Billett, 2003). There is often little support for resituating existing knowledge and skills in new contexts.

In many new pedagogical concepts in Dutch VET, inspired by a short-sighted version of constructionist learning theory, workplace learning is often seen as a way to motivate students and apprentices for theory, but theory is not conceptualised as a way to better make sense of work experiences. As stated earlier, there is, however, a growing number of projects and practices where different patterns of interaction between employers and vocational schools are being developed, with the aim of improving the connection between learning in school and in the workplace and between developing competencies for new professionals and innovation in occupational practice (Onstenk & Janmaat, 2006). An example of this development is 'achievement steered learning' (*prestatiegestuurd leren*). Rather than sending students as apprentices to a company, learning is organised around a series of real work tasks and assignments, formulated by companies and carried out partly in school and partly in the company. This kind of learning involves the implementation of context-rich project tasks from professional practice. Assignments fulfil requirements with regard to learning objectives (relevance, complexity, developmental quality), and guidance and reflection on learning and work processes and outcomes are improved. Teachers have an active role in this guidance, provided they regularly visit the company and the student and discuss progress and results. Students can take their work assignments to school, rather than the other way around. It is also expected that working on real assignments will stimulate learning questions with regard to theory and learning motivation in students. In a curriculum of this kind students participate in a number of company-provided innovative assignments, covering the whole range of learning objectives. In some innovative projects, students themselves can choose the assignments they will perform. Thus they have an opportunity to steer their own learning process and outcomes, which means chance of developing in the direction which interests them most and suits them best. In this way from the outset, learning could become more provocative and motivating as well as meaningful.

## Conclusions

Workplace learning in both pathways in Dutch VET contributes to the development of broad occupational competency (Onstenk, 2001, 2004). Learning in different settings, work as well as school, offers a variety of possibilities to apply and develop knowledge and skills, contributing to the capacity to adapt what has been learned to different situations, which is a key benchmark of rich learning in vocational education (Billett, 2003).

Several organisational models have been developed to monitor and enhance the quality of workplace learning in Dutch VET, by schools, national bodies, and support organisations. Workplace learning is an important way to concretise and 'tailor' the new, broad qualifications in Dutch VET (Onstenk & Janmaat, 2006). Workplace learning in many cases can be rich and is also much appreciated by apprentices and students (JOB, 2005). But research shows that the quality of workplace learning is not guaranteed and that learning in school and in the workplace are not sufficiently integrated. Different kinds of learning outcomes (i.e. disciplinary knowledge, tacit knowledge and work process knowledge) are often badly connected.

For this reason VET innovation should focus on quality improvement and the connectivity of work-based learning by establishing quality criteria for work-based learning places, by enriching learning in the workplace and by designing curricula which integrate different learning places as well as learning experiences. Vocational schools in the Netherlands should pay more attention to structuring, supporting and assessing communication processes between school, company and students and apprentices about what could and should be learned in a specific learning workplace, what the apprentice would like to learn, how this fits into the requirements of the qualification, and, of course, what actually has been learned.

There is a need to establish more connective relationships between workplace learning and learning in school, in order not only to ensure that practice helps to explain the meaning and value of concepts but also, and more importantly, that concepts and theoretical knowledge can become a tool to interpret and change the world (Guile & Griffiths, 2003). Learners in the VET system, should from prevocational to higher education, and in both school- and work-based pathways, have ample opportunity to interpret new situations in the workplace in the light of concepts they have developed in school or earlier practice encounters as well as to deal with counter-interpretations. If apprentices and students are ill-prepared for contributing to the development of new knowledge or new social practices, there is the risk of limiting educational objectives to adaptation to existing practices, rather than developing an intellectual basis for criticising existing work practices and taking responsibility for working with others to co-shape work by conceiving, and where possible implementing alternatives (Guile & Griffiths, 2003). This limits the possibilities for the contribution of VET to personal growth as well as to social and economic development and innovation.

# References

Billett, S. (2002). Workplace pedagogic practices. *Lifelong Learning in Europe, 2*, 94—103.
Billett, S. (2003). Vocational curriculum and pedagogy: an activity theory perspective *European Educational Research Journal, 2*(1), 6–21.
Blokhuis, F. T. L. (2006). *Evidence-based design of workplace learning*. Enschede: University Twente.

Blokhuis, F., Jellema, M., & Nijhof, W. J. (2002). *De kwaliteit van de beroepspraktijkvorming. Een onderzoek naar praktijken en ervaringen met de beroepspraktijkvorming bij ROC Eindhoven* [The quality of work-based learning at Eindhoven VET College]. Enschede: Universiteit Twente.

Cedefop (2004). *Vocational education and training in the Netherlands. Short description. Revised edition.* Thessaloniki: Cedefop

Cullen, J., Hadjivassiliou, K., Hamilton, E., Kelleher, J., Sommerlad, E., & Stern, E. (2002). *Review of current pedagogic research and practice in the fields of post-compulsory education and lifelong learning: Final report.* London: ESRC.

Dehnbostel, P., Holz, H., & Novak, H. (1992). *Lernen für die Zukunft durch verstärktes Lernen am Arbeitsplatz* [Learning for the future by improved learning in the workplace]. Dezentrale Aus- und Weiterbildungskonzepte in der Praxis (Berichte zur beruflichen Bildung No. 149). Berlin/Bonn: BIBB.

Eraut, M. (2000). Non formal learning, implicit learning and tacit knowledge in professional work. In F. Coffield (Ed.), *The necessity of informal learning.* Bristol: The policy press.

Fuller A., & Unwin, L. (2003). Fostering workplace learning: looking through the lens of apprenticeship. *European Educational Research Journal, 2*(1), 41–55.

Guile, D., & Griffiths, T. (2001). Learning through work experience. *Journal of Education and Work, 14,* 113–131.

Guile, D., & Griffiths, T. (2003). A connective model of learning: the implications for work process knowledge. *European Educational Research Journal, 2*(1), 56–73.

Inspectorate of Education (2007). *Competenties: kun je dat leren?* [Competences: Can they be learned?] Utrecht: Inspectorate of Education.

JOB (2005) *Rapport JOB Monitor 2005* [Report on VET students Monitor 2005]. Amsterdam: Jongeren Organisatie Beroepsonderwijs.

Lee, T., Fuller, A., Ashton, D., Butler, P., Felstead, A., Unwin, L., & Walters, S. (2004). *Learning as work: Teaching and learning processes in the contemporary work organisation* (Learning as work research paper No. 2). Leicester: University of Leicester The Centre for Labour Market Studies.

Marsick, V. J., & Watkins, K. E. (1990). *Informal and incidental learning in the workplace.* London: Routledge.

Nijhof, W. J., & Esch, W. van (2004) *Unravelling policy, power, process and performance. The formative evaluation of the Dutch Adult and Vocational Education Act.* Den Bosch: Cinop.

OCW (2005) *Kerncijfers 2001–2005* [Core Figures Education 2001–2005]. Den Haag: Ministry of Education, Culture and Science.

Onstenk, J. (2001). Broad occupational competence and reforms in vocational education in the Netherlands. *Australian and New Zealand Journal of Vocational Education 9*(2), 23–45.

Onstenk, J. (2003). *Werkplekleren in de beroepsonderwijskolom. Naar een integratie van binnen- en buitenschools leren.* [Workplace learning in the vocational education column. Towards an integration of learning inside and outside of schools.]. Den Haag: Onderwijsraad.

Onstenk, J. (2004). Innovation in vocational education in the Netherlands. *VOCAL, Australian Journal of Vocational Education and Training in Schools, 5,* 20–24.

Onstenk J., & Janmaat, H. (2006). *Samen werken aan leren op de werkplek. Op weg naar co-design en co-makership van scholen en bedrijven.* [Working together on workplace learning. Towards comakership and codesign between schools and companies.]. Den Bosch: Cinop EC.

Poortman, C. J. (2007). *Workplace learning processes in senior secondary vocational education.* Enschede: University of Twente.

Straka, G. A. (2000). Conditions promoting self-directed learning at the workplace. *Human Resource Development International, 3*(2), 241–251.

Walden, G. (2005). Lernortkooperation und Ausbildungspartnerschaften [Learning-place cooperation and educational partnership]. In F. Rauner (Ed.), *Handbuch Berufsbildungsforschung* (pp. 254–261). Bielefeld: Bertelsmann Verlag.

Wenger, E. (1998). *Communities of practice: Learning, meaning, and identity.* Cambridge: Cambridge University Press.

# Chapter 12
# Work Experience Constructed by Polytechnics, Students, and Working Life: Spaces for Connectivity and Transformation

Maarit Virolainen

## Introduction

This chapter discusses the role of the connective model of work experience (Griffiths & Guile, 2004; Guile & Griffiths, 2001) in the context of higher education and identifies some of the limits and challenges that may be encountered in seeking to implement connectivity in practice. The question considered here is that of organising placements through cooperation between working life and the polytechnics[1] in Finland. The process of introducing connective links appears to be somewhat contradictory but nevertheless negotiable, with plenty of room for improvement. As one teacher in social and health care put it: "*Our students, when they go on a placement and they have been given the task, like, to figure out the central processes of the workplace, those main rehabilitation processes, this is a task the existing employees would not be able to do. That's what it is . . .And our students will have to, they won't get any guidance at the workplace, they will have to invent and think and that is what it is all about. And when we ask the employees, they say that students' competences don't meet their requirements, and our students are thinking about completely different things. They are thinking holistically about processes and actions at the workplace and then they are expected to open doors, and serve food and that sort of mechanical work.*"

This chapter seeks to scrutinise the contradictions in the relationship between polytechnics and working life. The question to be examined here is: How does

M. Virolainen (✉)
Institute for Educational Research, University of Jyväskylä, Jyväskylä, Finland
e-mail: maarit.virolainen@ktl.jyu.fi

[1] The Finnish polytechnics (ammattikorkeakoulu in Finnish, equivalent to the German Fachhochschule) were established gradually during the 1990s on the basis of the former vocational higher education colleges. Law for them was given in 2003. Since 2006 the rectors have been promoting the English translation, University of Applied Sciences (UAS in short). In this article, however, the old English translation, the officially approved 'polytechnic' is used. It has been recommended by the Ministry of Education and, in addition, many of the data were collected at a time when only the term polytechnic was used. The author, however, finds the polytechnics' ambition to be known as 'Universities of Applied Sciences' wholly legitimate.

the model of connectivity conform to the patterns of professional higher education? In order to get a multivalent picture of the relations between working life and polytechnics the theme is approached from the following perspectives. First, the relevance of paying attention to the model of connectivity on the level of higher education is discussed. The connective model and arguments for and against it on the level of higher education are briefly described. The demands set by the global economy for the innovative systems and capacities of the nation state are taken as the most serious argument in support of the importance of connectivity in higher education. The value of the model of connectivity is seen especially in the emphasis it places on the question of the quality of interaction in organising relations between working life and educational institutions: how to move on from adaptation to a more active and progressive approach both on the student and institutional levels. Second, the concepts of integration and transformation are specified. The differences between them are found to be important because they are related to genuine, long-standing questions regarding differences in learning at school and learning at work (see e.g. Lewis, 2005). They describe how the confluence of learning at work and learning at school, and how the confluence of theory and practice take place. They inherently anchor the discussion on either the individual or organisational level. Third, the framework of organising placements in the interface of school and work in the Finnish polytechnics is discussed from two points of view: first, the national development and, second, research results on the experiences of polytechnics, workplace supervisors and students. The latter includes results from both the national follow-up organised by the Ministry of Education and studies completed by Institute for Educational Research. Finally the connective model is discussed in relation to these results. The further exploration and elaboration of the model with an emphasis on actors and actor network is recommended.

## Connectivity in Higher Education

The connective model for organising work experience as a part of education has come up in the context of a European project aiming at a new agenda for the provision of work experience (Griffiths & Guile, 2004; Guile & Griffiths, 2001). The connective model is based on the studies of expertise and critiques of existing models. In the project four different models already practised on the upper secondary level were described and their main features were characterised. These models are briefly described in Chapter 2 of this volume.

In contrast to the models already in practice, the connective model claims to pay careful attention to the context, the situated nature of learning as well as the organisation of work to support students' learning and development and to give opportunities for developing boundary-crossing skills. The term connectivity refers to the pedagogic approach required to develop learners' knowledge and skills both horizontally and vertically. Horizontal development refers to the expansion of fields of know-how from task to task and field to field, i.e. expansion of everyday forms of knowledge, while vertical development means deepening one's insight theoretically and developing autonomous expertise (Griffiths & Guile, 2004; Guile, 2006; Guile & Griffiths, 2001).

The connective model takes as its starting point the assumption that workplaces are not stable. On the contrary, the world of work is constantly changing. Changing workplaces do not self-evidently facilitate interns' learning. A very competitive climate in working life may even create an obstacle to newcomers' learning at the workplace. Purposeful action, aiming at the mediation of knowledge and skills and providing room for students to negotiate their learning is therefore needed. From the point of view of the nation state, the constant quest for change and innovation spurred by technological development and globalisation is an important reason for the need to adopt a new perspective on how work experience is seen as a part of education, and how learners should be enabled to see themselves as active participants in communities of practice at work and at school (Guile & Griffiths, 2001). For students the concept of connectivity can open up the perspective of work-based learning as meaningful for lifelong and life-wide learning.

In the connective model the purpose of work experience is reflexivity. In other words, work experience is not so much about becoming attuned to the work environment, about getting key skills assessed, about co-development between education and work or about launching students into the world of work, as it is in other models. Learning in placements is seen as both vertical and horizontal development. Acquiring work experience is seen mainly to consist in the collaborative application and development of knowledge and skills, with the aim of boundary crossing and entrepreneurial ability. Supervisors are expected to manage the work experience in a way that supports developing and resituating learning. The outcome of placements is expected to be the development of polycontextual and connective skills. The role of educational institutions in organising placements aiming at connectivity is to form partnerships with workplaces in order to develop environments for learning (Griffiths & Guile, 2004; Guile & Griffiths, 2001).

## For and Against Connectivity

The connective model can be criticised on several grounds for its overly optimistic goals. First, it is often stated that it takes from 10 to 15 years to become an expert in a field. Therefore it may be asked whether it is realistic to expect very much, especially on the upper secondary level: Can youngsters really be expected to acquire enough field-specific knowledge and experience to engage in a developmental dialogue that challenges existing practices. Second, everybody does not need and cannot become an innovative expert; therefore it may not be realistic or reasonable to set very high goals for placements. Third, not all workplaces and work routines are in a state of constant change. Thus, in accordance with this criticism, setting such high goals for every placement will eventually lead to disappointment and exaggerate the importance of work experience for learning.

Here, the connective model is seen as a reasonable ideal for work placements, also on the level of higher education, because of the focus that it has on the developing learner and because it takes seriously the challenge of changing learning environments. While it is true that the connective model presents an ideal on the upper secondary level, it can be thought of as an empowering concept which underlines the role of educational institutions as communities of practice, especially with respect to the UK context of upper secondary education (Green, Wolf, & Leney, 1999; Raggatt & Williams, 1999). It underlines the role of communities of practice that keep up with the development of theories and practices in a field and take responsibility for their delivery and further development. There are several further reasons for considering the connective model as beneficial with respect to workplace placements in higher education. Firstly, studies on situated learning have shown how the newcomers gradually move from the periphery to the centre in taking responsibility for tasks in working communities (Lave & Wenger, 1991). It cannot be foreseen which individuals and at what pace will move from the 'periphery' towards the centre of activities and take responsibility for their direction. Therefore those for whom high quality workplace placements should be planned and delivered cannot be foreseen and it is thus better to try and provide all possible students with high quality placements. Secondly, studies have shown that in the information age and in the flux of technological change newcomers may have a sound command of the skills needed in some areas and these capabilities may be very relevant to the core processes of the working place (Fuller & Unwin, 2003). Despite their skills newcomers cannot know the actual social processes or particular core processes of a working community. Therefore learning the reflective dialogue, underlined in the connective model, between members of the working community and learners is extremely important. In the past, during the industrial age, the organisation of work could be expected to follow the hierarchical and bureaucratic patterns described by Weber, but in the lean and networked production units of the information age workers cannot take for granted that they will have a boss to tell them what to do and where they are located in the processes of work according to a flowchart (Beck, 1992; Sennett, 2003; Toiviainen, 2003). It is important to learn to negotiate about the object of work, what kind of demands it sets for learning and what learners' own opportunities are in relation to it and co-workers in the working process as a whole. The connective model underlines an entrepreneurial orientation and reflexivity.

## Connectivity for Innovation

Global economic competition and technological and environmental change, not only demand adaptation but also pro-activity from citizens and workers. In the Finnish innovation system, the polytechnics are expected mostly to play an intermediary role in the process of knowledge creation and knowledge diffusion, while the universities are expected to produce that knowledge (Schienstock & Hämäläinen, 2001, p. 162).

On the one hand public policy demands from polytechnics active involvement in change and innovation, while on the other it tries to limit its role in order not to disrupt the balance between universities and polytechnics. However, research on the adoption of technological innovations has shown that innovations often are not used in practice in the ways foreseen by their designers. There is no straightforward linear process from an individually produced invention to a wave of expected technological change. Rather, innovations are incrementally adopted in social interaction in various communities of practice which, in turn, deal with identities, competences, production, shared meaning and appropriation, and where learning takes place (Tuomi, 2002). Thus the division of innovative labour envisaged in public discussion is often too linear. In the cooperation between polytechnics, workplaces and universities it is possible to build communities of practice which can transform knowledge and innovate, but the dynamic interaction of the different participants in such communities of practice should rather be supported than limited in advance.

Employers and representatives of educational institutions need through dialogue to construct workplace placements as a learning environment. They need to build up a specific, locally situated community of practice through this dialogue. When they set their goals, models like the connective model are needed for picturing the aims of placements. The co-construction of individual and organisational competences takes place by trying to reach an understanding of common goals. This attempt gains from utilising tools, approaches or procedures that are mutually recognised and agreed on (Boreham, 2006). Cooperation on organising working practices as learning environments for trainees may thus lead to a process, one outcome of which may be a transformation of working practices. This can take place as a result of the dialogue, where tacit practices and different types of implicit and explicit knowledge are mulled over and resituated to fit the pattern and give it an explanation (Boreham, 2006). In the very same process, the identities of interns and other workers participating, alongside teachers and employees, as producers of the change are also transformed (Billett & Somerville, 2004).

## From Integration to Transformation

Transformation is the second concept defining the approach of this book. It is also the second important concept used in this chapter in defining the aims and outcomes of the processes that take place when a learner, an intern participates in working practices. Here transformation is understood as an outcome of a collective endeavour that takes place in a specific socio-cultural setting. The difference between integration and transformation is understood as a shift of perspective with respect to time and the focus of actors. For example, Eraut (2004) pictures the transfer of knowledge from education to the workplace as a multifaceted process where the extraction and integration of previous and new context-specific knowledge are two separate stages. Whereas a student may integrate different types of knowledge acquired at the workplace and at the polytechnic, the outcome of such changed patterns of thinking and action may be that they are transformed not only for the learning student but for the other actors in the workplace as well. Transformation can only take place in communities of practice and for shared physical and conceptual artefacts. It involves a shift in how objects of thought and natural objects are seen. Thus transformation here means denaturalising the change in the patterns of thought that takes place as intern starts a workplace placement, enters the workplace and becomes a participant in the community of practice in that workplace. This process is also about identity construction as described by Beach (2003), and his concept of consequential transition. Compared to integration the concept of transformation is understood as less individualistic, more interactive and action-focused, underlining the concrete changes that take place in the conceptual changes as well as more open to the disparities between actors. It takes the disparity produced by the heterochronocity of actors, as described by Beach (2003), as a positive engine of change. People come to a specific situation each with their own developmental background, history and understanding for what is to be performed. Transformation is understood as a phenomenon shared between several actors while integration is seen as referring to more individually completed conceptual and analytic procedures where (changed) patterns are linked and connected to larger wholes. Both concepts concern the emergence of cohesion between different types of knowledge, information, experience, and understanding but have a different emphasis on the outcome, whether it is individual or social in the first place. While the concepts used to define learning in the interfaces of work and learning are heavily contested, this differentiation between transformation and integration is sufficient to define the approach of this chapter and how transformation is the expected outcome of connectively organised work experience (see e.g. Fenwick, 2006; Hodkinson, 2005).

## The National Framework for Workplace Placements in the Polytechnics

Placements form a relatively big part of the curricula in Finnish polytechnics. Study programmes are defined as 210, 240 or 270 credit points (ECTS), each of which includes a placement worth 30–120 credit points which is the equivalent of 20–80 working weeks, depending on the programme in question (Salonen, 2007). From the polytechnics' point of view they represent a considerable number of contacts between working life organisations and polytechnics. In some estimates based on statistics collected by individual polytechnics themselves over half of the contacts made annually between working life organisations and polytechnics are related to placements.

The polytechnics were introduced into the Finnish educational system gradually during the 1990s. At present they number 29 and form the second pillar of Finland's dually organised system of higher education next to the 20 universities. Since the legislation on polytechnics in 2003 the focus of their development has shifted. Before 2003, (i.e. during the experimental phase) much effort centred around developing the degree curricula, foregrounding the rise in standards compared to the previous vocational higher education institutions, and educating the personnel. At this point many individual teachers produced dissertations related to the development of polytechnic education (e.g. Liimatainen, 2002; Raij, 2000; M.-L. Vesterinen, 2002; P. Vesterinen, 2001). Since 2003, the main objectives for polytechnics have been promoting regional development, constructing their own research and development profile and developing the quality assurance systems required by the common European educational policy. In addition, the Ministry of Education has supported developmental networks organised around specific themes, such as placements and work-related learning (Salonen, 2004).

The national network for developing placements in polytechnics has issued recommendations for their organisation (HARKE, see Salonen, 2007). These recommendations are quality development tools, that is, they supply polytechnics with a more uniform reference format for use, when they are communicating with working life organisations. They also offer a common language that enhances the exchange of models between polytechnics, and in and between their different fields. The recommendations include guidelines for good practices regarding where placement can take place, how, ideally, it is connected to the curriculum and other study components like bachelors' thesis, the duration of placement, accreditations of prior work experience in adult further education, guidance by mentors at the workplace and tutors in the polytechnics, training tutors and mentors for guidance, making agreements, learning tasks and students' reports, and the evaluation of students' learning with respect to the objectives set. Furthermore the recommendations describe the roles and responsibilities of the different parties involved in placements.

The approach to quality assurance adopted in the national network for the improvement of workplace placements can be described in the terms suggested by Harvey & Newton (2004, p. 162). It underlines self-regulation and is enhancement-led. It has the learner and better outcomes of learning as its objects. It focuses on improving the learning infrastructure and learning experience. In contrast to the external quality procedures described by the same authors it takes a more constructive approach. The recommendations made for improvement, however, focus on features of provision. They do not help to picture the dynamics of individual student's learning in networks. Quality is approached from the point of view of its parts rather than holistically. While the national network has tried to serve all fields and promote the spread of good examples the multi-field approach has inhibited the development of more dynamic interplay within each curriculum. The responsibility for developing connections with curricula was left to field-specific sub-groups.

Nationally, students' experiences of placements have been followed up by a survey organised by Ministry of Education in which students still in education form the focus group. Students' experiences of workplace placements are investigated from two points of view (Ministry of Education, 2007). First, has the guidance received during the workplace placement been adequate? Second, have the tasks done by the student during the placement supported learning? The results indicate that most students have been rather satisfied with their placements. These results, however, do not offer a basis for a thorough critical evaluation of workplace placements since they do not propose very many criteria that students might measure their experience against. Their strength is that they enable differences between fields of study to be seen and individual polytechnics to be compared to the average. In addition to the national survey individual polytechnics have followed up the success of their placements through a variety of more or less formal procedures. These results are not, however, comparable. The studies by the Institute for Educational Research discussed below have tried therefore to attain a more multi-field and multi-polytechnic picture of the placement situation.

## Practice and the Building of Spaces for Connectivity and Transformation in the Polytechnics

### Three Studies, Three Interest Groups

Below, the challenges of connectivity are discussed in the light of the results of three studies completed in 2002–2006 by the Institute for Educational Research. First, some excerpts from the thematic interviews completed with teachers organising and guiding placements in five polytechnics in three fields in 2002–2003 ($n = 28$) are presented as examples. The degree programmes in question were bachelor of social services, bachelor of engineering and bachelor of business administration. The interviews were also transcribed and a theory-led content analysis performed as a method of obtaining a description of the different models practised (Virolainen, 2006, 2007). In the next section the factors that define the implementation of the models for placements are presented on the basis of the thematic analysis of the interviews with the teachers. Second, polytechnics students' views on their placements are described on the basis of a survey conducted among students who had graduated a couple of years earlier. The survey was completed in 2005. The focus group of this survey are students from two fields, bachelors of business administration and bachelors of engineering ($n = 1050$). Third, the workplace supervisors' views on what kind of aims they find important and how they think they have benefited from interns are examined on the basis of a survey conducted among the above mentioned three fields in 2005 ($n = 269$).

### Teachers

The Finnish models of placements produced on the basis of the teachers' interviews show that models having features of connectivity are included among them (see also Virolainen, 2007). However, the extent of their usage does not match the experiences of the majority of the students who participated in the survey (see Fig. 12.1, next section). Of course, the widespread prevalence of classic interpretations of the curriculum means that results like these do not come as a surprise. Even in research, a curriculum can be viewed, for example, in terms of its means (pedagogies) and

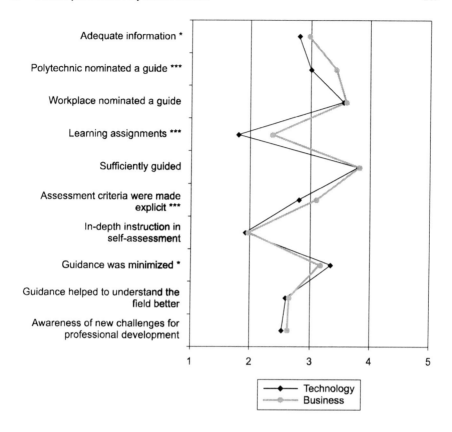

* p < .05. ** p < .01. *** p < .001.
Scale: 1 = totally disagree, ..., 5 = totally agree

**Fig. 12.1** Polytechnic students' (*n* = 1050) views on how guidance for learning in placements had been organised in practice

ends (what to learn) as well as students' personal knowledge construction or the existing learning material, like text books and tools that mediate the concepts to be learnt (Connerly & Lantz, 1985). Considering the numerous viewpoints available for research, it is hardly surprising that the results on participants' experiences in a multi-actor cooperative process, like workplace learning, emphasise different features.

The curriculum of workplace learning does not show the same face to all the participants even though it may be described as a process and a tradition for such presentations does exist (see e.g. M.-L. Vesterinen, 2002, p. 202). In addition to curriculum planning, a number of other factors are involved in building the cooperative framework between educational institution and workplace that define the outcome of the curriculum that polytechnics may plan for their students' placement. On the basis of the interviews with the teachers these institutionally structured factors defining the curriculum for workplace learning include the position of the placement in the overall curriculum, the contract between the polytechnic and the employer, the reward for the student and compensation for the employer, guidance at the workplace, students' reports and self-assessment, and assessment. Each of these features is anchored to institutional traditions specific to particular communities of practice and individual teachers alone cannot change them. Rather they have to be built anew and negotiated in between the participants in these networks. The effects of these factors are briefly characterised as:

- The position of the placement in the overall curriculum is dependent on the availability of internships. Mostly curricula have been built flexibly to allow for individual variety and to support opportunities for inserting placements in various parts of the curriculum. Such flexibility, however, may make building the connections between the overall curriculum and the placement a challenging endeavour, demanding either individualised teacher input or a very general framework regarding where to start with individualising the learning goals. The universality of the general approach is apparent in how students' reports on their placements have often been structured on the basis of general guidelines on how to write the report.
- Individualised learning assignments would be pedagogically more supportive of deepening understanding of specific subjects than merely writing reports on the placement as a whole. Constructing more of these assignments would, however, demand more input from the polytechnic side and its teachers. Many placements take place in the summer, when teachers are partly on their summer holidays but workplaces need temporary employees. This hinders the possibilities to negotiate personal learning goals under the guidance of a teacher and thus emphasises the need for student autonomy.
- The making of contracts between polytechnics and employers allows for the building of a broader framework between the partners. Experience of giving guidance and commitment to its development are meaningful determinants of its quality (see Fuller & Unwin, 2003). The benefits of making such a shift from organising individual students' placement to working within a larger cooperative framework are well understood among the polytechnics but doing this in practice requires commitment from both the polytechnics and workplaces. Likewise developing guidance at the workplace would demand long-standing commitment. In a situation of accelerating global competition for workplaces to find time for long-term commitment is difficult in itself.
- Students' remuneration and compensations for employers are dependent on field-specific traditions and agreements on wages between labour market organisations. While paying employers has constituted a financial burden to polytechnics, for example, in the field of social and health care, it has at the same time strengthened the position of polytechnics in negotiating on the need for developing the guidance given at the workplace. In contrast, students in the technology fields have often been very well paid but they have also been expected to survive with less guidance (see Fig. 12.1 for students' account).

- Self-assessment and assessment are procedures that for their part build students' abilities to see and plan their own growth as experts. Assessment of students' placements was often evaluated on a pass–fail basis. Sometimes discussions between student and teacher and student and mentor at the workplace did take place. Self-assessment was mostly included as a part of the structured report. On rare occasions teacher-led peer-group discussions had been organised to enhance reflections on the placement experience. Teachers' accounts of the procedures suggested that assessment of placements was often summative and the vision of the role of self-assessment was not especially strong. The results that emerged from the interviews with the teachers were in line with the students' feedback on self-assessment (see Fig. 12.1). Reflecting on practice would be strengthened by feedback on both reflection and practicing in situ. Learning both reflection and self-assessment might be enhanced by more developed thinking regarding the assessment of placements. The results for both the teachers' and students' experiences suggest that there would be room for introducing concepts like that of sustainable assessment as suggested by Boud (2000, see also Boud, 1999).

## Students

Comparison of the results from the national survey conducted by the Ministry of Education and the survey by the Institute for Educational Research showed a considerable shift in students' attitudes between leaving education and going to work. Views on the guidance and organisation of placements were much more critical among students who had been in working life for a couple of years than among students still in education. In the national survey by the Ministry of Education the majority of the students in education were positive both about the guidance and the learning that took place during their placement (Ministry of Education, 2007). In the survey by the Institute for Educational Research completed in 2005, on students who had graduated in 2002, the students were likewise positive about many features of the placements, like having a clearly nominated guide in the workplace. The majority of polytechnic students had also had a tutor at the educational institution. Many students felt that they had received enough guidance to manage at work. Accordingly, students reported in this survey that their professional competence had been strengthened during their placement (cf. Ministry of Education, 2007). All the groups of students in this survey, however, were negative about not having had learning assignments, or in-depth guidance in self-evaluation or guidance in deepening their professional insight. The results seem to suggest that students feel they learn a lot during their placements, but that learning takes place despite the lack of in-depth guidance. Guidance does not actively support identifying one's own developmental challenges. The results indicate that there is a demand for a more expertise-oriented curriculum with respect to placements.

The reason for the different views presented by the students in the two studies (Ministry of Education vs. Institute for Educational Research) may of course be partly due to phase of development the students were in. Further work experience and maturation may have made the students, who had already graduated, in the survey by the Institute for Educational Research, more critical about their education and more confident in expressing critical viewpoints. In addition the questionnaire format had a clear effect. The national survey quoted above did not ask about the support that guidance in the workplace or at school would have given in terms of deepening insight or learning self-assessment. Thus the progressive approach underlined in the connective model was initially omitted from the national survey. Furthermore answering questions put by a third, independent, party, the Institute for Educational Research, may have encouraged students to express more critical views.

## Employers

Workplace supervisors' (mentors) views on placements concerned their expectations of polytechnics as the organiser of placements and how they evaluate the benefits of having interns in their workplace (see Figs. 12.2 and 12.3). First, employers, as workplace supervisors and mentors of students, expected a positive input and active involvement on the part of the educational institution. They had high expectations with respect to all activities provided by the educational institution. On the one hand, this is good for the polytechnics, since they are relatively free to create their own profile. On the other hand, it suggests that workplaces do not have very specific expectations and have not had time to properly figure out what their demands should be. The responsibility for developing the goals of students' learning and cooperation between the partners is thus left to the polytechnics. Second, representatives of all fields reported it important that students should be trained to have the right attitudes towards work. The increased demand for the right attitudes is an outcome of the rise in the level of education (Chisholm & Hurrelmann, 1995). When the supply of students with the same formal qualifications is high, the 'right attitudes' towards work are thought to be an easy way of differentiating between students (Fig. 12.2). The right attitudes concern active willingness to adapt in performing tasks and good manners. These expectations about the right attitudes are somewhat problematic with respect to expectations about innovativeness and progressive development. Interpreted negatively, if it is thought that there is a shared, taken-for-granted understanding of what is needed in the workplace, there may not necessarily be much room left for discussion, criticism, and questioning of existing practices. Interpreted positively, critical thinking is what putting one's heart into something is all about and constitutes one essential component of the right attitudes.

Third, how the supervisors see the benefit interns bring to companies and workplaces seems to be field-specific (Fig. 12.3). The supervisors from the fields of technology and business and administration emphasised the benefits of temporary and possibly more permanent labour, whereas mentors in the field of social services and health prioritised the input interns have on the quality of work and its development. These differences are related to the respective corporate cultures. The fields of tech-

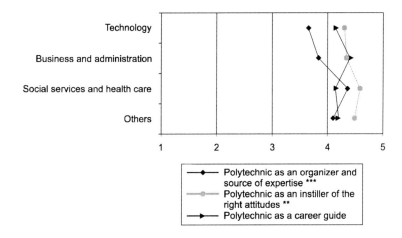

** p < .01. *** p < .001.
Scale: 1 = not important, ..., 5 = very important

**Fig. 12.2** Workplace supervisors' ($n = 269$) expectations of the role of polytechnics in organising placements. Mean variables are based on a factor analysis of 11 statements. Cronbach's alphas are 0.718, 0.618 and 0.642 according to order of description of factors

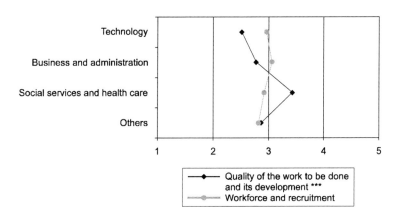

*** p < .001.
Scale: 1 = not at all, ..., 5 = very much

**Fig. 12.3** Workplace supervisors' ($n = 269$) views on how their company has benefited from having interns. Mean variables are based on a factor analysis of eight statements. Cronbach's alphas are 0.844, and 0.527 according to order of description of factors

nology and business and administration represent the private sector and, probably, more competitive cultures. The field of social services and health is publicly organised in Finland and is not competitive in the same sense. The field has been active in developing education for mentors, because it sees it as an investment in competing for future employees. The regional centres for excellence have also been active in developing the education and placements in the field (Ministry of Social Affairs and Health, 2003, p. 18). Other fields have not had similar networking partners on the national level, despite the existence of locally strong centres of expertise (Centre of Expertise Programme, 2007). Furthermore, in the field of social services employers are compensated for their guidance. However, although, interns in the field of social services and health have not traditionally been paid and the polytechnics have compensated employers nominally for their efforts, this has given the polytechnics the advantage of being able to negotiate over the quality of guidance. In the other fields it has been rather the other way around. Where interns are paid, full working input and autonomous performance may be expected from them.

## Challenges of Connectivity Calling for Transformation

The strength of the connective model is its focus on the learner and a changing societal context which demands a new, more dynamic approach to organising learning on the basis of work experience. It convincingly portrays the limitations of the earlier models in coming to terms with the new approaches to learning that arise out of late modernity and the changing world of work. It suggests that the new demands for structures, content and processes should be taken seriously (cf. Chisholm, 1999). In practice it provides the educational institutions like polytechnic with a tool for communicating with their working life partners about what the meaning of a placement should be. Such a tool seems to be in great demand (see Fig. 12.3). Trying to introduce new values and understanding regarding what is important about learning during placement may, however, be a conflicting process even on the level of individuals and local institutions.

### *Local Negotiations Between Polytechnics and Workplaces*

This chapter started by citing a teacher trying to express some of the problems he has encountered in organising placements. While teachers, as representatives of polytechnics, have tried to organise higher learning goals for placements and embed them meaningfully into curricula, some who supervise interns in workplaces have felt that schools are teaching something that has no relevance to practice. This contradiction is negotiable locally. Teachers can have meetings with their workplace partners to explain the meaning of the tasks that students have planned for enhancing their learning and combining theory and practice in the workplace. They also have to show that they do not disapprove of the goals that are meaningful to workplace and that both sets of goals are not contradictory but complementary. Achieving shared understanding demands local initiative and dialogue between the participants. Most importantly, participation on the working life side should not be understood as just one person nominated as a mentor in the workplace, but the working community more widely.

## Sharing Initiatives at the Workplace

Recent research results indicate that organising placements effectively might best be supported by what the researchers call 'distributed mentoring' (Paré & Le Maistre, 2006) and paying attention to 'workplace affordances' (Billett, 2004). In his systematic suggestion for workplace pedagogy Billett (2002) outlines the importance of what he sees as key processes for learning from work experience: participation, guidance at work and guidance in transferring knowledge. In practice distributed mentoring means constructing multiple opportunities for dialogue between the intern and the intern's colleagues throughout the workplace. Such spaces should give the students a chance to discuss solutions with colleagues at hand, to mull over the explanation that best suits the problem and conflates everyday and theoretical knowledge; and encourage the asking of questions. In addition these spaces should create occasions to shadow another worker and chances to represent and debate procedures in workplace. They should allow discussions on the tacit boundaries of the territory between different professional groups and going to lunch with more experienced colleagues and hearing they argue over cases. Distributed mentoring is about organising spaces for connectivity in the workplace and having an awareness of what the workplace affords. The concept emphasises that newcomers' work experience should take place across communities of practice. (Paré & Le Maistre, 2006)

In the study results presented in this chapter students were critical about the opportunities for self-reflection and self-assessment that guidance, either at school or at the workplace, had provided. In another study completed in the UK students have appeared rather vulnerable to the temptation of obtaining good grades and thus satisfying clients' sometimes short-sighted needs. Students have been willing to negotiate learning assignments easily by conforming to real work demands (Walters, Greenwood, & Ritchie, 2006). In the Finnish cases, grades are not a crucial question, as grades do not necessarily differentiate students. Placements are assessed mostly only on pass–fail criteria. The limited discussion on assessment may lead to a demand for the development of criteria that students might apply in self-assessing their performance. The provision of criteria for professional performance will otherwise have to be built into the curriculum.

## Different Actors have Both Contradictory and Compatible Goals

In the following, the effects of supra-organisational structures like field-specific cultures, field-specific networks of expertise, networks for developing placements and state interventions for developing higher education are discussed. Their dynamics do not necessarily work in predetermined ways but they bring the vested interests of parties in the labour market and on the state level to the fore. Despite good intentions, some interests may severely hamper implementation of the connective model. The teacher quoted in the beginning of this chapter was from the field of social services, where development of placements has been active and theory driven. In the previous section the effects of field-specific cultures were discussed. In fields other than health and social services similar field-specific state interventions do not exist, while the interest of technology and science parks has not focused much on education so far. Many projects on developing education in the field of technology are, however, under way. Some of these projects are financed by the Ministry of Education. According to the research results presented in the previous section, the field-specific cultures that typify working life in business and technology place a greater emphasis on the adaptation of interns to existing processes. The prevailing cultures of adaptation do not actively support the development of more 'progressive' placements.

In the previous sections, the positive outcomes of a national network for developing placements in polytechnics, organised as a project in 2004–006, were mentioned (Salonen, 2007). Also in the future, field-specific development might benefit from further support. At present field-specific development work may be partly hindered by competition between polytechnics. State interest in restructuring and developing higher education, which threatens to close some educational institutions may thus both lead to the stagnation of content-wise development in education as well as pre-empt the development of new models for placements. The model adopted in the first phase of building a national framework for placements placed emphasis on the role of individual tutors and mentors. Research suggests, however, that a more holistic approach to guidance would be more fruitful, that guidance should be better understood as distributed mentoring (for example, Billett, 2004; Paré & Le Maistre, 2006). The development of guidance and practices across the workplace should be taken as the goal. A new national guidance approach would be meaningful (see Scott, 1995). Fortunately, the general recognition of the need to educate workplace mentors provides for the taking of a holistic viewpoint in developing the workplaces and mentoring practices.

The assessment of the quality of placements has taken place through national surveys on students' experiences of placements organised by the Ministry of Education (2007) and by individual polytechnics' own follow-up studies. The national approach is rather general and it does not specify how the content, structure or process of placements should be developed. It seems that individual polytechnics would need to take responsibility for developing and making use of quality assurance tools by themselves. They may need to cooperate with each other for the purposes of comparison and deepening their field-specific approaches. Self-developed measures for evaluating success in organising placements have the advantage that they commit personnel to participate in an on-going quality process, which is characteristic of a learning organisation (Argyris, 1992). Introducing such continuing processes demands resources, which polytechnics have to find, at least partly by themselves and despite of the organisation of special projects for developing placements on the national level.

## Constructing Operating Spaces for Networks of Expertise

The connective model as an ideal type assigns somewhat dyadic quality to the partnership between the educational institutions and working life organisations. This ideal is valuable in that it underlines the positive input regarding placements that the two most powerful actors can make on the organisational level. In practice, in the networking society the categories of knowledge at work in communities of practice are multilayered. Therefore, it is argued finally, in this chapter that cooperation between educational institutions and working life partners should rather be understood as the building of networking communities of practice that together create the learning environment for the student (Hakkarainen, Palonen, Paavola, & Lehtinen, 2004). Networked communities of practice may adopt innovative approaches in unforeseeable ways. For example, the research results (Fig. 12.3) show that field-specific cultures are not present in education but also in working life. Typically in the male-dominated cultures of technology paying too much attention to guidance is labelled nursing, which is negative and contrary to autonomous self-fulfilling action. It may be joked about but in practice it is also about something that multi-field polytechnics have to intra- and inter-organisationally reconcile, when, for example, they are agreeing on the forms to be used for collecting feedback information from the local working life partners. In order to support students' learning from work experience, educational institutions can locally build up networked communities of practice in between themselves, their different fields and their working life partners. They can introduce new categories for understanding the meaning of learning at work, categories such as the connective model. Networked communities of practice need to share some meanings and values in order to find agreed goals on placements. Shared meanings and values are built locally in discussions which draw upon, and can invent on the basis of existing models and practices. Such networks are distributed across the communities of practice at work and communities of practice in the polytechnics. The initiative for change can also come from the side of working life, as the closing example shows.

Interviewer: *Have students done projects in relation to their placements?*
Coordinating teacher: *Some of them have. Let's say, they have mostly been done in cooperation with our contractual partners. . . .I think that the best example of cooperation between our polytechnic and firms is the cooperation we do with firm X. And the way we got into this cooperation and at the level it is now, about once a month for about year we had a meeting between people from our school and X and we wrote down all the possible things we could do together. And it was precisely projects related to placements that came out of it.*
Interviewer: *Were these kinds of developmental projects the outcome?*
Coordinating teacher: *Yes. Yes and why it was so good that such projects came into being is that it is a factory. And they have plenty of places for students in the field of technology, but not in business and administration. Well, they haven't had that many places. But now we have introduced placements as projects and we have clear intentions. Our students have created brochures for educating newcomers and all kind of knowledge-seeking tools with web-browsers and . . .*
Interviewer: *Where did the initiative come from?*
Coordinating teacher: *Well actually it came from them. I was asking for something and they said your requirements are coming up one by one, now we need this and now we need that.*

*'Have you ever thought that we could sit down at a table and create a long-term plan?' And so we did. I have found it very good as a system and there are a lot of nice people there. It is like you have a wish or an idea and we can find the right people between us and contact them.* (See Virolainen, 2004, pp. 231–232.)

This last quotation brings up many of the important features in constructing connectivity between polytechnics and working life: openness to new initiatives, commitment to building cooperation that satisfies all interest groups, goal-oriented discussion aiming at long-term planning, and trust. Discussion on mutual objectives without compulsion has been thought to be one important resource for building trust in the theoretical debates on social capital (Luhmann, 1979; Putnam, 1993; Ilmonen, 2000). Building networks of expertise to organise workplace learning involves creating social capital on the regional level.

# References

Argyris, C. (1992). *On organizational learning*. Cambridge, MA: Blackwell.

Beach, K. (2003). Consequential transitions: A developmental view of knowledge propagation through social organizations. In T. Tuomi-Gröhn, & Y. Engeström (Eds.), *Between school and work: New perspectives on transfer and boundary crossing* (pp. 39–61). Amsterdam: Pergamon.

Beck, U. (1992). *Risk society: Towards a new modernity*. London: Sage.

Billett, S. (2002). Toward a workplace pedagogy: Guidance, participation, and engagement. *Adult Education Quarterly, 53*(1), 27–43.

Billett, S. (2004). Workplace participatory practices: Conceptualising workplaces as learning environments. *The Journal of Workplace Learning, 16*(6), 312–324.

Billett, S., & Somerville, M. (2004). Transformations at work: Identity and learning. *Studies in Continuing Education, 26*(2), 309–326.

Boreham, N. (2006, September). *The co-construction of individual and organizational competence in learning organizations*. Paper presented at the Symposium: European VET and the Reflexive, Relational and Knowledge-Seeking Dimensions of Competence at the European Conference on Educational Research, Geneve, Switzerland.

Boud, D. (1999). Avoiding the traps: Seeking good practice in the use of self-assessment and reflection in professional courses. *Social Work Education, 18*(2), 121–132.

Boud, D. (2000). Sustainable assessment: Rethinking assessment for the learning society. *Studies in Continuing Education, 22*(2), 151–167.

Centre of Expertise Programme. (2007). *Centres of expertise – Key to efficient cooperation*. Retrieved April 27, 2007, from http://www.oske.net/in_english/centres_of_expertise

Chisholm, L., & Hurrelmann, K. (1995). Adolescence in modern Europe. Pluralized transition patterns and their implications for personal and social risks. *Journal of Adolescence, 18*(2), 129–158.

Chisholm, L. (1999). Education is more. The momentum for reform. In W. Bucherl, & T. Jansen (Eds.), *Globalization and social governance in Europe and in the United States* (pp. 87–92). European Commission Working Paper. Retrieved April 5, 2007, from http://ec.europa.eu/comm/cdp/working-paper/index_en.htm

Connerly, F. M., & Lantz, O. (1985). Curriculum. Definition of curriculum. In T. Husen, & T. N. Postlethwaite (Eds.), *The international encyclopedia of education* (Research and Studies Vol. 2, C, pp. 1160–1163). Oxford: Pergamon Press.

Eraut, M. (2004). Informal learning in the workplace. *Studies in Continuing Education, 26*(2), 247–273.

Fenwick, T. (2006). Tidying the territory: Questioning terms and purposes in work-learning research. *Journal of Workplace Learning, 18*(5), 265–278.

Fuller, A., & Unwin, L. (2003). Learning as apprentices in the contemporary UK workplace: Creating and managing expansive and restrictive participation. *Journal of Education and Work, 16*(4), 407–426.

Green, A., Wolf, A., & Leney, T. (1999). *Convergence and divergence in European education and training systems*. (Bedford Way Papers). University of London: Institute of Education.

Griffiths, T., & Guile, D. (2004). *Learning through work experience for the knowledge economy. Issues for educational research and policy*. (CEDEFOP Reference series No. 48). Luxembourg: Office for Official Publications of the European Communities.

Guile, D. (2006). Learning across contexts. *Educational Philosophy and Theory, 38*(3), 251–268.

Guile, D., & Griffiths, T. (2001). Learning through work experience. *Journal of Education and Work, 14*(1), 113–131.

Hakkarainen, K., Palonen, T., Paavola, S., & Lehtinen, E. (2004). *Communities of networked expertise. Professional and educational perspectives*. Amsterdam: Elsevier.

Harvey, L., & Newton, J. (2004). Transforming quality evaluation. *Quality in Higher Education, 10*(2), 149–165.

Hodkinson, P. (2005). Reconceptualising the relations between college-based and workplace learning. *Journal of Workplace Learning, 7*(8), 521–532.

Ilmonen, K. (2000). Sosiaalinen pääoma: käsite ja sen ongelmallisuus [Social capital: the concept and its problems]. In K. Ilmonen (Ed.), *Sosiaalinen pääoma ja luottamus* (pp. 9–38). (SoPhi No. 42). Jyväskylän yliopisto.

Lave, J., & Wenger, E. (1991). *Situated learning: Legitimate peripheral participation*. Cambridge: Cambridge University Press.

Lewis, T. (2005). At the interface of school and work. *Journal of Philosophy of Education, 39*(3), 421–441.

Liimatainen, L. (2002). *Kokemuksellisen oppimisen kautta kohti terveyden edistämisen asiantuntijuutta. Hoitotyön ammattikorkeakouluopiskelijoiden terveyden edistämisen oppiminen hoitotyön harjoittelussa* [Towards health promotion expertise through experiential learning. Student nurses' health promotion learning during clinical practice]. (Studies in Sport, Physical Education and Health). Jyväskylä: Jyväskylän yliopisto. Retrieved April 5, 2007, from http://selene.lib.jyu.fi:8080/vaitos/studies/studsport/9513913511.pdf

Luhmann, N. (1979). *Trust and power*. Chichester: Wiley.

Ministry of Education (2007). *OPALA student feedback system for polytechnics*. Retrieved April 27, 2007, from http://opalareport.ncp.fi

Ministry of Social Affairs and Health. (2003). *Sosiaalialan osaamiskeskukset* [Centres of Excellence in the field of social and health care]. Retrieved April 27, 2007, from http://pre20031103.stm.fi/suomi/pao/osaamiskeskus/esitteita2003_4.pdf

Paré, A., & Le Maistre, C. (2006). Distributed mentoring in communities of practice. In P. Tynjälä, J. Välimaa, & G. Boulton-Lewis (Eds.), *Higher education and working life: Collaborations, confrontations and challenges* (pp. 129–141). Amsterdam: Elsevier.

Putnam, R. (1993). *Making democracy work. Civic traditions in modern Italy*. Princeton: Princeton University Press.

Raggatt, P., & Williams, S. (1999). *Government, markets and vocational qualifications. An anatomy of policy*. London: Falmer Press.

Raij, K. (2000). *Toward a profession. Clinical learning in a hospital environment as described by student nurses*. (Helsingin yliopiston kasvatustieteen laitoksen tutkimuksia 166). Helsinki: Helsingin yliopisto. Retrieved April 5, 2007, from http://ethesis.helsinki.fi/ julkaisut/kas/kasva/vk/raij/

Salonen, P. (2004). Onko TUPA ratkaisu harjoittelun mitoituskysymykseen? [Is production-based education a solution to the problem of the amount of work-related learning required in polytechnics?]. In J. Keskitalo (Ed.), *Työelämä osana insinööriopintoja* (pp. 81–94). (Hämeen ammattikorkeakoulun julkaisu No. A:6). Hämeenlinna: Hämeenlinnan ammattikorkeakoulu.

Salonen, P. (2007). *Harjoittelusta amk-opintojen kuningas. Harjoittelun kehittämishankkeen 2004–2006 loppuraportti* [Placement as king of studies in polytechnics. Final report of the development project]. Kokkola: Keski-Pohjanmaan ammattikorkeakoulu.

Schienstock, G., & Hämäläinen, T. (2001). *Transformation of the Finnish innovation system: A network approach.* Helsinki: SITRA. Retrieved April 5, 2007, from http://www.sitra.fi/en/Publications/search/publication_search.htm

Scott, R. W. (1995). *Institutions and organisations.* London: Sage.

Sennett, R. (2003). *Respect: The formation of character in a world of inequality.* London: Allen Lane.

Toiviainen, H. (2003). *Learning across levels. Challenges of collaboration in a small-firm network.* Helsinki: University of Helsinki, Department of Education.

Tuomi, I. (2002). *Networks of innovation. Change and meaning in the age of the internet.* Oxford: Oxford University Press.

Vesterinen, M. -L. (2002). *Ammatillinen harjoittelu osana asiantuntijuuden kehittymistä ammattikorkeakouluissa* [Promoting professional expertise by developing practical learning at the polytechnic]. (Jyväskylä Studies in Education Psychology and Social Research No. 196). Jyväskylä: University of Jyväskylä. Retrieved April 5, 2007, from http://selene.lib.jyu.fi:8080/vaitos/studies/studeduc/9513913007.pdf

Vesterinen, P. (2001). *Projektiopiskelu- ja oppiminen ammattikorkeakoulussa* [Project-based studying and learning in the polytechnic]. Jyväskylä: Jyväskylän yliopisto. Retrieved April 5, 2007, from http://selene.lib.jyu.fi:8080/vaitos/studies/studeduc/9513911691.pdf

Virolainen, M. (2004). Työhön sopeutumisesta oppimisen tilanteiden luomiseen. Ammattikorkeakoulujen työelämäjaksot ja työstä oppimisen mallit [From adaptation to work towards developing learning situations at work. Workplace learning and its models at polytechnics]. In P. Tynjälä, J. Välimaa, & M. Murtonen (Eds.), *Korkeakoulutus, oppiminen ja työelämä* (pp. 213–233). Jyväskylä: PS-kustannus.

Virolainen, M. (2006). *Osaamista rakentamassa. Ammattikorkeakoulut harjoittelun ja työelämäyhteistyön kehittäjinä* [Building competencies. Polytechnics as the developers of work-related learning and cooperation with working life]. (Research Reports No. 27). Jyväskylä: University of Jyväskylä, Institute for Educational Research.

Virolainen, M. (2007). Workplace learning and higher education in Finland: Reflections on current practice. *Education + Training, 49*(4), 290–309.

Walters, D., Greenwood, A., & Ritchie, R. (2006). Work-based learning: Effectiveness in information systems training and development. *Higher Education Quarterly, 60*(1), 91–107.

# Chapter 13
# Connecting Work and Learning Through Demonstrations of Vocational Skills – Experiences from the Finnish VET

Marja-Leena Stenström

## Introduction

Historically, learning and work were inseparable during the pre-modern era, whereas during modern era a progressive differentiation took place between work and learning. In the late modern era differentiation has become fragmentation. Learning and work after post-compulsory education are organised in different forms such as educational establishments, teams and processes. Although many examples of separation can be found, these are also increasing example models of integration, from new kinds of apprenticeships to work-based learning, work-related learning, organisational development and so on (Boud, 2005). Nowadays, the fact that knowledge and skills are also provided outside formal education and training, is gradually leading to the formulation of a European educational policy (Tessaring & Wannan, 2004).

International comparisons (e.g. Stenström & Lasonen, 2000) of VET systems in the European countries revealed much of variation in how the relationship between education and working life is organised. Described as a continuum, at one end are countries such as Germany and Austria in which working life bears the main responsibility for VET, while at the other end there are countries where vocational education has been strongly school-based. For example, in Finland prior to the turn of the millennium initial vocational education was mainly organised by vocational schools with few links between education and working life. However, in recent years educational policy has emphasised the importance of creating closer relationships between education and industry in countries with as well as those without a school-based VET system. Consequently, since 2001, among the central reforms undertaken in Finnish upper secondary VET has been the incorporation into the curriculum of work-related learning lasting at least 6 months. Efforts to achieve closer cooperation between VET and working life also include what are known as *vocational skills demonstrations*, a procedure that was in experimental use in educational establishments from 1999 until autumn 2006, when it became established practice (Opetusministeriö, 2004).

M.-L. Stenström (✉)
Institute for Educational Research, University of Jyväskylä, Jyväskylä, Finland
e-mail: marja-leena.stenstrom@ktl.jyu.fi

M.-L. Stenström, P. Tynjälä (eds.), *Towards Integration of Work and Learning*,                221
© Springer Science+Business Media B.V. 2009

Vocational skills demonstrations are competence-based tests carried out in a work situation or as past work of a process which are designed, implemented and assessed by the education provider in cooperation with representatives from working life. Vocational skills demonstrations represent a new form of student assessment, in which cooperation between education and working life plays a central role and which brings together representatives from working life and *teachers* (Räkköläinen, 2005, p. 21; Stenström, 2001, 2005; Stenström, Laine, & Kurvonen, 2006). Competence-based examinations have been used mostly in countries where vocational education is driven by working life (Eraut, Steadman, Trill, & Parker, 1996; Wolf, 1995). The recent enhancement of the work-related[1] learning system in Finland and pilot projects to try out performance-based tests are developments reflecting the current process of change in the relationship between working life and VET. The effort to raise the level of VET participation has made the question of reorganising assessment to meet the demands of both HE institutions and working life an acute one in other European countries as well (Green, Wolf, & Leney, 1999).

The aim of this chapter is to describe how work and learning are linked in Finnish vocational education and training with particular reference to skills demonstrations. First, the context of work-related learning is described and everyday learning compared with formal learning compared. Second, the skills demonstration system as part of work-related learning and vocational study programmes in Finland is introduced. Third, the vocational skills demonstration as a tool for improving the interface between education and working life is discussed. This chapter is in fact based on a study the aim of which was to examine *students'* practice-oriented learning as a part of VET provision in authentic situations in the workplaces (Stenström et al., 2006). The context was the experimental phase of in the introduction of vocational skills demonstrations in Finland. Skills demonstrations were included in all initial vocational qualifications in autumn 2006 (Laki ammatillisesta koulutuksesta annetun lain muuttamisesta 15 July 2005/601). The data were collected by interviewing students in the fields of social welfare and health care and the construction industry ($n = 6$), their teachers ($n = 8$), and representatives ($n = 6$) of enterprises operating in these fields in central and southern Finland.

## Connecting Work and Learning: Background and Starting Points

In the modern industrial and post-industrial eras a clear divide between the context of production (work) and the context of reproduction (education) has become evident (Lundgren 1991; Marhuenda, 2000; Stenström, 2004). The two contexts develop their own language, rationale, needs and traditions. Schools specialise in teaching and learning, whereas the function of working life is to produce goods,

---

[1] Work-related means here a period of working as a component of formal education (see also Streumer & Kho, 2006).

services and nonmaterial products. The models according to which schools operate usually differ from those that prevail in working life. Also learning between the two contexts differs. Nowadays, the aim is to unite these two worlds, two systems, two markets (education and labour). School-based and work-based learning represent distinctive cultures and offer distinctive contexts for learning. Activities outside school are often socially shared, while in schools activities are based on the achievements of the individual. Further, schools also value abstract thinking while work-based learning presupposes a situational and contextual frame of reference (e.g. Tynjälä & Collin, 2000; Wenger, 1998). Both at school and in work-based learning, it is crucial that theory and practice are brought into interaction and integrated and that this is linked with personal reflection. This is an approach manifested, among others, in the experiential theory (Kolb, 1984; Schön, 1987; Tynjälä & Collin, 2000; Tynjälä, Slotte, Nieminen, Lonka, & Olkinuora 2006; Tynjälä, Välimaa, & Sarja 2003)

The interface between education and working life can be examined from different viewpoints. One way is to analyse learning situations in terms of the attributes of formality and informality. These are parallel and overlapping issues. The terms of horizontal or everyday learning, as opposed to vertical or theoretical learning have been used (e.g. Bernstein 2000; Guile & Griffiths, 2001; Young 2003). According to Bernstein (2000) horizontal discourses are local, segmental and context-bound, whereas vertical discourses are general, explicit and coherent. The former dimension focuses on workplace learning. Malcolm, Hodkinson, & Colley (2003) see two separate paradigms: (1) informal learning (horizontal within workplaces) and (2) formal (within educational institutions). They suggest four aspects of formality/informality: (1) process, (2) location and setting, (3) purposes and (4) content. All learning situations contain attributes of formality and informality, but their nature and the balance between them varies significantly from situation to situation. These attributes of formality and informality are also interrelated in different learning situations.

There has been an increase of interest in workplace learning among educational scholars (e.g. Billet, 2001; Fuller & Unwin, 1998; Griffiths & Guile, 2004; Lave & Wenger, 1991). One of the unifying themes in their work has been the learning context and the development of vocational competence. Guile & Griffiths (2001) also stress the learning context. According to them the concept of horizontal development refers to the internal process of change and development which occurs as an individual moves from one context (school) to another (workplace). Guile and Griffiths have analysed the concept of the learning context with reference to work experience. In particular, they argue that it is necessary to take different types of context (education and work) into account. They introduce a typology of work experience consisting of five models which describe the relationships between these contexts: traditional, the experiential, the generic, the work process and the connective. They highlight the need for new curriculum frameworks (see also Young, 2003) with which to introduce the last mentioned 'connective model' (see Tynjälä, Chapter 2). Such a new curriculum framework would enable students to relate formal and informal, horizontal and vertical learning. Therefore, learners need to be encouraged to conceptualise their experiences, as this serves different curricula purposes. This is the approach taken in Finnish vocational skills demonstrations, where students' reflection and self-assessment is emphasised as part of the assessment process. According to Guile (2002) work experience has to become part of learning programmes in order to assist students to connect their formal and informal learning. This can be also seen in the Finnish vocational skills demonstrations which have been developed pedagogically to form part of vocational study programmes and to improve the relationship between education and working life. Vocational skills demonstrations aim to ensure that the training meets the requirements of working life and brings the view of the latter to bear on assessment (Stenström et al., 2006).

## Demonstrations of Vocational Skills Demonstrations as Part of Work-Related Learning

In Finnish vocational education and training, the central competencies of each vocational study module are assessed by means of vocational skills demonstrations. The assessment targets and criteria used are defined in the national core curriculum (Opetushallitus, 2005). The central competencies, as targets of assessment, are command of the knowledge that forms the foundation of the work domain, command of work processes, command of working methods, tools and materials, command of occupational safety, common emphases, and core skills common to all fields (Kinnunen, 2005, p. 70; see Fig. 13.1). These assessment targets are the same for every initial vocational qualification, but not all of the above-mentioned targets of assessment are included in every vocational skills demonstration (Opetushallitus, 2005).

Eraut (2004) distinguishes five types of knowledge in vocational and professional education programmes (see Tynjälä, Chapter 2). The components of vocational competence presented in the Finnish VET curriculum are compared with this typology in Table 13.1.

This comparison has been made on the basis of the titles of the types not their contents. However, it can be seen that the contents of the Finnish curriculum resemble Eraut's typology, although the concepts are different. In general, the targets of assessment of Finnish VET largely cover the vocational competencies including key skills. Therefore, the focus of assessment in vocational skills in Finland seems to be broader than most other European countries (Stenström & Laine, 2006a).

According to Eraut, although most types of knowledge are described as transferable, there is little evidence that these skills are being transferred to the workplace. A vocational skills demonstration is an excellent opportunity for students to show how they have integrated their practical and theoretical knowledge. In a vocational skills demonstration students can, by doing practical assignments, show how successfully they have reached the targets of their initial VET and acquired the skills needed in working life (Räkköläinen, 2005, p. 21; Stenström et al., 2006).

**Fig. 13.1** Targets of assessment of vocational competence in Finnish VET (Kinnunen, 2005, p. 70)

**Table 13.1** Comparison between Eraut's typology of knowledge and targets of assessment of Finnish vocational competence

| Eraut's typology of knowledge | Targets of assessment of Finnish vocational competence |
| --- | --- |
| Theoretical knowledge | Command of the knowledge that forms the foundation of work |
| Methodological knowledge | Command of working methods, tools and materials, and command of occupational safety |
| Practical skills | Command of work processes |
| Generic skills | Core skills common to all fields |
| General knowledge about occupation | Common emphases |

## Assessment of Skills Through Demonstrations

The following sections focus on the assessment of vocational skills demonstrations, as these constitute one of the central events where cooperation between education and working life concretely takes place. This assessment was also termed practice-oriented assessment within QUAL-PRAXIS project (Grollmann & Stenström, 2005; Stenström & Laine, 2006c, 2006d).

## *Assessing Demonstrations of Vocational Skills*

Assessment and learning can be seen either as separate processes or as aspects of the same process (Poikela, 1998; Stenström, 2005). If learning and assessment are separate processes, then the function of assessment is to measure outcomes rather than foster the learning process. From this perspective, learning is assumed to take place along lines defined by the curriculum and by teachers. By contrast, if education is seen from the perspective of learning, assessment can, by the same token, be seen as a part of the learning process.

A description of the differences between traditional thinking on assessment and the idea of practice-oriented assessment based on work-related learning is presented in Table 13.2. The characteristics of practice-oriented assessment can be set against those of the traditional thinking on assessment (cf. Biggs, 1994; Black, 1999; Eisner, 1993; Stenström & Laine, 2006b).

It is possible to differentiate traditional from practice-oriented assessment according to their respective conceptions of learning and teaching. One essential difference concerns how the assessment context is understood. In the traditional model assessment sessions are arranged after the conclusion of a course as an event separate from the teaching process, while in practice-oriented assessment the stress is on

**Table 13.2** Central features of traditional assessment and practice-oriented assessment (Stenström & Laine, 2006b; adapted from Tynjälä, 1999a, 1999b)

| Traditional assessment | Practice-oriented assessment |
|---|---|
| Emphasises quantitative assessment | Emphasises qualitative assessment |
| Repetitive, emphasises rote learning | Emphasises connectivity between theory and practice and the transformation of knowledge |
| Artificial assessment settings | Assessment settings that are as authentic as possible |
| Assessment as separate from the learning process | Assessment as part of the learning process |
| Assessment by the teacher | Assessment by the teacher, the student and the workplace instructor together and also by other students (peer-assessment) |
| Focus on outcomes | Focus on the learning process, changes in the student's knowledge and skills, and learning outcomes |

the authenticity of learning assignments and their assessment. A further difference relates to the question of who are seen as the assessors. In traditional thinking on assessment, the task is performed exclusively by the teacher, while in practice-oriented assessment the teacher typically works in collaboration with other assessors (e.g. the workplace instructor, the student or/and other students). As pointed out above, the emphasis in practice-oriented assessment in on fostering the student's metacognitive thinking, self-directedness, learning-to-learn process, and interaction, all of which are found in the constructive learning theory.

## *Assessment as Part of Learning*

The constructivist learning theory forms one approach to vocational skills demonstrations. However, constructive learning is not enough on its own to explain work-related learning, which can be described using the concepts of reflective, transformative, contextual and situated learning (Lave & Wenger, 1991; Mezirow, 1991). The contextual nature of work-related and work-based learning lies in the fact that the student engaged in it learns and is assessed in an authentic context. Thus, learning of this kind can be described as a process of participating in communities of practice (Lave & Wenger, 1991; Wenger, 1998).

In vocational skills demonstrations, assessment is part of learning and its aim is to guide and motivate the student to learn and to acquire self-assessment skills (Stenström et al., 2006). The most important element is the assessment discussion, which occurs after every demonstration of vocational skills, the aim of which is to promote the learning process. During the assessment discussion the student, among other things, receives guidance and feedback from the teacher and the workplace instructor as well as gives feedback in turn.

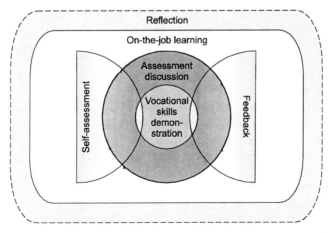

**Fig. 13.2** Assessment of vocational skills as part of students' learning process (Stenström & Laine, 2006a)

Moreover, student self-assessment and reflection are elements which link the assessment of vocational skills tightly to the learning process (see Fig. 13.2). The students assess their learning in relation to their skills test, and their self-assessment is one of the topics considered during the assessment discussion. Reflection is present throughout the on-the-job learning process.

## *Joint Assessment by Teacher, Workplace Instructor and Student*

The most prominent principle guiding the implementation of vocational skills demonstrations in Finland is their assessment by the student, the teacher and the workplace instructor (Stenström et al., 2006). Vocational skills demonstrations are controlled and supervised locally by a tripartite board consisting of representatives from local working life, the education provider, teachers and students. The board ensures that the vocational skills demonstrations are carried out in accordance with the legislation and local requirements. The education provider's plans and curriculum for vocational skills demonstrations should be approved by the board. It also nominates the persons responsible for the assessment of particular vocational skills demonstrations and issues the final certificates.

During skills demonstrations all the above-mentioned parties have their own roles and responsibilities. The tripartite basis of the assessment discussion enables a broad perspective to be taken on the student's skills since the different parties notice different things. The assessment discussion is, however, more than just an opportunity for grading students and enhancing their learning. At its best it evokes reflection and broader discussion and promotes the development of all the participants.

The assessment discussion plays a central role in the vocational skills demonstration process both as a whole and in relation to guiding the growth of students' vocational competence (Stenström et al., 2006). One of the reasons why the assessment discussion is so central is that other kinds of tripartite cooperation during on-the-job learning and vocational skills demonstrations are rather rare. The assessment discussion gathers together the viewpoints of the teacher, student and workplace instructor with the aim of arriving at a mutual understanding of the students' skills. This requires time and commitment from all participants, but a consensus is usually reached without conflict.

The teacher's role in the assessment discussions is that of an assessment expert. Teachers also have the main responsibility for the implementation of the assessment and must ensure that the grades given are based on the agreed criteria. The teacher's role is emphasised because *workplace instructors* may have widely differing educational backgrounds.

Moreover, especially in the initial stage of implementing vocational skills demonstrations, workplace instructors may also have inadequate information and may lack the skills required for assessing demonstrations (Stenström et al., 2006). Even if the new and more detailed criteria have made the assessment of work-related learning more objective, students and workplace instructors, especially, still feel that the criteria, as described, can be rather difficult to interpret. It seems that the feeling sometimes expressed by workplace instructors that there is a lack of clarity in how to go about the assessment is connected with whether they have taken part in the special training given to workplace instructors, their previous experiences of vocational skills demonstrations or their basic education.

Because of these problems, teachers' opinions are highly valued and their views carry a lot of weight. Teachers help in defining the level of the student's skills. Workplace instructors are again valued for their professional and workplace-specific expertise. Assessment by a professional is one of the main strengths of vocational skills demonstrations. Apart from their expertise in working life, it is equally important that these assessors have taken part in a sufficient amount of assessment training, since proper training can reduce human errors of judgement and increase inter-assessor reliability (Hoepfl, 2000, p. 56; McAlister, 2000, 30). This training unifies assessment practices, reduces different interpretations and helps to ensure objectivity in assessment.

The students' most salient task within the assessment process is to demonstrate their skills. Alongside their practical knowledge students also show their theoretical knowledge. Therefore they have to prepare a written plan of their demonstration before the demonstration itself. In addition, they assess their own skills on the basis of the relevant assessment criteria by filling in an assessment form. Furthermore, the students join the teacher and the workplace instructor in the assessment discussion (see Fig. 13.3).

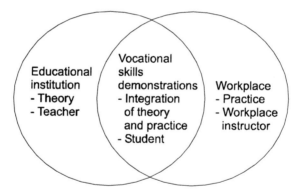

**Fig. 13.3** Connection between education and working life in vocational skills demonstrations

## Reflection

Being able to reflect on what has already been learned and what future learning needs are can aid in connecting work and learning, and in facilitating the learning which takes place during work. Reflective processes are also connected with the development of deeper thinking processes and expertise (e.g. Schön, 1983). Students should be encouraged to express their thoughts.

Our studies have indicated that vocational skills demonstrations and on-the-job learning periods have generated reflection not only among what may be called the primary learners, the students, but also among workplace instructors and teachers (Stenström et al., 2006). Supervising students has caused workplace instructors to rethink their own working methods and approach to instruction. On their own admission advising students helps them to find new perspectives on their work and prevent their job from being reduced to a routine. Functioning as a workplace instructor has also increased these employees' work motivation. Some workplace instructors have even become interested in developing themselves as workers by applying on the criteria against which their students are assessed.

Teachers, again, feel that the implementation of vocational skills demonstrations has broadened their perspectives and helped them to keep up to date. Conducting vocational skills demonstrations has forced teachers to get to grips with the essential issues included in a study module or qualification. This has given them a better understanding of the instruction they give. Moreover, teachers have played a central role in the process of introducing vocational skills demonstrations into working life. This has required them to find ways of convincing its representatives that the new procedure makes sense.

## Self-Assessment

Learners need information that will help them evaluate themselves so that assessment becomes integrated into the learning experience (de Rozario, 2002). Self-assessment is an extremely important tool for improving motivation and personal goal-setting skills. It helps students to become reflective practitioners. However, the ability to assess one's own learning is not easy to acquire. Therefore, external guidance and appraisal, such as from a workplace instructor or from a teacher, are of significant help (Brennan & Little, 1996).

Self-assessment is part of both on-the-job learning and vocational skills demonstrations. During the assessment discussion, the participants consider the student's self-assessment and the student is given an opportunity to justify it. An organised assessment discussion is a central essential means of fostering students' vocational development and the evolution of their self-assessment skills.

Many students find self-assessment difficult, particularly at the early stages of their studies, although in the opinion of teachers, today's students have better self-assessment skills than their forbears (Stenström et al., 2006). Despite the difficulty of self-assessment, students feel that it is essential that they were able to evaluate their own work. Self-assessment offers students a chance to identify their personal vocational strengths and weaknesses and become aware of their development needs. In addition, better skills in assessing themselves and in being assessed by others has made students more mature and thus better equipped to enter working life.

## Feedback

Research findings show that students consider the assessment discussion in vocational skills demonstrations useful (Stenström et al., 2006). In particular, the opportunity for getting and giving feedback during the discussion is considered very valuable. Feedback is a central part of the learning process and is related to the growth of vocational identity (Askew & Lodge, 2000; Wiggins, 1993). Getting to know the strengths and weaknesses of their own performance gives students the possibility to invest in the skills in which they have the greatest need of improvement. Assessment is most effective if feedback is given during the learning process itself, and not only after the evaluation has been completed.

During the discussion on their vocational skills demonstrations, the performance of students in the demonstration is examined. In this discussion, the teacher and the workplace instructor give the student feedback, provide guidelines for the student's future development and explain why they are proposing a particular grade. The assessment discussion offers also students an opportunity to present feedback of their own and share their thoughts on skills demonstrations and assessment situations. A carefully organised assessment discussion is a central means of fostering students' vocational development and the evolution of their self-assessment skills. Moreover, being able to arrange a shared assessment discussion promotes cooperation between education and working life.

## Conclusion: Skills Demonstrations as Integrator of Education and Working Life

The studies of skills demonstrations show that the implementation of this new assessment system has improved cooperation between education and working life (Stenström et al., 2006). Vocational skills demonstrations offer an excellent opportunity to connect formal school learning and more informal workplace learning and to integrate theory and practice. Skills demonstrations have also led all three parties involved – teachers, workplace instructors and students – to take their own learning-related duties more seriously as well as encouraged them to develop their occupational skills. Table 13.3 summarises the aspects of vocational skills demonstrations that foster cooperation between education and work.

The cooperation between educational institutions and workplaces has forced teachers to take into account the needs of working life. Teachers now invest more than earlier in the guidance they give students. Teachers have reoriented their teaching with the aim of helping students to achieve a good standard in vocational skills demonstrations. Vocational skills demonstrations have thus helped them clarify the central issues related to each study module. Teachers have channelled their teaching so that the topics taught are ones the students will be able to utilise during their on-the-job learning periods and vocational skills demonstrations. For students this means transferring their theoretical knowledge into practice in an authentic context. Furthermore, the link between theory and practice becomes realised in curriculum, teaching and assessment.

Furthermore, representatives from working life have taken part in the planning and implementation of the vocational skills demonstrations. The curricula of the · vocational institutions have had substantially to be modified. This has led workplace

**Table 13.3** Elements within assessment of vocational skills demonstrations which foster cooperation between education and working life

| Action | Teacher | Workplace instructor | Student |
|---|---|---|---|
| Joint assessment | Responsible for implementation of assessment and ensuring the grades are based on the agreed criteria, professional of assessment and theory | Valued for their professional field and workplace specific expertise, professional of practice | Show their vocational competence (theoretical and practical skills) in as authentic situations as possible, learner during the-on-the job learning (skills demonstrations) |
| Assessment discussion | Responsible for assessment, aware of learning theories | Motivate students' learning at the workplace | Guide and motivate students' vocational development and promote students learning |
| Reflection | Broaden their perspectives and help them to keep grip on the essential issues, help them to reflect on their own role within skills demonstrations | Make them think over their own ways of action and working, find new viewpoints on their work, help to reflect on their own role within skills demonstrations | Improve their professional judgments and their understanding of new situations, better understanding of vocational competence |
| Self-assessment | Teachers' guidance and appraisal is a significant help for students on their way to becoming professionals (skilled workers) | Workplace instructors' guidance and appraisal is a significant help for students on their way to becoming professionals (skilled workers) | Important tool for improving motivation and vocational development, helps students on their way to becoming professionals (skilled workers) |
| Feedback | Expert in vocational assessment, giving feedback for students | Expert in vocational practice, giving feedback to students | Feedback promotes students' learning, getting feedback from the teacher and workplace instructor |
| Curriculum | Responsible for the implementation of the curriculum | Participant in curriculum development process | Participant in implementation of the curriculum (vocational skills demonstrations) |

instructors to a greater awareness of vocational curricula. Taking part in curriculum planning is nevertheless somewhat difficult for them because acquiring familiarity with a curriculum takes a lot of time and work.

To act as a workplace instructor requires the ability to give guidance. As a consequence of their guidance duties workplace instructors have begun to consider their work more thoroughly and find new perspectives on it. They have also started to question some of their working methods. The instructors state that when trying to teach someone else, you yourself also learn during this process. Although workplace instructors' guidance skills have improved as a result of vocational skills demonstrations, they sometimes consider that their guidance skills are inadequate. Therefore, more training for the workplace instructors in guidance and assessment is needed. One of the most important questions related to vocational skills demonstrations is whether the resources of working life can be stretched far enough not only to enable an adequate number of representatives of working life to be recruited to the assessment of vocational skills demonstrations but also to provide a sufficient amount of training relating to their duties of assessing and guiding students (cf. Young, 2000).

Although Finland has followed the current trend to shift part of the teaching and learning process from educational institutions to the workplace, on-the-job learning including vocational skills demonstrations remains within the domain of formal education. This explains the central role played by teachers' assessment. They are primarily responsible for assessment, whereas elsewhere, e.g. in Australia a major shift towards the assessment of competencies in the workplace by staff of the employer organisation and away from teachers has been seen (Boud, 2005). This Finnish practice may derive from the school-based nature of the VET system and the egalitarian educational principle that governs assessment.

Students have been shown to invest more time and energy in their studies in order to perform well in their vocational skills demonstrations. Skills demonstrations have also helped them to better monitor their own development. Thus, students have become substantially more prepared to enter working life. Students feel that vocational skills demonstrations may have added value in terms of better employment opportunities, although they perceive that their performance during the on-the-job learning periods continues to carry more weight in that respect. Naturally, employers may be interested in giving a job to a well-performing student whose vocational skills demonstration they have had an opportunity to observe. Thus, performance in vocational skills demonstrations can be one way of proving one's skills.

Even if cooperation with working life has developed in a more positive direction, it still seems to have certain limitations. Cooperation between educational institutions and workplaces in relation to vocational skills demonstrations and students' on-the-job learning periods has been restricted mainly to discussions involving targets and assessment. Figure 13.4 describes the situation.

The current practice allows only little room for personal cooperative relationships. Furthermore, teachers feel that their special expertise is not being utilised adequately in the working life context. These problems are connected with the limited resources budgeted for these purposes. In the transfer of information between education and working life, the main channel is definitely the students. Their role is central: they are the ones who bring new ideas from the school to the workplace and vice versa. The role of information exchange on the other levels seems to be rather modest. Therefore, one of the biggest challenges in developing work-related learning and skills demonstrations is to strengthen the direct cooperation between teachers and workplaces.

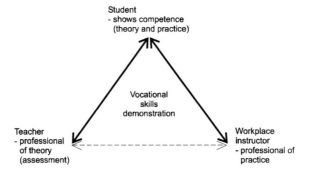

**Fig. 13.4** Student as mediator between education and working life

The vocational skills demonstrations appear able to measure a wide number of the vocational competencies defined in the national core curriculum and needed in working life. Use of vocational skills demonstrations also enables attention to be paid to the smaller details which relate to the tasks in question. Thus a skills demonstration seems to be reasonably valid instrument for measuring vocational competence (see Fig. 13.1). However, demonstrations alone may not be the most efficient method of gaining a deeper knowledge of a student's vocational skills. This might be better achieved, for example, by observing the students for a longer time during their on-the-job learning period.

Teachers and workplace instructors alike consider it is essential that vocational skills demonstrations are authentic. According to them a genuine working situation is best able to bring out a student's vocational skills. Learning at the workplace provides learners with learning environments where they can acquire knowledge and skills different from those delivered in the classroom. This presupposes, however, that adequate attention is paid to guidance and assessment (Oulujärvi & Perä-Rouhu, 2000; Stenström et al., 2006). Guidance and assessment are challenging aspects of the development of work-related learning. When young people start their work-related learning period, they are often without any work experience; but they can be guided towards vocational development and a professional identity (skilled worker).

The findings of the Finnish studies suggest that vocational skills demonstrations mainly follow the principles of the constructive learning theory. The theory is realised in the students' assessment. To approach closer to the connective model (Griffiths & Guile, 2003) cooperation between teachers and workplace instructors should be improved. At present, cooperation seems still to be following the traditional work experience model. The reason might be that the findings presented here are based on the experimental, implementation phase of vocational skills demonstrations, when the contexts between schools and workplaces were newly established. Furthermore, few resources have as yet been made available.

There is also the question of the reliability of vocational skills demonstrations. The conditions under which vocational skills demonstrations are implemented differ. First, workplaces are different and working practices are diverse. Second, it is natural that workplace instructors will vary: instructors are different in their basic education and differ in how much training they have as workplace instructors. Moreover, in guiding students their motivation and styles differ. Vocational skills demonstration tasks are also various, as are the demands they make on the student. At this stage, one of the most important questions related to vocational skills demonstrations is whether suitable workplaces as sites for learning will continue to be available for educational institutions and their students.

In sum, the system of on-the-job learning and vocational skills demonstrations has contributed to the creation of closer links between education and work, closer collaboration between teachers and workplace instructors, e.g. in assessment process and closer integration of theory and practice. However, there are challenges for developing assessment of vocational skills. The issues concern assessment criteria, targets, assessor training, assessment methods, resources and tasks of the skills demonstrations.

## References

Askew, S., & Lodge, C. (2000). Gifts, ping-pong and loops – Linking feedback and learning. In S. Askew (Ed.), *Feedback for learning* (pp. 1–17). London: Routledge Falmer.

Bernstein, B. (2000). *Pedagogy, symbolic control and identity*. Lanham, MD: Rowman Littlefield.

Biggs, J. (1994). Student learning research and theory. Where do we currently stand? In G. Gibbs (Ed.), *Improving student learning. Theory and practice* (pp. 1–9). Oxford: Oxford Centre for Staff Development.

Billet, S. (2001). Knowing in practice: Re-conceptualising vocational expertise. *Learning and Instruction, 11*(1), 431–452.

Black, O. (1999). Assessment, learning theories and testing systems. In P. Murphy (Ed.), *Learners, learning & assessment* (pp. 118–134). London: Paul Chapman in association with the Open University.

Boud, D. (2005). Work and learning: Some challenges for practice. In E. Poikela (Ed.), *Osaaminen ja kokemus* (pp. 181–199 ). Tampere: Tampereen Yliopistopaino.

Brennan, J., & Little, B. (1996). *A review of work-based learning in higher education*. London: Department for Education and Employment/Open University Quality Support Centre.

Eisner, E. (1993). Reshaping assessment in education: Some criteria in search of practice. *Journal of Curriculum Studies, 25*, 219–233.

Eraut, M. (2004). Transfer of knowledge between education and workplace settings. In H. Rainbird, A. Fuller, & A. Munro (Eds.), *Workplace learning in context* (pp. 201–221). London: Routledge.

Eraut, M., Steadman, S., Trill, J., & Parker, J. (1996). *The assessment of NVQs*. (Research Report No. 4). Brighton: University of Sussex, Institute of Education.

Fuller, A., & Unwin. L. (1998) Reconceptualizing apprenticeship: Exploring the relationships between work and learning. *Journal of Vocational Education and Training, 50*(2), 153–172.

Green, A., Wolf, A., & Leney, T. (1999). *Convergence and divergence in European education and training systems*. (Bedford Way Papers No. 7). London: University of London, Institute of Education.

Griffiths, T., & Guile, D. (2003). A connective model of learning: The implications for work process knowledge. *European Educational Research Journal, 2*(1), 56–73.

Griffiths, T., & Guile, D. (2004). *Learning through work experience for the knowledge economy*. Issues for educational research and policy. (CEDEFOP Reference series No. 48). Luxembourg: Office for Official Publications of the European Communities.

Grollmann, P., & Stenström, M.-L. (Eds.). (2005). *Quality assurance and practice-oriented assessment in vocational education and training: Country studies.* (Working Papers No. 55). Bremen: University of Bremen, Institute Technology and Education.

Guile, D. (2002). Work, skill and work experience in the European knowledge economy. *Journal of Education, 15*(3), 251–276.

Guile, D., & Griffiths, T. (2001). Learning through work experience. *Journal of Education and Work, 14*(1), 113–131.

Hoepfl, M. (2000). Large-scale authentic assessment. In R. L. Custer (Ed.), *Using authentic assessment in vocational education.* (Information Series No. 381, pp. 49–67). Columbus, OH: The Ohio State University, College of Education, Center on Education and Training for Employment, ERIC Clearinghouse on Adult, Career, and Vocational Education.

Kinnunen, E. (2005). Targets and criteria of assessment. In E. Kinnunen, & T. Halmevuo (Eds.), *Student assessment guide for vocational education and training* (pp. 66–76). Helsinki: Finnish National Board of Education.

Kolb, D. A. (1984). *Experiential learning: Experience at the source of learning and development.* Englewood Cliffs, NJ: Prentice-Hall.

*Laki ammatillisesta koulutuksesta annetun lain muuttamisesta* [Act to amend the Vocational Education Act] 15 July 601/2005.

Lave, J., & Wenger, E. (1991). *Situated learning: Legitimate peripheral participation.* Cambridge: Cambridge University Press.

Lundgren, U. P. (1991). *Between education and schooling: Outlines of a diachronic curriculum theory.* Geelong, Victoria: Deakin University.

Malcolm, J., Hodkinson, P., & Colley, H. (2003). The interrelationships between informal and formal learning. *Journal of Workplace Learning, 15*(7/8), 313–318.

Marhuenda, F. (2000). Rethinking education-work relationships. In M. -L. Stenström & J. Lasonen (Eds.), *Strategies for reforming initial vocational education in Europe* (pp. 239–249). Jyväskylä: University of Jyväskylä, Institute for Educational Research.

McAlister, B. (2000). The authenticity of authentic assessment. What the research says…or doesn't say. In R. L. Custer (Ed.), *Using authentic assessment in vocational education.* (Information Series No. 381, pp. 19–31). Columbus, OH: The Ohio State University, College of Education, Center on Education and Training for Employment, ERIC Clearinghouse on Adult, Career, and Vocational Education.

Mezirow, J. (1991). *Transformative dimensions of adult learning.* San Francisco: Jossey-Bass.

Opetushallitus. (2005). *Ammatillisen peruskoulutuksen opetussuunnitelman ja näyttötutkinnon perusteet. Opiskelijan arviointi, opetussuunnitelma.* Määräys 32/011/2005. [National core curriculum and competence-based qualification requirements for initial vocational education and training. Student assessment, curriculum]. Helsinki: Author.

Opetusministeriö. (2004). *Koulutus ja tutkimus 2003–2008.* Kehittämissuunnitelma [Education and research 2003–2008. Development plan]. Helsinki: Opetusministeriö.

Oulujärvi, J., & Perä-Rouhu, E. (2000). *Oppiminen työelämässä – työssäoppiminen opiskelussa. Koulutuksen ja työelämän yhteistyötä Leonardo da Vinci -projekteissa* [Learning in working life – Work-based learning during studies. Cooperation between education and working life in Leonardo da Vinci projects]. Helsinki: Opetushallitus.

Poikela, E. (1998). Oppiminen, arviointi ja osaaminen [Learning, assessment and practical competence]. In A. Räisänen (Ed.), *Hallitaanko ammatti? Pätevyyden määrittelyä arvioinnin perustaksi.* (Arviointi No. 2, pp. 35–46). Helsinki: Opetushallitus.

de Rozario, P. (2002). *European forum on quality in VET. Self-assessment as a quality approach.* CEDEFOP. Retrieved July 12, 2007, from http://www.trainingvillage.gr/etv/upload/projects_networks/quality/archives/techn_group/safinalreportgbnov2002.doc

Räkköläinen, M. (2005). *Kansallisen näyttöperusteisen oppimistulosten arviointijärjestelmän kehittäminen ammatillisiin perustutkintoihin. Arviointikokeilusta kohti käytäntöä.* [Developing a national skills test-based system of assessing learning results for initial vocational education. From assessment pilots towards practice.]. Helsinki: Opetushallitus.

Schön, D. A. (1983). *The reflective practitioner: How professionals think in action.* New York: Basic Books.

Schön, D. A. (1987). *Educating the reflective practitioner. Toward a new design for teaching and learning in the professions.* San Francisco: Jossey-Bass.

Stenström, M. -L. (2001). *Näytöt ammatillisessa peruskoulutuksessa. Kokemuksia ja tutkimustarpeita* [Competence-based assessment in initial vocational education. Experiences and research needs]. Helsinki: Opetushallitus.

Stenström, M. -L. (2004). Ammatin oppiminen ja työelämäyhteydet. [Learning of occupation and relationships between education and working life]. In M. Tuominen, & J. Wihersaari (Eds.), *Ammatti ja kasvatus. Ammattikasvatuksen tutkimuksia vuonna 2004.* (pp. 88–97). Hämeenlinna: Tampereen yliopisto. Ammattikasvatuksen tutkimus- ja koulutuskeskus

Stenström, M. -L. (2005). Assessment of work-based learning in VET as a subject for research: Quality assurance and practice-oriented assessment in vocational education and training. *Special edition of the Finnish Journal of Vocational and Professional Education,* 99–105.

Stenström, M. -L., & Laine, K. (2006a). Conclusions and discussion. In M. -L. Stenström & K. Laine (Eds.), *Quality and practice in assessment: New approaches in work-related learning* (pp. 155–172). Jyväskylä: University of Jyväskylä, Institute for Educational Research.

Stenström, M. -L., & Laine, K. (2006b). Practice-oriented assessment and quality assurance within the QUAL-PRAXIS project. In M. -L. Stenström, & K. Laine (Eds.), *Quality and practice in assessment: New approaches in work-related learning* (pp. 7–17). Jyväskylä: University of Jyväskylä, Institute for Educational Research.

Stenström, M. -L., & Laine, K. (Eds.). (2006c). *Quality and practice in assessment: New approaches in work-related learning.* Jyväskylä: University of Jyväskylä, Institute for Educational Research.

Stenström, M.-L., & Laine, K. (Eds.). (2006d). *Towards good practices for practice-oriented assessment in European vocational education.* (Occasional Papers No. 30). Jyväskylä: University of Jyväskylä, Institute for Educational Research.

Stenström, M. -L., Laine, K., & Kurvonen, L. (2006). Practice-oriented assessment in Finnish VET – Towards quality assurance through vocational skills demonstrations. In M.-L. Stenström & K. Laine (Eds.), *Quality and practice in assessment: New approaches in work-related learning* (pp. 89–120). Jyväskylä: University of Jyväskylä, Institute for Educational Research.

Stenström, M. -L., & Lasonen, J. (Eds.). (2000). *Strategies for reforming initial vocational education in Europe.* Jyväskylä: University of Jyväskylä, Institute for Educational Research.

Streumer, J. N., & Kho, M. (2006). The world of work-related learning. In J. Streumer (Ed.), *Work-related learning* (pp. 3–49). Dordrecht: Springer.

Tessaring, M., & Wannan, J. (2004). Vocational education and training – Key to the future. Lisbon-Copenhagen-Maastricht: Mobilising for 2010. Cedefop synthesis of the Maastrict Study. Thessaloniki: CEDEFOP.

Tynjälä, P. (1999a). Towards expert knowledge? A comparison between a constructivist and a traditional learning environment in the university. *International Journal of Educational Research, 31*(5), 355–442.

Tynjälä, P. (1999b). Oppiminen tiedon rakentamisena: konstruktivistisen oppimiskäsityksen perusteita [Learning as knowledge construction: Foundations of the constructivist conception of learning]. Helsinki: Kirjayhtymä.

Tynjälä, P., & Collin, K. (2000). Koulutuksen ja työelämän yhteistyö – pedagogisia näkökulmia. [Cooperation between education and working life – Pedagogical perspectives]. *Aikuiskasvatus, 20*(4), 293–305.

Tynjälä, P., Välimaa, J., & Sarja, A. (2003). Pedagogical perspectives on the relationships between higher education and working life. *Higher Education, 46*(2), 147–166.

Tynjälä, P., Slotte, V., Nieminen, J., Lonka, K., & Olkinuora, E. (2006). From university to working life: Graduates' workplace skills in practice. In P. Tynjälä, J. Välimaa, & G. Boulton-Lewis (Eds.), *Higher education and working life: Collaborations, confrontations and challenges* (pp. 73–88). Amsterdam: Elsevier.

Wenger, E. (1998). *Communities of practice. Learning, meaning and identity.* Cambridge: Cambridge University Press.

Wiggins, G.P. (1993). *Assessing student performance: Exploring the purpose and limits of testing.* San Fransico: Jossey-Bass Publishers.

Wolf, A. (1995). *Competence-based assessment.* Bury St Edmunds, UK: St Edmundsbury Press.

Young, M. (2000). Improving vocational education: Trans-European comparisons of development in the late 1990s. In M. -L. Stenström & J. Lasonen (Eds.), *Strategies for reforming initial vocational education in Europe* (pp. 147–162). Jyväskylä: University of Jyväskylä, Institute for Educational Research.

Young, M. (2003). Vocational knowledge. In H. Rainbird, A. Fuller, & A. Munro (Eds.), *Workplace learning in context* (pp. 185–200). London: Routledge.

# Author Index

# Subject Index

## A

Abstract knowledge, 97, 104
Academic education, 33, 39, 41, 42
Action research, 86, 141
Activity, 13, 22, 25, 26, 27, 29, 44, 45, 46, 47,
  48, 51, 52, 56, 65, 69, 70, 77, 80, 83, 88,
  89, 117, 121, 153, 157, 162, 167, 179, 180,
  181, 204
Activity system, 25
Activity theory, 22, 46
Actors, 5, 6, 8, 48, 72, 84, 85, 95, 122, 124,
  138, 140, 141, 142, 144, 145, 148, 149,
  153, 163, 167, 174, 175, 177, 180, 196,
  202, 205, 206, 208, 209, 210, 213, 217
Adaptation strategies, 8, 173–183
Adult education, 5, 25, 128, 129, 131, 188
Adult learning, 79, 85
Advanced beginner, 95, 106, 110
Agency, 66, 70, 105, 108, 109, 110, 194
Apprentices, 138, 139, 142, 147, 148, 160,
  190, 192, 193, 194, 196, 197, 198
Apprenticeship, 5, 8, 20, 29, 66, 89, 138,
  153–168, 187, 189, 190, 195
Apprenticeship training, 8, 138, 153–168
Assessment, 14, 20, 21, 33, 83, 84, 85,
  88, 117, 118, 128, 130, 144, 149, 187,
  193, 210, 211, 212, 215, 216, 222,
  224, 225, 226, 227, 228, 229, 230, 231,
  232, 233
Attributions, 155
Authentic context, 98, 129, 227, 231
Authenticity, 227

## B

Ba, 27, 29, 30, 117, 118, 120, 157, 158, 159,
  161, 165, 167
Baccalaureat professional, 40
Behaviourism, 96
Benchmarking, 140
Berufsmensch, 43
Bildung, 54, 55, 56, 147
Bodily performance, 105, 107, 109
Bologna process, 32
Boundary crossing, 22, 23, 24, 26, 102, 176,
  202, 203
Boundaryless careers/career, 176, 183
Business skills, 162, 165

## C

Career, 9, 64, 69, 80, 154, 155, 156, 163, 167,
  173, 174, 175, 176, 178, 180, 188, 192
Career development, 80
Citizenship, 41, 42, 78, 79, 83
Coaching, 9, 21, 130, 191, 192, 193
Codified knowledge, 15, 196
Cognitive constructivist view of learning, 25
Coincidental learning, 154
Collaboration, 3, 8, 12, 21, 22, 24, 28, 29, 31,
  40, 69, 117, 118, 126, 128, 130, 132, 133,
  137, 138, 139, 149, 227, 235
Collaborative climate, 31, 121
Collaborative work, 120, 130
Communication, 11, 15, 28, 30, 44, 47, 51, 54,
  66, 84, 87, 88, 121, 123, 124, 132, 133,
  138, 142, 143, 144, 145, 146, 147, 164,
  175, 178, 193, 198
Communication skills, 15, 88
Communities of practice, 21, 22, 23, 26, 27,
  28, 157, 158, 163, 174, 175, 177, 178, 196,
  203, 204, 205, 206, 210, 215, 217, 227
Community of practice, 25, 26, 27, 70, 161,
  164, 194, 195, 205, 206
Company, 5, 7, 31, 52, 66, 67, 78, 79, 81, 82,
  83, 84, 85, 86, 87, 88, 89, 90, 93, 94, 96,
  99, 105, 109, 118, 121, 138, 139, 140, 143,
  179, 182, 190, 191, 197, 198, 213
Company-based training, 93, 94, 96, 109

Printed in the United Kingdom by
Lightning Source UK Ltd., Milton Keynes
139263UK00008BB/4/P